# THE FRENCH SIDE OF HENRY JAMES

# The French Side of
# HENRY JAMES

E D W I N   S I L L   F U S S E L L

COLUMBIA UNIVERSITY PRESS NEW YORK

COLUMBIA UNIVERSITY PRESS
New York   Oxford
Copyright © 1990 Columbia University Press

Library of Congress Cataloging-in-Publication Data

Fussell, Edwin S.
    The French side of Henry James / Edwin Sill Fussell.
      p.   cm.
    ISBN 0-231-07070-5
    1. James, Henry, 1843–1916—Knowledge—France.   2. James, Henry,
1843–1916—Knowledge—Language and languages.   3. French philology
in literature.   4. France in literataure.   I. Title.
    PS2127.F7F8   1990                                89-24016
    813'.4—dc20           CIP

Casebound editions of Columbia University Press books are Smyth-sewn
and printed on permanent and durable acid-free paper

Printed in the United States of America
c 10 9 8 7 6 5 4 3 2 1

*For Mary*

# Contents

# Preface

I began this book, initially to be an essay on *The American,* immediately upon return from my longest stay in Paris ever, five whole
weeks. Inevitably what I still thought about was the setting of that
novel, chiefly the topography of Paris and the French language, as
re-experienced by myself more than a century later. I was luckier
than I knew, for topography and language have proved the two
richest aspects of James' French settings as well as the two aspects
most ignored by previous scholars and critics, I mean those who
even notice that James novels *have* settings. It is wondeful what
people notice and what they don't. As I went about for the next few
years carrying a volume of Henry James (most often one of the
Library of America volumes, they have so many pages), people
would ask, in their friendly impertinent American way, at a lunch

counter or in a restaurant, on the bus or on Amtrak, who *that* was. "Oh, *him*," I would say, in my best meet-the-public tone, "You know who Shakespeare is?" "Of course!" "Well, Henry James is the American Shakespeare." Alternatively, "You know how Mark Twain is the Lincoln of our literature?" "Sure!" "Well, Henry James is the George Washington of our literature"—sometimes Benjamin Franklin, for variety, mentioning Paris. *"That's* cool!" they would say, followed by appreciative silence.

James criticism tends to be almost as silent about particularities, textual and referential both; most of it reads like an interminable discussion arising from a plot summary or a character sketch; it is singularly inattentive to the main truth about the Jamesian textual œuvre, as succinctly put by Adeline R. Tintner: "James's imagination soared when it relied on facts" and "James is always tied to reality." [1] Articles on France and French in James are few and far between. Previous books on the subject—or *not* on the subject, not critically, they cover too much ground too superficially—fail adequately to get at James' French side either in depth or in detail. [2] I have attempted to do both. Specifically, I want to show how this French business of James is in the text, by way of reference or representation, of persons and personages real or made up (Napoleon and Noémie Nioche), of places real or made up (Paris and Fleurières) but mostly real, and mostly Paris—of French manners and morals and habits and habitudes and customs and culture and civilization and religion and history and landscape and politics and economics and more than anything else the French language, for French is also resplendently conspicuous *in* the text, either by way of direct quotation as ascribed to the personages or as reserved to narrative voice; French is part of the text; at times, French *is* the text—Italian and German much less frequently. Indeed, the James text inscribes French so much and so well that it is no exaggeration to say that readings of James which scant the fact of language are no readings at all but the merest selective reduction. Attention to France and French further compels attention to questions of literary patriotism and internationalism, the relations of languages and literatures, the relations of literatures and world politics, as well as deliberately sought cultural alienation, presence and absence, the oddity of "the other," comparison and contrast, the idea of differentiation, and perhaps more than anything else disjunction—all stemming from the fact, so clearly enunciated and incorporated by James, that the one human race does not all inhabit the same location or speak the same language. Disjunction of conflicted differences, celebration of their *interest,* diminution of their *threat,* movement toward the vision of a single many-voiced worldwide humanity—this is what Henry James is all about. It would be a pity to miss it; it is just what we need, and what we need so badly.

Almost everyone in the world knows, admires, subscribes to, and even pretends to act on, the trinitarian slogan of the French Revolution, *liberté, égalité, fraternité.* The slogan is pure French in inspiration, French in language, forever connected in our minds with the memory of Paris as *centre,* that secular shrine to which you repair, literally or in imagination, if you wish to be informed and happy, just as Rome is the sacral shrine to which you repair if you wish to be saved. I gladly record my allegiance to the two cities and I gladly recall how early and young Henry James came to his dream of that France. As he tells us in *A Small Boy and Others,* his first memory was of the Place and Colonne Vendôme, of being driven past, "in the second year of my life . . . as a baby in long clothes . . . a great stately square surrounded with high-roofed houses and having in its centre a tall and glorious column . . . while I waggled my small feet, as I definitely remember doing, under my flowing robe."[3] At the other end of his life, he raised and distributed funds for the Allied cause, labored in the home-front war effort, and ministered to wounded soldiers in hospitals, often in French, for who else could speak to them so well in that most heroic and beautiful of tongues?

The structure of my book is basically chronological, with obvious exceptions, e.g., *The Reverberator* is placed just after *The American,* to which it pertains, rather than just after *The Princess Casamassima,* to which it does not. Chapters 3 (Italianate Fictions), 6 (The English Period), and 8 (Selected Tales) unavoidably violate strict chronology for the purpose of surveying broad sectors of the Jamesian œuvre that ought not to be entirely overlooked. All along, the problem was to put sufficient emphasis on the major monuments—clearly discernible, I trust—while at the same time somehow including more, though not all. In a pocket notebook, I find the following entry (undated): "A short book wd be American Princess C. Tragic Muse Ambassadors" and then an afterthought: "That wd omit too much!"

and then another afterthought, evidently conclusive: "No, it wouldn't!" Thus the basic structure of four major monuments was mysteriously arrived at, but then there had to be subsequent compromises, in order to cover the ground.

Alice James records in her diary her brother H.'s response to a friend's plea for help in commencing a book, "to which H. replied 'that there is no difficulty in beginning, the trouble is to leave off.' "[4] The same may be said of prefaces. And still there are acknowledgments to be made. Looking up from the clutter on my dining-room table, street maps and old Bædekers and French dictionaries and French reference books, and glancing one final time at my notes to *The French Side of Henry James* I make the discovery, not new, that most of them allude to works by James made available by the lifelong labors of Leon Edel—editions of novels and tales and plays and travel books and criticism and letters and notebooks (and surely I have overlooked a few more categories). How can you say a decent thank-you for a gift so capacious when you can scarely imagine where you would be without it? You would probably not be writing a book about Henry James—certainly not this one. I also wish to thank Adeline R. Tintner for spirited and kindly correspondence on these and related matters; Daniel Mark Fogel, editor of *The Henry James Review,* for interest and assistance in regard to the chapters about *The American;* Alvin M. Katz of Continental Book Search, New York, who found me all those Bædekers and Galignanis; Kim Bloemke and Barbara Horner of Star Girls, Encinitas, California, for endlessly good-natured typing and retyping; various scholarly and literary friends, Bett Miller, Kathryn Shevelow, Patricia Terry, and most of all the one to whom the book is dedicated. The first chapter on *The American* is reprinted from the *Henry James Review* with the permission of the editor and of The Johns Hopkins University Press.

"How can I thank you?" said M. Nioche. "My English does not suffice."
"I wish I spoke French as well," said Newman, good-naturedly.

*The American*—May 1868, the Louvre

# I.

# Contes de Lieu et de Langue

## 1. The Art of Fiction

In *The American Scene* (1907), Henry James records what must have been a hugely enjoyable moment for himself at Independence Hall, Philadelphia. He is a British colonial on the verge of imagining a new national definition:

> One fancies, under the high spring of the ceiling and before the great embrasured window-sashes of the principal room, some clever man of the period, after a long look round, taking the hint. *"What* an admirable place for a Declaration of something! What could one here—what *couldn't* one really declare?" And then after a moment: "I say, why not our Independence?—capital thing always to de-

> clare, and before any one gets in with anything tactless. You'll see
> that the fortune of the place will be made."[1]

It is James' most amusing word on the close yet varying relations of
character, action, and place. There are many others, for as he remarked in 1865, more than forty years earlier, in what was only his
second published book review, "All writing is narration; to describe
is simply to narrate things in their order of place, instead of events in
their order of time."[2] That is a partial truth or truism. Another is a
remark in *The Bostonians* (1886) that "a figure is nothing without a
setting."[3] There are many partial truths or truisms about the relations of figures (mostly in action, not in static poses) and where they
are apprehended as being.

James' first (1875) Balzac essay speaks of the indissolubility of
personages and the *mise en scène:* "This part of his story had with
Balzac an importance—his rendering of it a solidity—which it had
never enjoyed before. . . . The place in which an event occurred was
in his view of equal moment with the event itself; it was part of the
action."[4] An 1878 review of a popular novel alleges the opposite,
while incidentally furnishing us a term of the day, now lost—quite
suggestive: "the book comes under the perilous head of that class of
literature which is vulgarly known as 'scenery novels.' "[5] An 1882
review of Daudet happily splits the difference: "The new fashion of
realism has indeed taught us all that in any description of life the
description of places and things is half the battle."[6] Among these
citations, and among citations to come, the reader will easily notice
an ever present possibility of *place,* literally understood, passing over
into metaphor, that is to say *situation,* as (back to *The American Scene)*
the comical bleat of "the American girl" for an ambience adequate to
her charm: "Ah, once *place* me and you'll see—I shall be different, I
shall be better . . . what do I know, helpless chit as I can but be,
about manners or tone, about proportion or perspective . . . other
forms of existence than this poor little mine." And so on. Earlier in
*The American Scene,* James had remarked, playing verbal games with
his favorite French saying (by far), how a "place may abound in its
own sense, as the phrase is, without bristling in the least—it is liable
indeed to bristle most, I think, when not too securely possessed of
any settled sense to abound in."[7]

Sobersided observations found in the late novels conduct us more directly to the strictly literary aspect of our problem, namely the connection of setting (however construed) and "what goes on 'there.' " In *The Tragic Muse* (1890), "He [Peter Sherringham] had *seen* Miriam now; he had never seen her before; he had never seen her till he saw her in her conditions." Perhaps she has not quite existed, or was not the same, outside her "conditions." In *The Awkward Age* (1899), we are told that Vanderbank, in this respect emulating his creator, "had the kind of imagination that likes to *place* an object, even to the point of losing sight of it in the conditions," that word again. Merton Densher in *The Wings of The Dove* (1902) is made to ponder the inextricable reciprocity of Milly Theale and where she happens to be, which happens to be Venice; this is what he takes in, and how he takes it: "Her welcome, her frankness, sweetness, sadness, brightness, her disconcerting poetry, as he made shift at moments to call it, helped as it was by the beauty of her whole setting and by the perception at the same time, on the observer's part, that this element gained from her, in a manner, for effect and harmony, as much as it gave—." It is just that kind of observer that James' fictions call us to be, for, as we are further admonished in *The Ambassadors* (1903): "The text was simply, when condensed, that in *these* places such things were, and that if it was in them one elected to move about one had to make one's account with what one lighted on." In plain English, if one elects to read James at all one is required to make one's account with what one lights on and that is, among other things, specifically, *places,* specific places, e.g., Paris, France. That is especially so if one is an American reader, for whom the whole disconcerting poetry was primarily constructed, as we may learn from Charlotte Stant musing on behalf of us all in London: "It was as if it had been waiting for her, as if she knew it, placed it, loved it, as if it were in fact a part of what she had come back for. So far as this was the case the impression of course could only be lost on a mere vague Italian; it was one of those for which you had to be blessedly an American—as indeed you had to be blessedly an American for all sorts of things: so long as you hadn't, blessedly or not, to remain in America."[8] And "there" it all is, in embryo, our apprehension of James' European text as place—not only European in what it represents but European in what it *is*—France more than London, however, much more.

Regardless of their opinions, convictions, prejudices, preferences, concerning other literary matters, most readers of fiction, and most James critics, tend to assume that a work of narrative art properly consists of three distinctive elements, traditionally called "character," "plot" (or "action"), and "setting"; they further assume that these three elements are "ideally one" (they speak with much fondness of "organic unity") but that for practical purposes they are separate and equal, so that you can endlessly analyze and discuss Isabel Archer as if she were your sister-in-law or someone at the office, quite over-looking the fact that Isabel Archer is no more than certain effects caused by certain prose sentences found in certain sequences in a particular text—were it not for the invention of printing you would probably never have heard of her. It is surely true that there is only the one text—in the case of Henry James, more than one, but one at a time—and that everything we want to say about it must be some sort of abstraction from the readerly apprehension of that text. It is also true that character and plot, as elements abstracted from a text, are easily and quickly shown to be the same thing in different, reciprocating, lights. In "The Art of Fiction" (1884), James demon-strated this identity in a few simple sentences: "What is character but the determination of incident? What is incident but the illustration of character?" What, indeed? To argue otherwise is to quibble about terms. "It is an incident for a woman to stand up with her hand resting on a table and look out at you in a certain way; or if it be not an incident I think it will be hard to say what it is. At the same time it is an expression of character."[9]

Thus our three elements of fiction are effectually simplified to two, character-in-action or action-of-character on the one hand, and setting on the other, what I call *narrative* and *setting,* the *what* and the *where* of the fictive representation. At that point simplification ceases, for narrative and setting are by no means identical reciprocating aspects. Their relations to each other are various and loose and flexible and imperfect, so that "organic unity" is a limit to approach (if you wish) rather than a condition to take for granted.* Narrative

---

*Needless to say, there is always some connection between the what and the where (as referenced, I mean); see James' 4 December 1912 letter to Edith Wharton about *The Reef,* quite baffled: "something *qui me chiffonne* throughout; which is why the whole thing, unrelated and unreferred save in the most superficial way to its milieu and background, and to any determining or qualifying *entourage* takes place *comme cela,* and in a specified, localised way, in France—these non-French people 'electing,' as it were, to have their story out there." Leon Edel, ed., *Henry James Letters,* 4 vols. (Cambridge: Harvard University Press, 1974–84) 4:645.

and setting are nonidentical and intrinsically different by virtue of a very simple distinction in the ways that textual language behaves toward its referents. Narrative referents are indeed as reflexive as heart (of recent critical theory) could wish, they have no being beyond or outside the text from which we abstract them. Christopher Newman and what he is alleged to do in relation to other imputed personages or happenings and what is said to befall him in consequence: none of these persons or happenings have any prior or subsequent or verifiable independent existence apart from the text of *The American.* Not so however with questions of setting. Paris as a referent of the text of *The American* exists both inside and outside that text. Paris was there, irrelative to the text of *The American,* and if one may be so crass as to say so, quite indifferent to the text of *The American,* centuries before Henry James was ever thought of, much less his critics. More than a century later, Paris is there still. Would it make a fascinating test case for "theory" if you should suddenly leap from your chair, grab your copy of *The American,* and rush off to Paris to read it at a sidewalk café? It might bring you to your senses.

Because of this basic distinction between the capabilities of textual language to refer both inside and outside itself, the *what* of a fiction (for the most part imaginary) and the *where* of a fiction (for the most part not) tend to be separable. As separable, they are detachable. In fact, most readers and critics of James give no thought at all to the way they detach narrative from setting, which they largely ignore. My intention is naturally to do the opposite but not merely as an exercise in compensation. I happen to want my narratives where I believe they are, in fact, *at,* viz., the confluence of geographic, demographic, political, and linguistic considerations of prime import in the real world and hence, as I also believe, in the literary work as well, especially if that work be a novel or tale by Henry James. It is indeed these extra-literary (as who should say) considerations which constitute a chief reason for reading Henry James. It is clearly impossible to read *The American* at all, I further dare to think, without noticing at least the following facts: *France* is a political entity and a geographical space; *French* is the name of the collective people who comprise that entity by inhabiting that space (and not only those living, those dead, also, and those to come); *French* is the name of the language spoken by them, there, and with varying degrees of success by outsiders entering that linguistic space; *American* is the (better part of the) title of that novel, which commenced serial publication during the centenary celebration of national independence from the British Empire; *American* designates the national status of the novel's centralizing, typifying personage; *American* is the nationality of the author, for the greater part of the novel's composition resident in France and for the greater part of that time with intentions of permanency. I too am an American national. Like most readers of *The American* most of the time, I am not resident in Paris but somewhere else. Reading *The American* I can hardly not know that it is about French-American relations. And I can hardly not know that Paris is *not*-where-I-am, that where-I-am is *not*-Paris, an instructive and pleasurable exercise in negation. Perhaps that is *why* I am reading Henry James. It is certainly *how* I am reading Henry James. His personages and their doings are unreal, imagined, invented, nonexistent, conventional, improbable, melodramatic, I can do with them what I will. I can much less do what I will with that Paris which *is* and *is not* "in" the text. Where I *sit* is not where *The American* is *set*. The setting and the narrative are separable, detachable, and disjunct. The setting and I are disjunct. The disjunction is the basis of my reading.

## 2. The International Theme

What is sometimes called in the pages to come the Magic Land of Elsewhere is simple shorthand for a complex of human desires, rife among Europeans and Americans, especially the latter, during the nineteenth century and continuing down to the present—for your Americans of sufficient leisure and means can hardly wait to "get out" or "get away" from wherever it is that they are, be that place never so wonderful in the eyes of persons who wish they were there! —to take their pleasure, not pain, from intentional geographical and cultural disjunction. This complex of human desires is clearly related to literary romanticism, increased interest in realistic milieux for fictions, foreign travel, travel writing, international fictions. And this obsession with Elsewhere is particularly powerful in Henry James, literary conventions of the day deriving extra support from his personal character, as revealed chiefly in his correspondence. If it is impossible (I have tried) to arrive at any judicious view of what he "really" thought and felt about such a place as France—he adored it one year and loathed it the next—it is comparatively easy to make a few fairly definite generalizations about places in general as they struck Henry James early and late. In general, then:

1. He was perpetually changing his mind, and the more so as the place in question was a real possibility for him as a residence; he is most changeable about Paris and London, least changeable about Boston-Cambridge and Venice.

2. Wherever Henry James found himself, he soon wished to be some place else.

3. Any two places (e.g., where he was versus where he wanted to be, or might be, or had been) almost automatically formed in his mind a dramatic contrast, what is called an invidious comparison. The invidious comparison might be against any place whatsoever but it was most often against the United States (particularly Boston-Cambridge), London and England, and, surprisingly, Paris, France, the French people, and even on occasion French Literature, but never, that I can recall, the French language.

4. He preferred to dwell for extended periods in places where it was easy to work, even if this meant places he disliked (for a lessening of distraction).

5. For practical reasons, he preferred to live in places with easy access to contemporary means of literary production (fellow writers, editors, publishers, etc.).

6. Other things being equal, as they seldom were, he preferred to be in places felt as glamorous for a literary-intellectual-aesthetic past.

Needless to say, these criteria failed to coincide: for consideration 6, Italy would have been best; for consideration 5, it was worst.

The places he lived or often visited and which he also wrote about a lot are not so unlimited as is sometimes supposed. They are pretty well exhausted by New York, Newport, Boston-Cambridge, and Washington, D.C., in the United States; London, beach resorts and health spas, country houses, Scotland, and Rye, in Great Britain; Paris, Geneva (French-speaking), Rome, Florence, and Venice on the continent. That was Henry James' real-life and representational beat. It did not include Berlin, Athens, Madrid—and the rest of the world. According to my list of six generalizations about place chez James, it is easy to see that he must have lived in either Paris or England, and that whichever he chose he would be gone a great deal of the time. Like your true cosmopolitan, James thoroughly enjoyed and deliberately cultivated the art of alienation. No one ever more wilfully, consciously, assiduously, and fruitfully worked the romanticism of the self-determining exile. He liked being "away"—from wherever; then he could feel homesick; so long as he was homesick he knew himself in good shape, "being of a nature eminently constructed for homesickness" (16 June 1883 letter to Lady Rosebery).[10] He aspired to "the beautiful openness to the world-relation" and the "disprovincializing breath."[11] Naive persons full of Americanism think his only joy was to live in Europe, forgetful what a pleasure it was not to live in the United States (of that time). It was perhaps an even greater joy not only to escape his compatriots but the limitations of the English language. Always, the romantic was the unfamiliar, the different, the other, so that in the end even the United States came to be romanticized: "Nothing could be of a simpler and straighter logic: Europe had been romantic years before, because she was different from America; wherefore America would now be romantic because she was different from Europe."[12] Anticipating that first trip to his native land in twenty-one years, he wrote on 19 January 1904 to Edward Lee Childe how he was "already gloating over the sentiments with which I shall expatriate myself here," meaning England.[13] Expatriation was easy. All you had to do was leave any place you had stayed too long; too long was about the time required to write a novel or a story or an essay or even a book review.

Such of those points as want buttressing may find their account in a few highly selected (one in a hundred) epistolary gems, in chronological order, without undue comment, save for a couple of indispensable passages by way of introduction, one from a 21 March 1879 letter to Mrs. F. H. Hill, the other from a 20 September 1889 letter to Edwin L. Godkin, both in defense of inconsistency: "Nothing is my *last word* about anything—I am interminably supersubtle and analytic—and with the blessing of heaven, I shall live to make all sorts of representations of all sorts of things. It will take a much cleverer person than myself to discover my last impression—among all these things—of anything"; "I am an incurable pessimist and have no comfort for any man. I would no more generalize than I would slide down the banisters." The gems: "Paris, vulgarized as it has become, haunts my imagination. It may be that it is better so, and that in the very interest of joy, I had best never go there"; "At last—for the first time—I live! . . . I went reeling and moaning thro' the streets" (Rome); "I certainly have not travelled a year in this quarter of the globe [Europe] without coming to a very deep sense of the absurdly clumsy and transitory organization of the actual social body. The only respectable state of mind, indeed, is to constantly express one's perfect dissatisfaction with it"; "you feel the interest of Italy with redoubled force when you begin to turn away from it and seek for the rare and beautiful in other lands. Brave old bonny England of ten short months ago—where are you now?"; "London is the same terrible great murky Babylon as ever. Blood-drenched Paris seemed as a glittering bauble beside it"; "Dear People [letter home] all—I take possession of the old world—I inhale it—I appropriate it!"; "The simplest thing to tell you of Venice is that I adore it"; "I find Italy peaceful for writing so long as it's not about its bescribbled self"; "The solution, of course, is to be in Italy when one can—not to live, in short, where one *does* live! . . . I can work better in other places (especially abroad)"; "How much more amusing is France than any country of the earth whatsoever, and how dreary would the human family be if it were not for that distinguished—the only distinguished—member! . . . When you get tired of 'distinguishing shades of difference'—'curious' or other—between the quartier latin and the quartier Montmartre, come back here [London] where there are no shades to be distinguished—*pas de nuances, pas de nuances!* Come back all the same and revel in chunks and lumps"; "Italy is almost as convenient as she is beautiful, and I don't know what I should do without her. She has wholly ceased to be exciting to me—which is a part of the convenience." And, finally, one passage from the *Notebooks,* which as chance would have it was written at the Hotel Del Coronado, near San Diego, only a few miles from where I sit, in fact; under date of 29 March 1905, thinking of Lamb House, Rye, England, and then of Cambridge, Massachusetts, "the ghostly old C. that I sit and write of here by the strange Pacific on the other side of the continent, *l'initiation première* (the divine, the unique) . . . that inward romantic principle which was to determine, so much later on (ten years!), my own vision-haunted migration . . . vision-haunted as I was already even then."[14]

There are distances in time as well as of space. Among the numerous significant events and changes which interpose themselves between the Jamesian text as it was originally read and our latter-day reading of it we easily think of the two world wars and the "cold war" resulting from emergence of the United States and the Soviet Union as preeminent powers, of the formation and continued existence of the United Nations with its agencies, of the instauration and development of worldwide travel by air, of the recession of Paris as the capital of the world and the substitution for it of multiple world capitals (or of none, some will say), of the recession of the French language as the world's second language, for diplomatic, social, and travel purposes, in favor of English. We are far from the world of even so late a date as *The Ambassadors* in 1903. We need an intercessor, an intermediary, a mediating principle, a go-between, for which role I have invented a Tourist Reader of that epoch, an appropriate and typical reader of the Tourist Fictions which were at the time so avidly consumed, a Tourist Fiction being simply the kind of fiction James, and many others, regularly served up, a fictive narrative about imagined personages in an actual setting "foreign" both to the personages and to the Tourist Readership. Vicariously substituting for the experience of actual travel or residence abroad, the Tourist Fiction almost inevitably incorporates large chunks of travel writing, subtly or otherwise, within the fictional text. Normally the shift from genre to genre is signaled by a switch from the customary past tense of fictive narrative to the present tense of travel reportage—for reasons yet to be discovered, events which did not happen go best when recounted *as history*.

For us, now, not only readers in our own right but readers *of*—and by way of—the Tourist Reader, the present-tense travelogue passages are inevitably subordinate to the past-tense narrative structures which contain them. (But to the Tourist Reader then? Who can say, with any real assurance?) Present tense interrupts, interpolates itself, as it were, intertextually, like a citation of something else, disrupting for the space of a word, a phrase, a few sentences, seldom more, the narrative business at hand. In the following passage from chapter 7 of *Roderick Hudson* (1875) you can virtually watch the Tourist Reader changing gears from sentence to sentence as the mode shifts from fictional narrative to travel-book presentation: "He was particularly fond of this part of Rome, though he could hardly have expressed the charm he found in it. [Therefore Henry James will express it; going over to the present tense, he continues:] As you pass away from the dusky, swarming purlieus of the Ghetto, you emerge into a region of empty, soundless, grass-grown lanes and alleys," exactly as you might read about the same in your Bædeker or Murray or other guidebook telling you where to go and what to see and what to think and feel about it. In *The American,* a weary protagonist sits exhausted in past tense before a painting which James then undertakes to describe in present tense: "In the left-hand corner of the picture is a young woman with yellow tresses confined in a golden head-dress; she is bending forward and listening . . ." While all this is going on, Newman obligingly sits, or, more accurately, he *sat.* Sometimes a Tourist Reader is more directly invoked, invited (ordered) in: "Newman took his way to the Avenue de Messine . . . The street in question, as some travellers will remember, adjoins the Parc Monceau, which is one of the prettiest corners of Paris. The quarter has an air of modern opulence and convenience," and on and on in the vein of a newspaper supplement. Sometimes a double-gaited Tourist Fiction sentence begins in present-tense description and silently passes into past-tense narrative: "The Parc Monceau is a very pretty piece of landscape-gardening, but Newman, passing into it, bestowed little attention." As for actual human beings, we will never directly know the Tourist Reader himself or herself, more often the latter, we suspect, but we may make intelligent inferences from what pleased them. The Tourist Reader was English or more likely American, definitely Anglophonic but with a gift for foreign languages, especially French (or if not will never dare to confess the lack), preponderantly but not exclusively middle class or better, reasonably affluent and leisured; at the very least, would fancy herself so. She or he has been a visitor to or a resident of France, especially Paris, has been there once, or more than once, is in possession of fond memories asking to be rekindled. Or: she or he has not yet been to Paris but is dying to go. Or: she or he may never make it to Paris but will compensate by reading about people who are luckier. Each type of Tourist Reader would have been pleased, but in different ways, by the opening of *The American* in the Louvre, with the ridiculous bilingual fumbling of a typical American tourist abroad with Mademoiselle Noémie Nioche who is clearly no better than she should be. The Tourist Fiction was decidedly not what might be called "working class literature" and I am under no delusion that "everybody" read it then or reads it even now.

In my irregular yet curious questings in search of whatever light may be made to shine on Henry James and his French fictions, I have happened upon, and looked over with a considerable interest, an anthology evidently acquired in 1947, edited by two notable scholars of the day, Harry R. Warfel and G. Harrison Orians, entitled *American Local-Color Stories*.[15] "American" in the title means stories *about* America as well as *by* Americans and "local" in the term "local color" means the same. It is a representative bit of post–Depression chauvinistic sentimentalized Americana, which, while confessing foreign sources and influences, nonetheless insists on viewing the local-color phenomenon as ineluctably a patriotic *American* expression of *America*'s diversified uniquity (and self-sufficiency, too). In the general introduction, Henry James is cited for *Washington Square* and *The Bostonians*. That he might have been more American in Paris or Rome is a possibility not entertained. In a headnote, his friend Fenimore (Constance Fenimore Woolson) is said to have "later adopted the technique of Henry James" and it is even admitted that she wrote about Italy, but not until after a listing of the five *American* regions she wrote about has been duly entered.

It has consequently been a surprise and a refreshment to discover that in a letter of 8 May 1883 Henry James was proposing to his publisher in London a volume entitled *Sketches and Studies in Local Colour,* apparently quite unAmerican.[16] Almost by definition, local color portended the romantic, the exotic, the foreign, the different, the other—it was naturally sought, and easily found, abroad rather than at home. Typically, in a 27 December 1869 letter to his brother William, James tells of finding it in the streets of Assisi: "Never have I seen the local color laid on so thick. They reek with antiquity."[17] A letter to his sister Alice, 24 May 1876, from Paris (whence *The American* was about to emanate) shows him handling the term in a lighter, broader way: "With this, sweet child, I have scraped together all the local color I can think of: may I not have labored in vain."[18] Reference is to literary, political, social gossip; the letter reeks with French words and phrases. At least three times in *The Portrait of a Lady,* Isabel Archer is said to go in search of local color, twice in England, once in Rome. As a literary emphasis and technique, local color was, according to James, virtually an invention of Balzac's: "His landscapes, his 'local colour'—thick in his pages at a time when it was to be found in his pages almost alone—his towns, his streets, his houses . . . his rooms, shops, interiors, details of domesticity and traffic . . ."[19] It would seem that for Henry James the term local color connoted the urban rather than the rural—no mention here of Sir Walter Scott or James Fenimore Cooper. Local color is mainly French; it is especially Parisian.

On the other hand (two other hands), local color was not what you looked for or found in the United States nor was that estimable nation exactly the best place to look for it. Such "impressions" are of course highly subjective but it can hardly be doubted that a powerful ingredient in James' weariness was revulsion from American self-regard, that overweening American preoccupation with such questions as whether "we" are, at bottom, the salt of the earth, or, perhaps, the scum of the earth. Americans are always willing to hear how dreadful they are but they cannot tolerate being told that they are ordinary. That was one of the things James had to say to his compatriots in his Hawthorne book, which was naturally resented. Of Salem, Massachusetts: "Mr. Lathrop has much to say about the ancient picturesqueness of the place, and about the mystic influences it would project upon such a mind and character as Hawthorne's. These things are always relative, and in appreciating them everything depends upon the point of view. Mr. Lathrop writes for American readers, who in such a matter as this are very easy to please. Americans . . . are so fond of local colour that they contrive to perceive it in localities in which the amateurs of other countries would detect only the most neutral tints."[20]

Letters of 1880 to Grace Norton (20 September and 7 November) discuss the lack—the deliberate omission, James wants to persuade her—of local color in *Washington Square,* "a slender tale, of rather too narrow an interest,"[21] as may also be said of many additional

James performances set in the United States. A passage in the *Note-books* shows him first thinking to inject "Impressions of a Cousin" with local color and then falling back in defeat: "But that would be pale—the heroine living in 37th St., etc. The New York streets are fatal to the imagination."[22] They ought to be named the Rue de Bellechasse or something French like that. In a letter of 16 October 1882 to his sister-in-law, the great philosophic brother in absentia, James commiserates her, half mockingly, half not, less on the missing husband than on her having to be in Cambridge, where he "used to walk about the byways . . . and endeavor to invest its habitations with a certain local color,"* a lost cause, the houses being mostly the same, *and* American, and so, *sans intérêt*. In an 1877 review of Gustave de Molinari (French, not Italian), *Lettres sur les Etats-Unis et le Canada,* James again frets the relativities of international "interest" or its opposite: "He says somewhere that every people has certainly its quantum of national vanity, but that that of the Americans towers far above all others. Granting the truth of this assertion, we must yet say that we have in this country [he is writing in the *Nation*] this symptom of modesty, that we are always rather surprised when an entertaining book is written about us. Addicted as we are to lamenting the absence of 'local color' within our borders, we are astonished to see a foreigner find so many salient points and so much characteristic detail."[23] That is a good phrase—"symptom of modesty" is good. A furious paragraph of the *Daisy Miller* preface to the New York Edition assaults the American local-color movement broadside and wholesale along with its credulous appreciators, the "thousands of celebrated works . . . from the vast wild garden of 'unconventional' life in no matter what part of our country," all smirched with Dialect (the capital is his), "the riot of the vulgar tongue . . ." Catching his breath, only to explode again: "Grand generalised continental riot or particular pedantic, particular discriminated and 'sectional' and self-conscious riot," amounting to "the bastard vernacular of communities disinherited of the felt difference between the speech of the soil and the speech of the newspaper, and capable thereby, accordingly, of taking slang for simplicity, the composite for the quaint and the vulgar for the natural."[24] *The American Scene*

---

*Henry James Letters*, 2:385. Leon Edel's note (386) is not to miss: "This was the second occasion on which WJ had taken off for Europe shortly after the birth of one of his children."

alludes to "the little tales, mostly by ladies, and about and for children romping through the ruins of the Language, in the monthly magazines."[25] *(Infantine* is a favorite word of Jamesian displeasure). In all American Literature no other work even approaches *The American Scene* for stylistically fascinating denunciations of American civilization as apparently the least fascinating spectacle yet tolerated by a presumably all-knowing yet suspiciously too-permissive Providence.

## *3. French in the Texts*

At last it is time that we shift attention to the bilingual, or even the multilingual nature of the Jamesian text, for on occasion there will be a third and even a fourth language in question but always there will be French—and how better to transcend or evade or bootstrap up the Americans in their more vulgar tendencies of patriotic monolingual partiality, simultaneously bypassing the more vulgar of the British, in fact all speakers of English only, by flight into a disprovincialized international *monde* where people change their languages as readily as their facial expressions? Very roughly speaking, there are four necessary areas for critical inspection in the extra-American extra-English and basically pro-French aspects of the *soi-disant* international theme: first, the general, the inclusory idea which for want of another term may be called "the attachment of literatures," especially French; second, James' bilingual behavior in his extensive criticism, taking Balzac as an example; third, certain language lessons to be learned from an easygoing wallow in the *Notebooks;* fourth, and finally, proposal of a model in linguistics capable of underwriting the rest of this book.

Even if somewhat indefinite, the term "the attachment of literatures" is essential to any full understanding of Henry James as a literary producer. What it points to are certain tendencies, on his part, for example, to regard the literature of a nation, a civilization, a culture, a people, as each one metonymous of the others, so that who shall take the literature takes all, together with a tendency to regard each and every national literature as a single coherent entity, whether to be grasped and assimilated or silently passed by. American Literature he appears to have considered as on the whole not yet quite in existence, so that there was almost nothing to seize or to leave alone, but in the meanwhile he, Henry James, was clearly in the process of becoming *it,* American Literature, so that all will be well if we only cultivate a bit of patience. But at the same time that he is in the process of becoming American Literature he is also in the process of attaching other, foreign literatures to itself (himself)—you can just as easily say he is attaching himself to them and you can just as easily say that the development of himself as American Literature and the attachment of extra-American literatures to it (himself) are one and the same process.

English Literature—mainly for satiric, social content—and French Literature—mainly for form and style—are obviously the two literatures James attaches. Inevitably he will end by bequeathing us a triangular construction, English, French, and American, of his own triangular devising and more or less equivalent to his own "works." We may hear a faint echo of all this in a 15 avril 1878 letter addressed to "Cher monsieur Flaubert" and containing, with much else, such curious tonalities as "Voici le second hiver que je passe à Londres, mais je me promets d'année en année le plaisir de me retrouver à Paris au moment où vous y serez et de frapper bien discrètement à votre porte. Tout à vous, cher Monsieur Flaubert, d'admiration et de reconnaissance. Henry James Jr."[26] It is hardly necessary, at this point, to dwell on James' fabulous French, written or spoken, as attested by many expert witnesses, nor on the absurdity of his name suddenly obtruding at the end its patent Anglo-Irish-American origins. What we might do, instead, is listen, and try to hear, the comparatively young Henry James—he is just thirty-five years old and it is his birthday—imagining himself back in Paris, listening in advance for the sound of his closed hand on that door which opens to Flaubert and to more than Flaubert. Other James critics have heard something of the same, though we may all phrase it variously and perhaps not in any instance to our entire satisfaction. Thus at least twice Leon Edel, "He would create a kind of imperium of letters, annex Europe to his native American domain, achieve a trans-Atlantic empire larger than that of other novelists," and "Thus in the midst of his great fertile years, when he summoned to his work the greatest powers of his maturity, James interrogated the literary reputations of the great novelists of France, in the interest of his own literary reputation. He was like a Napoleon of literature surveying conquered territories."[27] Thus John Carlos Rowe, omitting Napoleon but also, unfortunately, France, "In order to become a 'true' modern, *the* cosmopolitan novelist, James would have to internalize and thoroughly sublimate not only the figures of Hawthorne and Trollope but also the national literatures and formal modes that each represented."[28] Naturally I prefer my own formulation. It designedly escapes political and linguistic patriotism, both.

The attachment of French Literature occurs in a number of ways, explicit and devious alike, as will duly appear. It will of course appear in James' lifelong mission of bringing French Literature to the Anglophones in the genre of literary criticism. But does it not appear more obviously still in his jubilant use of the French language throughout his œuvre? You can apprehend both phenomena at once in his criticism of Balzac. Indeed, James' persistent positioning of Balzac as originator and specialized saint to all fiction worth bothering about amounts to the positioning of French Literature as a kind of umbrella benevolently overarching the rest. But it is Henry James who holds the umbrella aloft, for the protection of the unenlightened, and who gladly calls our attention to such wonders as may be glimpsed beneath. So early as 9 August 1864, he wrote, in all innocence, to Charles Eliot Norton, coeditor of the *North American Review,* that "if at any time you wish a particular work briefly reviewed, on learning your wish I shall be glad to undertake the task," adding, the modest young man who had never been to college and scarcely even to school in any systematic fashion, "I am frequently in the way of reading French books."[29] And stayed so. In the collected edition of his literary criticism, the proportionate page-counts are:

| | |
|---|---|
| French Writers | 891 |
| English Writers | 703 |
| American Writers | 514 |
| Other European Writers | 130 |
| General Topics | 177 |

Among other European writers we find thirty-seven pages on Gabriele D'Annunzio and fifteen pages on Matilde Serao, a total of fifty-two pages, a splendid illustration of a modern literature *not* attached by Henry James; when he wrote fiction about Italy or Italians he tended to French them (see chapter 3).

Surprisingly, there is less French in the French criticism than in the French fiction and James is more accommodating about it—except, of course, when he is warning the reader to get up his or her French if she or he expects to read—something really good. Most of the time, he abounds in a happy sense of bilingual *confort,* hinting, helping, pointing, explaining, apologizing, flattering, soothing. He will give a Balzac phrase in French, and then interrupt—the interruption here signaled by a dash—with an English equivalent. The Balzac phrase is in roman type, not in italics, as originally found in Balzac, perhaps implying that Balzac, albeit foreign, hence fascinating, is, like us, just folks:

> The attempt was, as he himself has happily expressed it, to "faire concurrence à l'état civil"—to start an opposition, as we should say in America, to the civil registers.[30]

James not only appears to complete Balzac's French sentence in English translation but he also adds "as we should say in America" rather than in the English language worldwide. The American reader in 1875 not charmed by such insouciance must have been both rare and impossible and the same may be said of the reader in the British Isles peering over the thin nervous American shoulder.

They are almost endless in their subtlety the little devices by which James renders a sense of French texts to a readership conceivably monolingual (but willing to improve). Quoting a Balzac letter, James first gives an English translation (his own) and only then the French original, in parentheses, as if some French person (Balzac) were explicating Henry James or as if Henry James were tactfully supplying to a French audience the French equivalent of an English phrase which might not be clear to them. Thus, almost unbelievably: "the worship of woman *(le culte de la femme).*"[31] If you knew no French, but studied that phrase good and hard you could learn five (four) French words and a bit of grammar. Or James will weave part of a Balzac phrase in French into his own English rendering, "I must go over things, correct them again, put everything *à l'état monumental.*"[32] The French is in italics (lest you miss the treat of exoticism) but it is not in quotation marks for the simple reason that the whole passage is a quotation from Balzac's French but most of it is presented in James' English, for convenience, and only the tail end of the quotation is presented in French, for flavor. The French words sound like an afterthought supplied by the kindly Henry James when in fact they are the only part of the quotation Henry James has not translated into his own English. Still another Balzac letter, as ever in English, concludes: "for a thousand francs what can one get in modern furniture? *Des platitudes bourgeoises, des misères sans valeur et sans goût.*"[33] In this little piece of bilingual ventriloquism we are, in effect, asked to suppose that Balzac addresses Henry James a question in English which Henry James then answers in French, thus reversing the native languages of the two (interchangeable) great writers. Does that amount to the attachment of French Literature to (by) Henry James? So that Balzac and all that stems from him now range themselves under the benign control of the clever young American? I think so. I think it might even, once in a while, be more forcefully put: French Literature has practically disappeared down the maw of the Western barbarian.

One last example of James politely leading his Anglo-Saxon reader, all tremulous, down the primrose path of French realism, up to the very edge of indecency. The following passage, plot summary of *Le Député d'Arcis,* is in James' English prose; it contains five interpolated quotations, two in English and three in French; it concerns a moral problem of Madame de l'Estorade, who writes to a lady acquaintance:

> on the question whether "it will be given" (as she phrases it) to a certain gentlemen to make her "manquer à ses devoirs." This gentlemen has snatched her little girl from under a horse's hoofs, and for a while afterward has greatly annoyed her by his importunate presence on her walks and drives. She immediately assumes that he has an eye to her "devoirs." Suddenly, however, he disappears, and it occurs to her that he is "sacrificing his fancy to the fear of spoiling his fine action." At this attractive thought her "devoirs" begin to totter.[34]

You could write a whole book about Henry James' linguistic handling of French Literature in his criticism—here, perforce, only a few words, by way of introduction to another topic. Whatever the topic, in James, the fact of language is the string to hang onto.

With James, as with many another person who scribbles, there are three distinct categories of writing which survive, whether according to or against the wishes of the writer, and in order from the most public to the most private: writing intended for everyone (and therefore published), writing intended for certain persons only (letters, which James ardently hoped the recipients would be so good as to destroy, but they did not; he should never have written so well), and writings intended for himself only (which he neglected to deal with and so nobody dealt with them and in 1937 Leon Edel chanced upon them at Harvard).[35] In the various documents known as the *Notebooks* we have James' linguistic internationalism relatively pure, personal, at home, in undress, and of a charm scarcely to be surpassed or matched in any other corner of the vast sprawling Jamesian œuvre, as when there now leaps from the page such a phrase as *"comme qui dirait,"* the French equivalent of James' familiar interpolation "as who should say." Again and again, his penchant for phrasing things in French, especially aesthetic things, interrupts his basically English text—thus producing yet one more form of disjunction—and at least once he directly speaks of his desire to cross over from the one language to the other—in doing so, he gives the reason, "oh, the common, general French *art de dire." Voyons, voyons,* he is forever saying to himself (and *un temps* and *mettons*): *"Voyons, voyons— arrangeons un peu cela,"* the point being *"produire* L'ŒUVRE, and L'ŒUVRE is, before God, what I'm going in for." In another entry, "I must," he admonishes himself, "have a long *tête à tête* with myself," and the entry concludes *"A bientôt."*

Citing a *Notebooks* passage commencing *"Causons, causons, mon bon" (mon bon* is James' pet name for himself in his tender or kittenish moods), Leon Edel translates the French words (back?) into English and curiously remarks that James "lapses, as he did earlier, into French."[36] I should rather say "as he does all the time" and instead of "lapses" something more like "escapes into," i.e., the Henry James who so obviously took pleasure in talking to himself in French is the same Henry James who shook the American dust from his feet in favor of the Old World and then shook the dust of England from his feet as often as possible in favor of the continent and its romanticism of many languages—if *elsewhere* is one indispensable word for Henry James, *multiplicity* is another. He positively doted on complication and change: in a 25 March 1878 letter to his father he told how at a party a "Russian girl was clever and interesting, and talking French with her was a pleasant momentary lift out of British Philistinism."[37]

The linguistic model assumed for the chapters which follow is basically the familiar triad of signifier, signified, and referent—through a range, for the referent of *Paris* is relatively exact whereas that of *truth* is less so and the referent of *God* is clear enough to whoever believes but to others not and Isabel Archer, poor thing, has no referent at all. Here my intended originality, such as it is, is to shift attention away from the second term toward the first and the third, so that we may see more clearly both how the text comports itself and what it leads outward to, rather than spending our days and years with the imputed frigidity of Isabel Archer or the arguable good nature of Christopher Newman. Then, also, there must obviously be, with a James text, a certain looseness for the accommodation of more than a single language—it amounts to an easy and almost automatic doubling, or further multiplication, depending on the number of languages involved. For the most part, French and English are involved. Take the word *ouvreuse* in chapter 17 of *The American,* an usherette, an opener, one who opens (at a theater). What we see on the page is the scripted signifier in French. It has eight printed characters. At the same time, we hear (in our mind's ear) the five phonemes of the word. Soon after, we doubtless translate the word into English phonemes from the French phonemes, English phonemes "meaning" one who opens. We may, if we like, transfer that phonic signifier into written form. Thus there are, all told, four signifiers, two French, two English, two voiced, two scripted. But all this while, the signified, in the usual sense of the term, the concept corresponding to the signifier(s) holds constant, *une ouvreuse,* an opener; and all this while there is only the one young lady who stands tapping her foot until people cease this nonsense and take their seats.

In effect, voiced and scripted signifiers stand in a second signifier-signified relation vis-à-vis each other. Each calls the other to mind. (For two languages, double the recipe.) In *A Small Boy and Others*

(1913), there is a trivial reference to matters not in the least trivial, "straw-covered bottles of the essence known in old New York as 'Cullone'—with a very long and big O."[38] *There* are the two kinds of signifier: the O is long when spoken, and so it might well be big if written. (Amusingly enough, the word, here given in its mangled English form, is French, and refers to a place in Germany.) I insist on the distinction of voiced and scripted signifier because James does (as also because, as it turns out, the insistence is itself French), e.g., in "Notes For the Ivory Tower": "I want her name moreover, her Christian one, to be Moyra, and must have some bright combination with that; the essence of which is a surname of two syllables and ending in a consonant—also beginning with one." It is the kind of precise question James was ever concerned with, James criticism not. And there is good reason to think James' concern—call it an obsession albeit quite reasonable—is one more debt to the French, in this case to a particular French person. In his 1888 essay on the Goncourts' *Journal,* James is quite essentially personal: "There was no style worth speaking of [!] for Flaubert but the style that required reading aloud to give out its value; he *mouthed* his passages to himself."[39] So, apparently, did James. And so we should likewise do, as adjured by the *Golden Bowl* preface, James' parting instructions to us, Flaubertian to the very end:

> It is scarce necessary to note that the highest test of any literary form conceived in the light of "poetry"—to apply that term in its largest literary sense—hangs back unpardonably from its office when it fails to lend itself to vivâ-voce treatment. . . . The essential property of such a form as that is to *give out its finest and most numerous secrets* [cf. the 1888 phrasing, "give out its value," indirectly quoting Flaubert], and to give them out most gratefully, under the closest pressure—which is of course the pressure of the attention articulately *sounded.* Let it reward as much as it will and can the soundless, the "quiet" reading, it still deplorably "muffs" its chance and its success. . . . I have nowhere found vindicated the queer thesis that the right values of interesting prose depend all on withheld tests—that is on its being, for very pity and shame, but skimmed and scanted, shuffled and mumbled. *Gustave Flaubert has somewhere in this connexion an excellent word—to the effect that any*

*imaged prose that fails to be richly rewarding in return for a competent utterance ranks itself as wrong through not being "in the conditions of life."* (Emphasis added.)

Among other conditions of life is the way voiced and scripted signifiers in English, and in French, have a habit of going off in different directions, as in the case of Paul Muniment's Christian name (see below, p. 80), or of Maisie's earliest nurse, in *What Maisie Knew*, whose written name is Moddle (suggesting *coddle*), but if you heard it first or without seeing the written word you would think of something else again *(model)*, as surely the small girl did.

As for texts in the written form, James demands closest attention *(Golden Bowl* preface again) "even to that of the shade of a cadence or the position of a comma"; as for Americanism of the very best, Aurora Coyne in *The Sense of the Past* (chapter 1) to Ralph Pendrel "I want in short to be an American as other people are—well, whatever they are" and he "Yes, it's the new cry, and what can be more interesting than to hear it sounded more or less in French?" (she has just sounded *"en fin de compte"*); as for the desirable necessity of more than a single language, James on the American people in *The American Scene*, "It seems odd to have to borrow from the French the right word in this association *[honnête]*—or would seem so, rather, had it been less often indicated that that people have better names than ours even for the qualities we are apt to suppose ourselves more in possession of than they";[40] as for deific arrangements on high, we may think of the French language as reservoir of formulas and phrases concerning *amour*, James wonderfully writing to Edith Wharton on 13 March 1912, how this consideration "by the way convinces me that Providence thinks and *really* expresses itself only in French, the language of gallantry."[41]

# II.

# Mise en scène: The American (1876–1877)

## 1. Time and Topography

The opening sentence of *The American* obligingly reads: "On a brilliant day in May, in the year 1868, a gentleman was reclining at his ease on the great circular divan which at that period occupied the centre of the Salon Carré, in the Museum of the Louvre."[1] Perhaps the phrase "at that period" catches our eye; perhaps it does not. The sentence in question first came to the attention of the original Tourist Reader in June 1876, eight years later than the alleged time of action, and several thousand miles to the west of the Louvre, for in its first publication *The American* was available only in the pages of the *Atlantic Monthly*. "Why 1868?" that original reader might well have asked and might well have found an answer more easily than we, so much more distanced from the original text. Yet surely the pristine contemporaneity of that occasion can be recovered, not by retrospective denunciation of Christopher Newman's "political *ignorance*,"[2] but by recuperation of how the political climate of France was related to Henry James' inscription of a novel about an American in France which James for the most part wrote while also living in France. The last installment appeared in May 1877. Five months after that, in October, the *Nation* printed James' review of Auguste Laugel, *La France Politique et Sociale* (1877), in which James wrote: "There are no people of any pretensions to liberal culture, of whatever nationality, to whom the destiny of the most brilliant nation in the world [not the United States] is a matter of indifference; and at a moment like the present, when she seems to stand at the parting of the ways and to be about to make a supreme choice between the habit of revolution and the experiment of tranquility . . ."[3]—and there we may let the citation trail off, having found something of what we need. The "habit of revolution" versus the "experiment of tranquility," violence versus democracy, may serve as the rubric for all of James' fictional dealings with France—she has been the one, she is now the other, and how long will tranquility last?

For *The American,* as a work by itself, we want something even more particular than that, as follows. In the dispatches he was writing for the New York *Tribune* concurrently with installments of *The American,* James makes quite clear his uncertainty about the stability to date of the Third Republic, still slowly, painfully, and belatedly establishing itself after the disasters of 1870–71, the Franco-Prussian War and the Commune.[4] That was no reliable setting for a novel ambitiously titling itself with the author's own nationality and commencing to show itself in public during the centenary year of that nation's independence. For his fictive setting James wanted something more fixed; 1868 gave him that fixity, for if there was one thing certain vis-à-vis contemporary France it was that the Second Empire was dead beyond recall. Even before the first installment of *The American,* James was describing, in a long essay-review of "The Two Ampères" (*Galaxy,* November 1875), just the kind of society he needed for his setting, "a society which by this time has pretty well passed away and *can know no more changes. It is motionless in its place; it is sitting for its likeness*" (emphasis added).[5] But then, 1876–77, James must be cunning about temporal details. The old Opéra fictively attended by Newman and the Bellegardes is not the new opera building *now* available to later Tourist Readers but young Madame de Bellegarde may *then* aspire to a court appearance at the Tuileries. The new Opéra is described in the *Tribune* letters, the Palais des Tuileries naturally not.

James' desire to have *his* Paris motionless in its place, sitting for its likeness to *him,* makes even more sense if we compare the Paris of *The American* with the Paris of contemporary guidebooks—these are invariably more conservative, at times almost hysterically so, these invariably lay claim to a much broader readership, and these are structured according to a sort of planned obsolescence, whereas James was obviously furnishing his novel with long views respecting the definitely recent past, the vaguely defined present, and the more-or-less predictable future. After that opening sentence of *The American,* where Newman reclines on a divan at the Louvre, we proceed to the second sentence, which begins "This commodious ottoman has since been removed," at some unspecified time between May 1868 and June 1876 known only to the author and to certain highly specialized Paris-fanciers, and then we proceed to the third sentence for the information, not surprising, that Newman is equipped with "a little red guide-book," and a few sentences further on the guidebook is finally identified as "his Bädeker," which is not how Bædeker spells his name but how Henry James spells it.

James' fictive control of Paris is epitomized in the removal of a comfortable couch. With that tranquilizing tonality we may, with much profit, compare the agitated tonalities of Bædeker himself (itself). Bædeker gives us more or less what we may presume to have been the views of such readers as consumed Bædekers, views of Paris and of France lurid, calamitous, and opinionated, views which James as a novelist seems determined to preclude from the Tourist Reader's apprehension of *The American*'s setting. I quote at length from the wonderfully revealing preface to 1872 Bædeker, after which we may compare 1872 Galignani and then 1874 Bædeker, noting how the agitation is gradually in the course of time dying down. From the 1872 Bædeker preface, the fifth and sixth paragraphs:

> Probably no city in the world ever underwent such gigantic transformations in its external appearance as the French metropolis during the reign of Napoleon III., and few cities have ever experi-

enced so appalling a series of disasters as Paris since the declaration of the Republic. Many unwholesome purlieus, teeming with poverty and vice, were swept away under the imperial régime, to make room for spacious squares, noble avenues, and palatial edifices. Paris was then in a transition state, and its grand metamorphosis was nearly complete when the gay, splendour-loving, pleasure-seeking city was overtaken by the signal calamities of 1870–71. Since the restoration of peace the city has in many respects resumed its former aspect, but in others it has sustained such irreparable losses that it must necessarily again pass through a protracted period of transition. The Editor has therefore found the preparation of the present edition of the Handbook a task of unusual difficulty. He has endeavoured to accompany the traveller to the chief attractions of Paris as he found them in the autumn of 1871. Many changes must, however, necessarily occur within the next few years; ruins will be restored or superseded by entirely new structures, museums and galleries will be remodelled and opened to the public under new auspices, and the ex-imperial palaces, châteaux, collections, etc. will be consecrated to 'national' purposes. Meanwhile it may be stated generally that the changes which have as yet taken place have been less considerable than might have been anticipated, and that the intention of the present government is to restore everything as far as possible to its former condition.

It need hardly be observed that it would be far beyond the scope of the Handbook to record all the momentous events of 1870–71, to describe the sieges of Paris by the Prussians and by the French, to give an account of the Communist insurrection, or to enumerate in detail the stupendous disasters and revolting crimes which characterised the second 'Reign of Terror' in May (20th–28th), 1871. Frequent allusion, however, to these events will be found in the following pages, and the Editor may here supplement his description of the 'principal attractions' of the city by a brief enumeration of the buildings, public and private, which have suffered most severely, and many of which, but for their misfortunes, would have failed to arrest the traveller's attention. It may be premised that there is hardly a single public building, or street, or park in Paris which does not bear numerous traces of the recent devastations, or to which some melancholy story does not attach; the following list, however, will be found amply sufficient for the guidance of all ordinary visitors to the sadly mutilated metropolis.[6]

Lists of ravaged monuments follow. Of particular interest to readers of *The American* is the Palais Royal to which Newman and Tom Tristram repair for drinks and conversation in chapter 2, well ahead of the Communists. Young Madame de Bellegarde wants to go there, too, as well as to the Palais des Tuileries (the palace Strether will remember in *The Ambassadors*).

Bædeker and James agree on one point, the continuing instability of the Third Republic. They differ radically in their attitudes toward the Third Republic, James wishing it nothing but well, Bædeker wistfully recalling the good old days of the Second Empire. Adoration of Louis Napoleon was no part of James' political baggage nor did he participate in Bædeker's obvious contempt for the new "national" government. Bædeker, clearly, is caught between a desire to make as much as possible of "the stupendous disasters and revolting crimes" of the recent revolutionaries and the necessity to portray Paris as a nice safe place to which the tourist may now return. From a literary standpoint, what is even more intriguing is that Bædeker's view of Paris is melodramatic while James' is the opposite. In *The American* James will pursue melodrama in his narrative and the opposite of melodrama in his setting. He will require for his setting a Paris more or less opposite to that of the guidebooks.

The preface of 1872 Galignani adopts the same generally conservative tone of horror, supplemented with a promise of special visual interest:

> As in happier times, the magnificent improvements effected during the late reign [guidebook writers are fond of "reigns"] were carefully chronicled in this volume [in its previous editions], so, after the recent political disasters, will the reader find recorded in its pages the places rendered memorable by military operations, bloody engagements or popular fury. The plates, executed by Mr. Outhwaite, which accompany this volume, are now doubly valuable, as showing the previous state of the edifices that have fallen a prey to the reckless incendiarism of the Commune.

And sure enough, facing p. 175 are two views of the Palais Royal. Better still, facing p. 127 are two views of the Palais des Tuileries,

the second (lower) of them with the caption, no doubt hastily revised: "(BURNT) PALACE OF THE TUILERIES (VIEW FROM
THE GARDEN). MAY 23$^D$ 1871." Was the picture of the Tuileries
Palace retained because so much money was invested in it that it
would be a shame to take it out even if no such palace now existed
or was it retained as a moral warning for prospective hotheads? (In
later editions, the Palais des Tuileries is no longer to be found.
Perhaps it finally became too embarrassing.) We should love to
know, and will never know, if James noticed this curious business of
representing in public a material object which once was but which is
now gone, so that what you see is the space it used to occupy and
what you think about may be quite imaginative. Representation of
objects (events, feelings, lives) destroyed or otherwise lost will figure
as a major element of *The Ambassadors.*

Meanwhile the Galignani prose: the opening paragraph of the 1872
edition shows again by sharp contrast the fundamentally democratic
(if not quite red-flag) assumptions of *The American,* its protagonist,
and its perpetrator. Newman at worst is a populist angel compared
to what the Tourist Reader was lapping up in the guidebooks (but
the guidebooks' Tourist Reader is not the same as the Tourist Reader
now in the course of construction by Henry James). Galignani:

> PARIS, although a great sufferer by the overwhelming events of
> 1870, and still more by the atrocious deeds of the Commune of
> 1871, has, in an incredibly short space of time, retrieved its losses
> and regained that ascendency in the world of literature, art, and
> fashion, which it may justly consider as its inalienable birthright,
> *however unsettled the country may still be in a political point of view.*
> (Emphasis added.)

And what may we now expect? Pretty much business at the same
old stand: "Princes and Ambassadors have again opened their man-
sions to the aristocracy, and English and American families flock in
as before, selecting this hitherto unrivalled capital for their temporary
or permanent abode."[7] Among the latter was our author. During
the composition of most of *The American* he was indeed considering
Paris as his permanent abode. But he can hardly be imagined as an
American family flocking in; nor was he received by Princes and

Ambassadors, only by Turgenev and Flaubert. He lived modestly at Rue de Luxembourg 29, near the Madeleine, a good inexpensive location for tourist-watching as well as for native Parisian ambience.

Keeping up with events, and bating no jot of retrospective and doomed conservatism, 1874 Bædeker in his preface continues to laud Louis Napoleon and to deplore the "disasters" of 1870–71. The phrase "since the declaration of the Republic" is dropped: it was never clear which Republic was meant. The unwholesome purlieus continue to have been swept away by the glorious Second Empire, whose grand "metamorphosis" of Paris is now further described as "from brick to marble." The "signal calamities" are now specified as "the Franco-Prussian war and the Communist rebellion." The unusual difficulties of the editor traipsing around the city are forgotten. The threat of "a protracted transitional state" is retained. The jeer about "national" purposes is dropped. The statement that "the intention of the present government is to restore everything as far as possible to its former condition" is rephrased in a more kindly style as "the present government has done its utmost to restore everything." The sixth paragraph is likewise abbreviated and toned down, "stupendous disasters" becoming "terrible disasters"—but the crimes of the Communists remain "revolting," surely no pun intended.[8]

At Rue de Luxembourg 29, Henry James was soon to concoct the moving of an ottoman as a token tossed in the direction of the memorable and violent changes of Paris induced by foreign war and native insurrection. The Paris of *The American* was not to be disturbed or disrupted by any such flamboyant behaviors or descriptions as were found in the guidebooks; *The American* is not a novel about war and revolution or about their aftermaths. Whether or not James expected or desired the Tourist Reader in 1876–77 or later to respond to the irony of pre-1870 Paris in its doomed complacency is another thing that we may never know; he could hardly keep awareness of subsequent events from his readership, try as he might to throw his narrative and setting backward into that past which can know no more changes. But if Newman is to be convicted of the irony of ignorance so must be the other personages of *The American,* along with millions of persons not personages of *The American,* including millions of French persons. The wonderful Bellegardes reveal no more political prescience than their despised American businessman-on-leave. Ignorant as they are, it is doubtful if the Bellegardes even know how their name is also the name of the last stop in France before the train gets into Geneva, but the Tourist Reader who consults the back pages of Bædeker may know it—and, turning the bygone informative pages, much, much more.

For the duration of *The American,* then, the temporality of its textual taking in, the Second Empire is still in place, securely and permanently so, for the simple reason that it *was not* and would not be again. It had become Never-Never Land with respect to time but not with respect to place, for in fact, Bædeker and Galignani not-withstanding, most of the monuments survived. The most salient fact of all about James' use of his 1868–69 setting is literary: it successfully excludes from his text any and all trace of melodrama attributable to setting. We may almost hear him saying to us: "There are two things going on here, quite different things, melodrama in the narrative and in the setting whatever it is you choose to call the antithesis of melodrama. *I* call it Paris. Please do not confuse the two things. Please do not neglect to notice that just as I am entirely responsible for conducting the melodrama so I am entirely responsi-ble for supplying the Paris which is to contain, as who should say, and counteract it. It is, after all, don't you see, *my* Paris." The narrative is thus melodramatic, the setting the reverse, call it realistic, and the two terms subsist in dialectic relation. It is a primary aspect of *The American,* often neglected, that the Paris represented in its text also exists outside the text and could care less what Henry James says about it, i.e., James' textualized Paris has for referent the real true-to-life actual city of Paris, but no such referent exists for Newman or any of the other fictive personages. This is of course true for any literary work "set" in a "real" place. What is unusual about *The American* is the degree to which it inserts as much space as possible into the disjunctive chasm between what is real and what is not.

Nothing, consequently, can be more bizarre than James' attempts, in the New York Edition preface, to gloss over this huge disjunction in terms of repeated claims to propriety, near cousin to necessity, in turn near cousin to "organic unity." It is all one, James makes out, how it all came back to him ("This resurrection then took place") at Paris, "where I was at the moment living," that much being true, and, most precisely, "in December 1875," somewhat miraculously, as will surprise no one, "with an immediate directness at which I now marvel," Paris personified offering "everything that was needed to make my conception concrete"; questions, however maddening, suddenly "gathered their answers in the cold shadow of the Arc de Triomphe." James fondly reimagines his setting, "the life of the splendid city," as if it were somehow mysteriously contained by, inside of, his narrative, "my particular cluster of circumstances," each situationally necessitating the other (narrative and setting), reciprocally, unitively, "playing up in it like a flashing fountain in a marble basin." Paris being, further, a stage and a medium, "Christopher Newman rose before me, on a perfect day of the divine Paris spring, in the great gilded Salon Carré of the Louvre," Anodyomene Herself an Urbanized Male. James keeps insisting on the "organic vastness of the city," "the great Paris harmony," "so huge an organism," all these things well enough in their way but irrelevant to his problem, as if the spirit of Paris were still in 1907 bewitching him— "my affront to verisimilitude" is one of his minor confessional concessional phrases, a better one being "The way things happen [in *The American*] is frankly not the way they are represented as having happened, in Paris, to my hero," the phrase between commas especially to be noted, and the best one of all concealing itself in James' final figuration of himself in relation to the conception of Christopher Newman as "clinging to my hero as to a tall, protective, good-natured elder brother in a rough place.★ But William James, still alive in 1907, could then no more than ever mitigate our incredulity over Valentin's duel and deathbed revelation, the attitudes of the reactionary Bellegardes both early and late, the unseemly conventualization of the diaphanous heroine, or the prolonged narrative recollections of Mrs. Bread. Over against all that stands Paris and realism, James' inscription of locale not unrelated to the travel sketches he had been writing and would continue to write, and not *altogether* unrelated to the non-narrative prose materials found in contemporary guide-books. Was the novel weak in plot and character? James would

---

★ The preface is cited from *French Writers*. James' prefaces have a way of throwing the reader off, not only his claim that *The American* is a romance when it is a melodrama, but also that *The Princess Casamassima* is about concealed depths when it is about flaunted surfaces; and, most misleadingly of all, in *The Wings of the Dove* preface, the allegation that "the poet essentially *can't* be concerned with the act of dying," a pretty sentiment, to be sure, but it steers us away from what happens to be *the* point of the novel as well as of *The Ambassadors* and perhaps even *The Portrait of a Lady*.

conceal the faults, he would more than make them up with solidity of ambience, the solid unchangeable ambience of 1868–69 Paris, "this serviceable city," "the most comfortable city in the world." Both remarks come from narrative authority, who should know. Paris was serviceable and comfortable mainly to a young novelist seeking common ground at once exotic and reliable with a readership eagerly seeking the same.

James works closely—perhaps not literally—with a Plan de Paris. The Tourist Reader with map spread out, or even with a notion of it in mind, would easily recognize the points of significant action (Louvre, Opéra, Notre Dame) and perhaps admire how nicely they are stationed at certain strategic well-known parts of the city. Once Newman in shock wanders as far as Auteuil but he soon returns to his senses and to our haunts by way of "the fantastic embankment known as the Trocadero" and in the very next sentence he proceeds to Mrs. Tristram's apartment *près de l'Etoile* and everyone knows where that is. Everyone also knows rather exactly how Newman proceeds when it is said that he "walked across the Seine, late in the summer afternoon, and made his way through those gray and silent streets of the Faubourg St. Germain," just as everyone knows how he will end on the Rue de l'Université, where predictably dwells in seclusion that cynosure of transatlantic longing Claire de Cintré. However *exotique,* Madame de Cintré lives within easy walking distance. Indeed, everyone lives within easy walking distance, the distance of the Tourist Reader. Related to the idea of a *centre,* the Parisian landmarks and the residences of the personages in *The American* form a lopsided polygon heavy to the Right Bank, for the sake of Americanism; virtually the same polygon continues to be used in subsequent Parisian fictions by James, most notably in *The Ambassadors.* What we fatally lack, in all James novels, are street numbers, a special loss in the case of the Bellegarde hôtel, the Rue de l'Université being so unusually, for Paris, long. Mrs. Tristram gives Newman Claire de Cintré's address, for how else shall he find his way, all alone, to the right house? But it is not given to the Tourist Reader, who might have been tempted, without invitation, to call.

Inevitably we find in *The American* superimposition of melodramatized characterization and behavior upon topographically and touristically plausible backgrounds—plausible in their own right, I mean, and indeed almost (one would think) inviolable in their extra-textual sanctity, but now in James' text serving as literary contrast to luridity rendered even more lurid by the place where it is said, in the wonderful English locution, "to take place." Perhaps the most revealing example of such contrast in all James "takes place" in chapter 24 of *The American,* at the Parc Monceau, "a very pretty piece of landscape-gardening," as James calls it, and within the confines of which the Tourist Readership is asked to imagine such theatrical passages as the following:

> The marquis gave three short raps on the ground with his stick. "I demand of you to step out of our path!" he hissed.

Upon which our spokesperson from the Western world, giving back as good as he gets, confronts the marquise:

> And he approached nearer to her, looking her straight in the eyes. "You killed your husband," he said, almost in a whisper.

The contrast between the spoken lines, with their accompanying physical gestures, and the presumed placidity of the public recreational space is grotesque, an apt miniaturized image of *The American* in its overall confrontation of generic tones.

At Château Fleurières, Newman is said to have "crossed the threshold of a room of superb proportions, which made him feel at first like a tourist with a guide-book and a cicerone awaiting a fee." So may the Tourist Reader of *The American* sometimes feel, trotted about Paris (but almost always within certain limits!) and from time to time conveniently whisked off to Poitiers, Switzerland, Belgium, Italy, San Francisco, New York, London. (The locales are only less globally far-flung than those of *Confidence,* published serially in 1879–80). *The American* is preponderantly a Parisian novel, however, with its central events neatly laid out on a centralized east-west axis from Notre Dame to Arc de Triomphe, taking the Louvre and the Opéra by the way. Other places are sketched in lightly: Mrs. Tristram runs into Claire de Cintré coming out of St. Sulpice, "she herself having journeyed to that distant quarter in quest of an obscure lace-mender"; M. Nioche recommends that Newman frequent the Théâtre

Français, "to cultivate refinement of diction," but James, who knew the Théâtre Français better than anything else in Paris except his own rooms, for one reason or another declines the suggestion (he will give it exhaustive treatment some years later in *The Tragic Muse*). The night before the opening of the novel Newman has "supped" at the Café Anglais—"someone had told him it was an experience not to be omitted." Someone may have been Galignani's 1872 guidebook, which has it as one of five "principal restaurants"; Bædeker supplies the address, Boulevard des Italiens 13 (S. side; "principally a restaurant, expensive"). M. Nioche's favorite neighborhood hangout, the Café de la Patrie, is "round the second corner to the left" from his lodgings in the Rue St. Roch. "Out of many hundreds" of cafés, says Bædeker, "a few of the best only need here be enumerated." Café de la Patrie is not among them. Neither is it enumerated in Galignani, which notes that the "number of cafés in 1870 was 4,730." If it ever existed, it must have been modest. And reasonably near, Rue St. Roch being about three blocks east of Rue de Luxembourg where dwelt our author in his modest expatriated frustrations and frissons.

Considerably up the economic scale, Christopher Newman first lives at the Grand Hotel, designated by Bædeker as one of the two largest hotels in Paris "and perhaps on the entire continent." The address of the hotel, if anyone cared, was Boulevard des Capucines 12. According to an ad in 1872 Galignani, the highest first-class room rate (including fires, lights, and meals) was 38F, with which price the Tourist Reader might compare the 10F Newman pays for his French lessons and the 3,000F the Nioches finally obtain for a bad copy of a painting plus varnish and frame. About six months later, Tom Tristram establishes Newman in rooms selected by himself on the Boulevard Haussmann (often spelled *boulevart* by the guidebooks and maps but not by Henry James). We do not know where along the Boulevard Haussmann the rooms are (were); it is, like the Rue de l'Université, a long street. We are free to imagine both Newman and the Bellegardes as far west or east as we like, so long as we keep them on opposite sides of the Seine. Newman's 1868–69 rooms, "gilded from floor to ceiling a foot thick" by a French not an American interior decorator (be it noted), may have been inspired by James' 1875 reaction to the new Opéra: "It is nothing but gold—

gold upon gold: it has been gilded till it is dark with gold. . . . If the world were ever reduced to the dominion of a single gorgeous potentate, the *foyer* would do very well for his throne room."⁹ On his first visit, Valentin de Bellegarde eyes the "great gilded parlour . . . from cornice to carpet"; and once, from these "theatrical-looking rooms on one of the new boulevards," Newman is by us glimpsed looking at "the reflected sunset fading from the ornate house-tops on the opposite side of the Boulevard," which might be a clue to his more exact location if only the Boulevard Haussmann had more of a north-south inclination than in fact it ever did.

When not at home in the family hôtel, Valentin lives "in the basement of an old house in the Rue d'Anjou St. Honoré," a nice short mainly north–south street extending from Boulevard Haussmann to the Rue du Faubourg St. Honoré and crossing the Boulevard Malesherbes, subsequently to be celebrated in song and story for the wondrous or mystic troisième there occupied and enjoyed by Chadwick Newsome and his motley associates. Valentin may or may not live right around the corner from Christopher Newman; we are not told. Valentin's rooms are at any rate full of collectibles (of a more masculine order than Maria Gostrey's) suitable to the "penniless patrician." The rooms themselves are damp, gloomy, cluttered, and, in a word, "picturesque." Newman naturally thinks it a shame that a man who might stroll about between New York and San Francisco "should think it a large life to revolve in varnished boots between the Rue d'Anjou and the Rue de l'Université, taking the Boulevard des Italiens by the way" but that locale happens to be the fundamental topographic extent of the novel within which he too revolves.

As *The American*'s representatives of the American Colony in Paris, the Tristrams obligingly live in an apartment with balcony which "enabled you [Newman, the Tourist Reader] to look up the broad street [the Avenue d'Iéna] and see the Arch of Triumph [here given as English] vaguely massing its heroic sculptures in the summer starlight," a picturesque view, surely, and for once a reasonably definite location: the Tristrams, we may rather easily ascertain, live along the northern stretch of the avenue before it curves too far to the westward at some point and loses that straight view. Otherwise, the Tristram apartment is the westernmost point of the polygonic *centre* (topographic and literary) for *The American;* the northernmost point (northwesternmost) is the Parc Monceau; the southernmost point (but outside the basic polygon) is Rue d'Enfer, Claire de Cintré's final incarcerating convent, clearly (on the 1872 Galignani map) the Couvent de la Visitation, a name James must have relished; but in the Galignani text it is identified as Couvent des Dames Carmélites (No. 25, rue d'Enfer), "where Mlle. de la Vallière, the beautiful mistress of Louis XIV., took the veil in 1675, as *Sœur Louise de la Miséricorde,* and was soon joined by Madame de Montespan,"[10] romantic fatalities, one thinks, compared to James' abrupt disposal of Claire de Cintré as Sister Veronica. The easternmost point is Notre Dame on the Ile de la Cité.

In his *Tribune* letters James outlined the "classic region" of American tourism as "about a square mile in extent, which is bounded on the south by the Rue de Rivoli and on the north by the Rue Scribe, and of which the most sacred spot is the corner of the Boulevard des Capucines, which basks in the smile of the Grand Hotel."[11] For the fictivized Paris of *The American* James furnishes the Tourist Reader a domain more spacious and more various than that, but not one likely to strain the touristic experience or imagination. It is after all one prime purpose of *The American* to give that fellow national, along with a frothy tale of lost love, a vicarious sojourn in Paris without the trouble or expense of actual locomotion.

The Bellegarde hôtel (even for lexical and circumflexed romanticism) is of course the pièce de résistance, precisely the kind of private residence the American abroad (tourist, expatriate, Tourist Reader) most desires to penetrate, but *hélas!* of all *The American*'s places it is predictably the most tenebrous in tone and the most obscure in semantics. It is the sort of place where exchanges occur which are impossible to interpret, a collection depôt for unanswered and perhaps unanswerable questions, such as these (all provoked by a couple of pages in chapter 5): (1) what is the significance of the date 1627 in relief on the Bellegarde paneling (something to do with the family past; important; perhaps vaguely Huguenot)? (2) why does the conversation shift from architecture to "theology"? (3) why does Newman then ask Claire de Cintré if she is a Roman Catholic (he knows perfectly well that she is)? (4) why does Valentin offer to show Newman the house, why does Newman regard the offer as French impudence, and why does Valentin's sister prevent the tour? Valentin calls his proposal a "scheme," Newman says he doesn't understand (neither do we), Valentin replies that "Perhaps some day I shall have a chance to explain it," but text never does, and Claire de Cintré terminates the conversation by saying "Be quiet, and ring for the tea." As often in fictions of James, much is withheld; here, perhaps, more annoyingly than usual (or is the lapse to be blamed on the *impudeur* of our touristical curiosity?). Details of the interior are also selective. Old Madame's salon is old, faded, familial, dark. It strikes Newman (he of the gilt rooms) as "rather sad and shabby." The hôtel remains as vague as the object of desire it encloses, that "extraordinarily graceful and delicate, and at the same time impressive woman, who lived in a large gray house on the left bank of the Seine." It is the fable itself which is vague and which sheds a vague light on all it touches, including prose style, here reveling in generalized adjectives. But on the occasion of the Bellegardes' ball the old house "looked strangely brilliant" and the uninvited excluded populace gawks. Flaring torches and crimson carpet are specified. Second Empire politics are also supplied in small dosage: "There were no uniforms, as Madame de Bellegarde's door was inexorably closed against the myrmidons of the upstart power which then [1869] ruled the fortunes of France," and against their lady friends as well, one surmises from the delicate language of that same company's being "not graced by any very frequent suggestions of harmonious beauty." At the ball Mrs. Tristram kindly quotes to Valentin two choice lines from Keats' "Belle Dame Sans Merci," a nice French title to a nice English poem. And in the course of *The American* the crisscrossed plots of divestiture painfully release Valentin and Newman from the two women they think they want, as many years later in *The Ambassadors* Chad Newsome and Lambert Strether will be relieved (or deprivated, as the reader chooses) of two more women.

And then there is death–in–life! And with what furious ambivalence! For the Tourist Novel no habitation so wonderfully excludes the visitor as a good old–fashioned continental Roman Catholic convent *(for women)* and especially in the degree that the Tourist Readership may be conceived as rather unCatholic. Assuming *on the other hand* a decent sort of cosmopolitan tolerance in that same Tourist Readership, the kindly Tourist Fabulator will gladly make liberal use of an educational kind of convent as an indispensable early meeting ground for out-of-country and in-country female personages whose acquaintance from girlhood, otherwise impossible to explain, is so desirable for the elaboration of narrative action. Examples run from "Madame de Mauves" in 1874 to *The Golden Bowl* in 1904. In *The American* Mrs. Tristram is thus given to know Claire de Cintré, not otherwise of her *monde*. So regarded, the convent is the key that opens European "society" to the eager outsider, and it is therefore, almost inevitably and invariably, in the Jamesian text, "good," good in the sense of useful or even necessary, an aspect of fable, an entry-point past real-life exclusion.

But when convent suddenly turns 180° around and locks *up* instead of *un*locking, then woe betide! Tone turns unremittingly dark, bleak, melodramatically foreboding, and more than all else exasperated. Pansy Osmond in Rome, Claire de Cintré in Paris: nothing, the Tourist Novel virtually shrieks at us, can be so wicked as to remove from the world, hiding it for even a day, if not indeed forever, that which the Tourist Novel would most particularly be at and avail itself of. Whether on the Avenue de Messine or the Rue d'Enfer, Claire de Cintré's convent represents communicational blockage and representational disaster. What we are given to see are *walls* (as in James' 30 March 1877 letter to Howells about what separates Newman and Claire de Cintré).* What we are given to hear are *wails,* even though to the analytic mind the sounds in question reduce to the probability of intoned Latin mass and Gregorian chant. What turns up on the page "from behind the inexorable grating" is a spate of language most unpleasant: "a strange, lugubrious chant . . . more of a wail and a dirge . . . the strangeness of the sound . . . the tuneless harmony . . . mechanical and monotonous . . . dismal repetitions and despairing cadences. It was hideous, it was horrible . . . this confused, impersonal wail . . . the dreary strain," and so forth, not one word of the spate in French. Among other things, the chant of the Carmelite nuns is Henry James' failed year at making a permanent home for himself in Paris, a year during

---

*Leon Edel, ed., *Henry James Letters* (Cambridge: Harvard University Press, 1974–84), 2:105. "It was cruelly hard for poor N. to lose, certainly: but *que diable allait-il faire dans cette galère?* We are each the product of circumstances and there are tall stone walls which fatally divide us. I have written my story from Newman's side of the wall, and I understand so well how Mme de Cintré couldn't really scramble over from *her* side!"

which he was neither American nor French but a little of each, a year in which he mostly spoke French to people—to concierge, waiter, passersby, but also to Turgenev, Flaubert—while writing a novel mainly in English about a representative man going down to defeat in strikingly similar circumstances (waiving a desire to marry into a French family). Significantly, in the Rue d'Enfer, where Newman finally gives over his quest, he "found himself in a part of Paris which he little knew—a region of convents and prisons"—but of the latter, I find only one on the maps of the day—far, indeed, from the well-known purlieus of the Café Anglais. Significantly, in Notre Dame, Newman's "last thought" is said to be unspoken: "If he had spoken it aloud he would have said . . ."

## 2. *Learning French*

Now equipped with a somewhat recuperated and renovative sense of that particular place at that particular time as together they serve for the context of a quite extraordinary performance in improbability (the adventures of Christopher Newman in a world he never made), we arrive, as we might have known we would, at the consideration of language, especially to confront the evident fact that not all the world's people speak our language. It is not a change of emphasis but an extension of emphasis, however, for topography and language are equally and relatedly aspects of what is called, in literary discussion, setting. In the case of *The American,* and of the works which follow, each of these two aspects of setting is actual, material, extra-textual, and consequently verifiable. What they are disjunct from, and in counterpoint with, is the narrative of *The American,* the ado got up by a fictional text about the goings-on among Christopher Newman and *les autres,* all of these personages imaginary, all of their actions and connections decidedly flaunting themselves against every conceivable likelihood, yet all of them alleged to have transpired in a place quite real on the map, during a historical epoch susceptible of numeration, 1868–69, which is both real and unreal, in the sense that the Second Empire represented in *The American* is backdated from a time when it clearly does not exist to a time when it did.

Inescapably, most of the inhabitants, especially those most at home in the serviceable the comfortable city speak French rather than the (Americanized) English of the author. French therefore constitutes a second source of vraisemblance, of extra-authorial intertextual distancing from the melodramatic, the "romantic" (as James would have it, in his preface), the theatrical, the positively stage-toned narrative (personages-in-their-behaviors) which is so contained and counteracted. But as fictional creations of internationally bent bilingually-equipped Henry James, certain inhabitants of Paris are the beneficiaries of special arrangements. They speak English and French about equally well, their dual proficiency duly explained and accounted for, or, if they do not, then the monolingual limitation is in the opposite direction made much of. With respect to languages, *The American* is more like "Madame de Mauves" (1874) than *Roderick Hudson* (1875) for reasons having little or nothing to do with the basic fables of these works, and not a whole lot to do with Henry James, either, but a great deal to do with the relation of the Tourist Reader to "foreign languages." There had been a lot of French, and some Italian, but not an overplus, in *Roderick Hudson,* the French language (even unto Rome) being the mark of verbal sophistication and international wit, with very little additional justification. Only one brief passage suggests any linguistic complication; it happens to concern Italian (otherwise the fact of people speaking Italian is blithely ignored): "Rowland assented, ungrudgingly fumbled for the Italian correlative of the adage 'Better late than never,' begged him to be seated, and offered him a cigar."[12] From the beginning of his career to the end, James counts on his audience either knowing French or on their being decently embarrassed (too embarrassed to admit it or to complain) if they do not; but Italian tends to be limited to such obvious matters as *mia cara* and *che vuole?* (the latter is perhaps the best-loved Italian-ism in the James œuvre, sometimes given as English, sometimes even in the form of its French equivalent). Language is not a major matter in *Roderick Hudson.* The issue of Italian is elided, the issue of French not pressed.

In *The American* the question of national language difference is central, thematized, and well-nigh overwhelming. I have already given, at some length, one very good reason, perhaps the best reason of all, why this should be so: the comparatively young author was desperately in want of something powerfully actual to balance out, or to draw attention away from, certain high (but not necessarily inexpressive) conspicuities of unlikelihood in the motivation and performance of his major personages. There are other good reasons; James asks, and receives, much from them. Newman's initial lack of French is the opening note in a comedy of errors (comedy of manners and morals both) featuring that disjoined miscommunication which is always at least potentially at the heart of the international theme; people who decline to stay home where they belong are conceived as taking chances of intentionally going awry—not only Christopher Newman but notably Isabel Archer, Lambert Strether, Milly Theale, among the Americans. At the same time, James must contrive for the Bellegardes to speak English, for how else shall Newman converse with them (insert himself into their social discourse) in the early stages of acquaintance; but he will also allow them to speak English with certain differences, which often include a crossing of the linguistic divide. "I know your secret," says young Madame de Bellegarde to Newman, "in her bad but charming English"—the point of charm being one, of many, for which we are obliged to take the author's word—"you need make no mystery of it. You wish to marry my sister-in-law. *C'est un beau choix.* A man like you ought to marry a tall thin woman. You must know that I have spoken in your favour; you owe me a famous taper!' "—and thanks to William T. Stafford's note we know that in that final sentence "Urbain's wife translates the French idiom *devoir une fière chandelle* literally—'to owe a proud candle'; that is, to owe a debt of gratitude."[13]

Another very good reason is that the French language, even more than the famous landmarks and spaces of Paris, is the best possible way for James to represent Newman unavoidably and of course by his own determined volition alienated from his earlier existence. His inability to speak and to understand French (written *or* spoken, the latter being much the most important) surely stands behind such remarks as "I feel as simple as a little child" and, in narrative voice, "The complex Parisian world about him seemed a very simple affair." It is not Newman's inherent simple-mindedness that is in question here, or even his national origins, except as the latter are coterminous with his monolingual limitation. It is because the American misses so much that Paris seems simple; it is because of his not having French that he misses it.

One last reason for James' emphasis on French in *The American* is that partial acquisition of it through persistent if not exactly heroic effort witnesses a growing sophistication in our representative national protagonist (didactically recommended, no doubt) as well as his perpetual willingness to meet other people more than halfway, his notorious and perpetually referenced "good nature." It is Newman alone who in the beginning knows almost no French. It is Newman alone who in the course of the novel takes lessons in a foreign language, meanwhile picking up what he can. It is Newman alone who makes modest headway. "I am not cultivated, I am not even educated," Newman needlessly and perhaps even wrongly declares. "I know nothing about history, or art, or foreign tongues. . . . But I am not a fool, either, and I shall undertake to know something about Europe by the time I have done with it." Among other things, what he shall know is a bit of French; and perhaps he shall also know that a bit of French is not sufficient for a permanent residence in France. Like Lambert Strether, Newman goes home of his own free will, in contradistinction from such badly behaved persons as Serena Merle and Charlotte Stant who must be *sent back* to the fate that is worse than death. Linguistically and otherwise, Newman is a progressive characterization, albeit in very modest terms, and perhaps that is why as the text of *The American* progresses in parallel with him the problems of the French language decrease. And yet, in the latter third of the novel, amid the wildest whirls of melodramatic posture and utterance, we may well imagine the French language still going on, even when what is quoted to the eye, and ideally into the ear, of the Tourist Reader, is English. Well trained by a close reading of the earlier pages, the Tourist Reader will make allowances for what is after all only a literary convention, namely the inscription of a fictional text almost entirely in a single language. From time to time, the Tourist Reader may even suppose that he or she is reading a novel originally written in French, translated into English, yet curiously double-tracked, perpetually reverting to the language of choice (French) in little tags and mannerisms.

Tourist Reader then, or Tourist Reader now, may well disagree about the possible over-interpretation of Oscar Cargill's source-tracing *The American* to Alexander Dumas, *fils, L'Etrangère*.[14] Dumas or not, semantic ambiguities concerning such words as "stranger" and "foreign," in two languages, were bound to play a major role in the international multilingual work of art. James must have noticed how Galignani guidebooks regularly, and without irony, refer to the tourist as the "stranger." In the Bædeker introductions, he might have read, as might anyone else, adjuration on the subject of getting up your language. In 1874 Bædeker, the opening sentence of the first paragraph is quite striking:

> LANGUAGE. For those who wish to derive instruction as well as pleasure from a visit to Paris, the most attractive treasury of art and industry in the world, some acquaintance with French is indispensable.

We might also notice the phrase "art and industry" as it applies to the thematics of *The American*. Accustomed as we are to think of Paris as a "treasury" of art only, we have quite forgotten that it was once regarded as the "treasury" of industry as well. There is much to be thought about in the way James has Newman, on vacation from business, go to Paris for art, he himself unwittingly bearing, from the United States, industry along with him (as if to say Paris has no monopoly of *that*), only to find that Paris (the Bellegardes) does not want even the proceeds of his "industry," having plenty of its own.

In more general terms, James would have been well pleased by the fact that by definition a "foreign" language is any language that happens not to be yours, a purely relativistic notion by most persons absolutistically held. But the best games of all are those involving *strange, foreign,* and *étranger,* as their denotations and innuendoes wobble back and forth from one language to another. "Have you any objections to a foreigner?" Mrs. Tristram asks Newman, meaning a French woman as a wife. "As a foreigner, no," Newman replies, syntax rendering it impossible to know if he means himself or a possible mate; "other things being equal," he continues, just as ambiguously, "I should prefer one of my own countrywomen. We should speak the same language, and that would be a comfort." Now what we don't know is whether "speak the same language" is to be understood literally (English, Americanized English) or figuratively (agree on basic modes of thought, metaphorized as linguistically ascertainable). It is then that Mrs. Tristram, ever-useful spokes-person for a manipulating author, providentially explains how Claire de Cintré is at once "foreign" (that is to say, mainly French in social and cultural tone) and, for a miracle, English-speaking: "she speaks English as well as you or I—or rather much better," not, presumably, because of her genius for talk but because for her English is a second language, learned by lesson, including grammar, and the like. Novelistically, what counts is the mixed linguistic proficiency, the same as is later undertaken for Madame de Vionnet in her dealings with Strether, whose adequacies or inadequacies in French are not so closely looked into (but once or twice made mild fun of).

*The American* is naturally fond of bilingual wordplay concerning *foreign-strange-étranger*. To Newman, who has been in Paris three days, Tom Tristram in the Louvre seems "a stranger to the gallery," a modest little lexical twisting which would go unnoticed were the word less loaded throughout the text. To M. Nioche, Newman is a "free-handed stranger," i.e., *un étranger,* i.e., a foreigner who by virtue of that condition is somewhat strange, peculiar. The joke depends on the way *étranger* connotes more peculiarity to an Anglophone than to a French person (who would probably say *bizarre.)* What is most useful of all, up to a point, is of course miscomprehension and even incomprehensibility, as when young Madame de Bellegarde idly remarks ("in a low voice, in French"): "So Claire receives strangers, like that?" and we shall never be sure if she means foreigners, e.g., Americans, or peculiar people (their Americanism a possible cause), or just persons hitherto unreceived at the Bellegarde hôtel. We may as we like think all three things and as many more as ingenuity can invent.

As for verisimilitude, of which *The American* is always in such crying need, and of which the supply is more or less equal to the need, French words and phrases abound, most of them ridiculously easy, many of them cognates, or words otherwise shared by English and French, or words in process of passage from one language into the other. Normally, in *The American* and throughout James, words which are given, and which the Tourist Reader is to take, as French are in italics, but that rule does not apply to the names of streets, buildings, places, or to common forms of address, such as monsieur and marquise. Nor is consistency perfect. At Fleurières a room is first given as a *salle* in French and then later the selfsame room is given as a salle in English. The word list which follows is limited to words and phrases not cited elsewhere in this chapter, and of course it may be easily skipped by those with small appetite for such curios: connoisseur (given as English), portemonnaie (given as English), *très-supérieure, artiste, Pas de raisons!, esprit, Hélas, oui, homme de monde, commerçant, caprice de prince, cocottes, Voilà ce qui s'appelle parler!, sang-froid* (given as French), *finesse* (given as French), sou (given as English), *Voyons!, café, demitasse, charcutière, franche coquette, coup de tête, quartier, dame de compagnie, Quelle folie!, comme il faut, fiancée* (given as French), *Je le veux bien!* ("said Newman, proving that he had learned more French than he admitted"; and not long after he manages " '*L'appétit vient en mangeant,*' says the French proverb," in his letter to Babcock, conceivably a phrase picked up in restaurants), *maîtres de cafés, dilettante* (given as French), *malaise* (given as French), *morgue, roturière, de notre bord, grande dame, Parbleu!, petite noblesse, improbable* (given as French), *Touchez-là, naïf* (given as French), *beaucoup de cachet, Monsieur mon frère* ("he looked much like an Englishman"); *En voilà, de nouveau; ennuis* (given as French), *valet de place,* rendezvous (given as English), the Corps Législatif (not in italics but with accent mark), *talon rouge, vielle roche, Ce que c'est que la gloire!, les gens forts, portière, naïveté* (given as French), salon (given as English), *Arrivez donc, fête champêtre; " 'Je suis triste,*' said Valetin . . . 'You are sad, eh?' " says Newman; *en somme, mots, papier-mâché, chère belle,* toilet (given as English but with the French meaning), *disponible, beaux noms, C'est positif, légende, bizarre* (given as French), *rez-de-chaussée, coiffure* (given as French), *drôle, raffiné, hôtel, enceinte* (of Paris) curé (not in italics but with accent mark), *commode, procès-verbal, cabinet de toilette, bonne, Savoir-vivre,* sabots (given as English), *que diable!, va!, Voilà, petit bourg,* calèche (not in italics but with the accent mark), Sœur Catherine, *Le misérable!,* Mamselle (given as English), *femme de chambre, le cœur tendre, Le reste vous regarde, partie, mêlée, il en resterait quelque chose, charmante, fadaises.* And such others, probably of the same sort, as I may have missed, although I have cast the net more than once. Most of these words and phrases appear in James' text without translation or comment, and they require none (except in Norton Critical Editions and other American college texts designed for the unFrench young). They are the linguistic constituent of local

47

color, the written but representationally voiced complement of referential topography, the whole designed to persuade us that we are
reading about, or are even "in," a very real and particular place
where our author may be presumed to know exactly what he is
doing, even if he evidently does not. He is most persuasive with
respect to languages and sites, least so with respect to what people
do with them there, i.e., narrative improbability, melodrama.

In comparison with vraisemblance, difficulties of communication
are always at least potentially thematic rather than merely environ-
mental. Or they can be both, as when M. Nioche inquires of Newman at the Café de la Patrie, "Will you do us the honour to *seat?*" Is
the word *seat* in italics for emphasis or because it is "French," or
anyway "not English?" He is said to inquire "timorously, and with
a double foreignness of accent." Among other things, we are probably to suspect mispronunciation. So in Switzerland when Valentin's
second says Newman's name (in French, of course) we are surely
expected to hear the name unusually stressed (for an English-lan-
guage name) on the final syllable. When Newman's French servant
shows in Mrs. Bread, he ceremoniously announces "Madame Brett"
while Newman continues to lounge in one of his fauteuils (given as
English). The following conversation, slightly obscure—with the
best will in the world it is difficult to keep shifting languages when
in point of fact the entire passage is printed in English—is doubtless
designed to illustrate Newman's progress in French (it comes in the
tenth chapter of twenty-six); young Madame de Bellegarde speaks
first:

> "What were you calling me just now, madame?"
> "I called you a gad-about," said the old lady. "But I might call
> you something else, too."
> "A gad-about? What an ugly word! What does it mean?"
> "A very beautiful person," Newman ventured to say, seeing
> that it was in French.
> "That is a pretty compliment but a bad translation," said the
> young marquise.

"Seeing that it was in French" appears to define the alleged language
of discourse except that the word *it* has no antecedent. The best

passages of bilingual dubiety are clearer than that, often functioning as occasions for the display of international wit on the part of the protagonist and the author alike. It is Henri-Urbain (parody-name of the author) de Bellegarde who speaks with his usual supercilious insipidity:

> "You are in—a—as we say, *dans les affaires.*"*
>
> "In business, you mean? Oh no, I have thrown business over-board for the present. I am 'loafing,' as *we* say. My time is quite my own."
>
> "Ah, you are taking a holiday," rejoined M. de Bellegarde.
> " 'Loafing.' Yes, I have heard that expression."
>
> "Mr. Newman is American," said Madame de Bellegarde.
>
> "My brother is a great ethnologist," said Valentin.

Maybe he means etymologist. Maybe not.

If *The American* had a subtitle it might be *Learning French*. The title and the subtitle would be interchangeable, both of them in reference to Christopher Newman. His first reported word in the novel, not altogether ridiculous or satiric but highly probable to the situation, is *combien*. The word is accompanied by authorial comment and novel-istic business, it is "the single word which constituted the strength of his French vocabulary," strength not being equivalent to entirety, and it is uttered "holding up one finger in a manner which appeared to him to illuminate his meaning. *'Combien?'* he abruptly demanded." It is Mademoiselle Nioche of whom he demands, who in turn knows no English, and so the conversation proceeds bilingually in such a manner as thoroughly to recommend itself to the memories or imag-inations of the Tourist Reader past or to come:

> "How much?" said our friend, in English. *"Combien?"*
>
> "Monsieur wishes to buy it?" asked the young lady, in French.
>
> "Very pretty, *splendide*. [Newman suddenly finds himself with a second word of French.] *Combien?"* repeated the American.

---

*And as Gilbert Osmond says to Casper Goodwood, "Am I assuming too much when I say that I think I have understood from you that your occupations have been—a—commercial?" *Henry James Novels 1881–86* (New York: The Library of America, 1985), p. 711. Perhaps Osmond's use of pronouns needs more critical attention, his character less.

> "It pleases monsieur, my little picture? It's a very beautiful subject," said the young lady. [All this in French, of course.]
> "The Madonna, yes; I am not a Catholic, but I want to buy it. *Combien?* Write it here."*

Tourist Reader is pleased that Newman is so good a guesser, but Tourist Reader must also know that "The young lady seemed as good a guesser as himself," i.e., Newman. Frustration and attempted remedy is the same on both sides: "Don't you understand a little English?" (Newman); "She fixed him with her conscious, perceptive eye, and asked if he spoke no French." In addition to what I have quoted, Newman manages to get out *"pas insulté," "Pas beaucoup," "Comprenez?"*, and *"beaucoup, beaucoup,"* while she offers in return nothing more formidable than *"Donnez!," "biscuit,"* and *"Bien sûr!"* They are both relieved by the arrival of M. Nioche, who translates back and forth between them for the rest of the scene, thus creating a situation where nearly every remark is an aside, as in the theater. Yet the upshot of comic theatricality is a return to realism, the young lady arranging for her father to give Newman French lessons, even while her own lack of English continues on display:

> "How much French can I learn in a month?"
> "What does he say?" asked Mademoiselle Noémie.
> M. Nioche explained.
> "He will speak like an angel!" said his daughter.

If neither instructor or pupil is unusually brilliant, at least the latter is amenable. " 'Oh yes, I should like to learn French,' Newman went on, with democratic confidingness. 'Hang me if I should ever have thought of it! I took for granted it was impossible. But if you learned my language, why shouldn't I learn yours?' " The point about Americans is at least double: linguistic limitation together with inappropriate humility (yet also a willingness to change).

Informally and sporadically, Newman's French lessons go on; he

---

*As happens with many passages of *The American*, obscurity abounds. I do not hear anything Mademoiselle says in French that should cause Newman suddenly to announce that he is not a Catholic, any more that I know why he asks Claire de Cintré if she is (of course she is) and Mrs. Bread the same (of course she is not), any more than I know why in the New York Edition Newman's remark "I am not a Catholic" was changed to "I'm not a real Catholic." Maybe he is a Tourist Catholic.

acquires the rest of his French in the usual pragmatic way (haphazard and osmotic). "Listening to your English," he says to M. Nioche, "is almost a lesson in French." Several times he is shown making a valiant effort:

> "Monsieur offers me my coffee, also?" cried M. Nioche. "Truly, my *beaux jours* are coming back."
> "Come," said Newman [not directly responding, so that we do not know if he has understood *beaux jours;* my guess is that he does, but, as happens all too often with the text of *The American,* most guesses are no better than most others], "let us begin. The coffee is almighty hot. How do you say that in French?"

We are not enlightened.

Another day, back in the Louvre, now with Valentin in tow, Newman attempts response to Mademoiselle Noémie's question, surely in French (unlike Newman, she does not appear to be learning a foreign language as part of her career), "Tell me something about your travels." Newman lists some places and then they converse as follows:

> ". . . the regular round. How do you say that in French—the regular round?" Newman asked of Valentin.
> Mademoiselle Nioche fixed her eyes an instant on Bellegarde, and then with a little smile: "I don't understand, monsieur," she said, "when he says so much at once.* Would you be so good as to translate?"
> "I would rather talk to you out of my own head," Valentin declared.
> "No," said Newman gravely, still in his bad French . . .

By chapter 15, Newman is said to be reading the *Figaro,* as all James (male) protagonists tend to do, even though James' private opinion

---

*The comma between *understand* and *monsieur* is an obvious error, corrected in the early American and the later New York Editions. Earlier in the same scene (Tuttleton edition) we find " 'I came here on purpose to see you,' said Newman in his bad French." In the New York Edition this is changed to " 'I came here on purpose to see you—*seulement vous,* expray, expray,' Newman said in his fairest, squarest, distinctest French," *expray* being of course *exprès.* It is possible that the adjectives describing Newman's French are sarcastic. Moreover, "expray, expray" is out of italics, as if it were English or at least not French.

of the paper was low: "Either in good humor or in bad it is, to my sense, a most detestable sheet."[15] When at the Bellegardes' ball he repeatedly says "Happy to make your acquaintance, sir," we are surely to suppose—that is, we are to *hear*—the conventional French phrase. In the deathbed scene, Valentin says to him, in French, but given as English (a perpetual trick of bilingual style in *The American* and elsewhere): "You are not alone. I want to speak with you alone," which is not much of a linguistic challenge but at least Newman understands it, as he probably also understands that Valentin speaks in French because his message to Newman must also be understood by the curé and the doctor, who know no English, and that his waning strength advises him not to say it twice.

It is that kind of small, subtle touch that largely accounts for the realism which I spoke of as constituting about half the effect—the better half—of *The American*. Realistically, too (not "just" thematically or psychoanalytically), Newman is relieved when it is all over. In London "he went to the theatre and found a surprising charm in listening to dialogue the finest points of which came within the range of his comprehension"; later, for the special polemic purposes of *The Tragic Muse,* James will decide to do without that charm. Also in London he catches the voice of Noémie at a distance, "a few words uttered in that bright Parisian idiom from which his ears had begun to alienate themselves," as in Paris his ears (and all that the ears lead to) had begun to alienate themselves from the bright idioms of San Francisco and New York. She says to him, *"Tiens,* how we keep meeting!" but there is no *Tiens* about it, James is nearing his end and verbally stitching his fabric back to that opening *"Combien?"* in the Louvre. Also, it is not only "people" (personages) who keep meeting but languages; James has now removed French and English to English soil but the difference of languages is unchanged. And even though it is only in reference to Franco-American gossip, it is "pleasant"—*agréable, aimable,* another word game of *The American,* presumably related to Newman's "remarkable good nature!" as Mrs. Tristram says in her contribution to clôture—to observe that the last French word of the novel's text is *résumé*.

In order to achieve such effects, our international novelist had to be both meticulous and practical about who speaks what. As we have seen, the Tristrams and the Bellegardes are virtually perfect bilingualists, with the difference that the Tristrams' second language is learned and the Bellegardes' is (in a manner of speaking) inherited. M. Nioche speaks a kind of bastardized French English, which James disdains to represent. Mademoiselle Nioche appears to speak French only and is thus the only significant Francophone among the dramatis personae. Mrs. Bread, who thanks God she is not a Frenchwoman and is more British than ever after forty years in Paris, is the most complex character of all, linguistically considered. She *speaks* both English and French; she can *read* English only; she can *write* neither tongue. One might say that her linguistic complication exceeds her novelistic use, except for one instance when her inability to read French obliges Newman to promise that he will translate for her the accusatory note of old M. de Bellegarde (which "consumes" itself in the last sentence of the text, thus establishing itself as coterminous with if not exactly tantamount to *The American;* it is naturally signed "Henry-Urbain"). The Tourist Reader may judge it a suitable reward for Newman's French lessons and overall improvement. The note is of course written in French but cited in the text as English, with no further word about translation, a kind of sleight-of-hand available to the author in the late stages of *The American* as his own reward for linguistic preparation in the earlier parts.

Small mistakes or even differences in language make for ongoing bilingual comedy of a modest nature, as when Valentin tells Newman he thinks his sister is "visible," a usage perfectly acceptable in French but not in English. Many pages later we are informed how Frenchified Newman has become when we hear him ask Mrs. Bread "She is in the house? She is visible?" When Noémie says to Newman presumably in French but rendered by James in (very bad) English, "we will pass the review" we are doubtless to know that what she "really" said was *passer la revue.* "You speak French to-day like a charm," she tells him, which can't be quite true, so that we wonder what she is up to. Still, it is notable that Newman has learned her language and she has not learned his, which is reasonable enough, considering where they (we) are: language in *The American,* let us remind ourselves once more, is not only a people and a culture and a view of the world but it is a function of place, and the place is Paris, France. Perhaps because of the old joke about all good Americans going to Paris when they die, we tend to slide over the irony involved in the disjunction of James' title and James' setting. If the novel were written by anyone else, and called *The Frenchman,* and if it "took place" in, say, Philadelphia, we might be more perceptive. On other occasions James indicates French not by bad English but by odd English. " 'You should have referred Claire to her mother, my brother,' said M. de Bellegarde, in French. 'This is very strange.' " Of course, it is strange (one more joke on *étranger),* especially the adjectival pronouns, which are not quite as they are with us (therefore *bizarre).* The texture of discourse throughout *The American* is strange and yet it is in the strangeness that the realism resides. *The American* is eminently true to life at least on the conversational side, as remembered or imagined, by the Anglophone in relation with France, the Tourist Reader momentarily lost in a Dream of Otherness (those places, that talk). *The American* is the work of a young novelist still weak on his pins in such areas as fable and characterization, but an old hand at setting. As recently as 1875 he had published a travel book entitled *Transatlantic Sketches.* The cleverness of the title may have escaped us: we all know where the Atlantic is but from which side of it are we to understand the prefix *trans-?*

Numerous scintillant scenes, mainly comic, turn on the question of languages, and I have glanced at several of these. Another is the conversation at the Café de la Patrie where M. Nioche invites Newman to *"seat."* Mademoiselle Nioche is also present, so we presume the entire scene to "take place" in French even though it is "given as English," as if it were a translation, but of course no such term is ever used: rather, we are asked to delude ourselves into thinking we read French (a wonderful, exotic, romantic language) instead of English (a familiar, pedestrian, boring language). The English text is spruced up to a sort of "French tone" by the insertion of French words and English phrases which sound "strange" (and must therefore be "foreign," thus French): monsieur, Garçon (both given as English), *aplomb* (given as French), *Quelle horreur!,* little father (twice), *dot, galant, Au revoir.* As usual there is little here to disturb the equanimity of the rankest amateur in French. Wherever Noémie goes, this young lady who knows only French, the French language pours, even if it is not she who speaks all of it—in her monolingual ignorance, as who should say, French is attracted to her. At the opera, we find "the small boxes which in France are called, not inaptly, 'bathing-tubs,' " the same as *baignoires,* and *coiffure* (given as French) and *foyer* (given as French) and *au sérieux, Vous parlex d'or, feuilleton,* the *Figaro, drôle, contrat, raffiné, naïveté,* entr'acte (given as English); *Mon Dieu, oui; ouvreuse, C'est ça qui pose une femme!, galant, Que voulez-vous (che vuole* in French form). Again the Anglophonic Tourist Reader is given a splendid sense of knowing French as it is spoken in Paris, without, in fact, having been put to much trouble.

"As they say here," or variants of it—"here" being Paris and "they" the French—is naturally a frequent phrase in *The American,* especially useful in that it clearly joins and more than joins the topographical and the linguistic aspects of realistic setting. Language *is* place. The French language *is* Paris. Paris is the fictive scene of the novel but this fictive scene perpetually refers itself outward from the text to the preexistent city which constitutes its ground. It almost seems as if Paris exists for the pleasures, whether direct or vicarious and literary, of the Americans, exists for the purpose of being imitated, represented, at times in the most literal fashion (street names), at times more suggestively in the way James gives conversations in English while convincing us that they are "really" in French. The "as they say here" formula naturally uses both languages. So Tom Tristram, quite early, to Newman:

> "*C'est le bel âge,* as they say here."
> "What does that mean?"

What does *what* mean, the French phrase or the English? The two men go on to talk about French lessons. Newman won't need them. French will come naturally. "It's a splendid language. You can say all sorts of bright things in it"—"here," that is, not necessarily in San Francisco. The conjunction of language and locality is seldom far from our attention. "Valentin was what is called in France a *gentilhomme";* Valentin to Newman, "All that is rather stiff, as we say," but what is it they say, *dur?;* Valentin to Newman again, "*vous m'imposez,* as we say"; Valentin to Newman, shifting languages and continents, "Time is money! Is that what you say in America?"; Mrs. Tristram to Newman, "Should you like me, as they say here, to marry you?"; Mrs. Tristram to Newman, "She belongs to the very top of the basket, as they say here"; still Mrs. Tristram to

Newman, "Her brother is the *chef de la famille,* as they say; he is the head of the clan"; Claire de Cintré to Newman, "Do you go *dans le monde,* as we say?"; Valentin to Newman, "He [M. Nioche] has had losses, *des malheurs,* as we say"; Valentin to Newman, "Mademoiselle Noémie has thrown her cap over the mill, as we say," or, in the nonexistent original, *elle a jeté son bonnet par-dessus le moulin.*

In virtually all these brief citations, Newman is the center of interest, the personage to whom what "they" say "here" is addressed. It is he who is learning French, he who is being educated out of or into more than "America," he to whom is being offered a more comprehensive and a more complicated world, and yet a world in which he, like his creator, will still be an, or even the, "American." For Henry James as well, *The American* was an education. One way you can tell is by the appearance in it of certain French sayings which would recur in his fictions to the very end and very few of which had appeared in his writings before. Tristram says to Newman in *The American:* "Well, if I'm not the rose, as they say here, I have lived near it." [16] In *Watch and Ward* (1871), "if he was no longer the rose, he stood too near it to be wantonly bruised"; in an 1875 book review, "Mr. Greville was not the rose, but he lived near the roses"; in *The Portrait of a Lady,* "Ah, yes, if she isn't the rose, she has lived near it"; in "The Author of 'Beltraffio' " (1884), "she was not, after all, though she had lived so near the rose, the author of *Beltraffio*"; in *The Awkward Age* (1899), "Mrs. Grendon, though not perhaps herself quite the rose, is decidedly in these days too near it" (meaning an adulterous fragrance); in a letter to Jessie Allen of 19 September 1901, "such a living—almost—*near* the rose!"

Mrs. Tristram says to Newman, "You must remember that, as the French proverb says, the most beautiful girl in the world can give but what she has," another favorite James quotation. Just before serialization of *The American* began, James wrote Howells from Paris (28 May 1876) that he could give him no news for there was none to give, i.e., as he went on, *"La plus belle fille du monde ne peut donner que ce qu'elle a."* Whatever our suspicions about the French phrase being perhaps less innocent than James seems to think it is, he continues to give it, in one or the other language, with no apparent sense of indecency, as, in *A Little Tour in France* (1884): " 'La plus belle fille du monde,' as the French proverb says, 'ne peut donner que ce qu'elle a'; and it might seem that an egg which has succeeded in being fresh has done all that can reasonably be expected of it. But there was a bloom of punctuality, so to speak, about these eggs of Bourg, as if it had been the intention of the very hens themselves that they should be promptly served."

Finally, James' favorite French saying of them all, lifelong: "Newman was, according to the French phrase, only abounding in her [Mrs. Tristram's] own sense," that is to say *abondant dans le sens de,* here more or less translatable as "was in agreement with," usually with a pejorative nuance of excessive length. That is not what it always means, however, there is no one equivalent, indeed there is no equivalent at all, but the phrase can mean just about what you want it to mean, and it always sounds awkward in English. James is mighty fond of this little device, he uses it freely in either language, we bump against it, early, middle, and late, in novel, tale, travelogue, criticism, notebooks, letters. After collecting examples of "abound in the sense of" for several years, I now have about thirty-five examples—but each day brings a fresh revelation. Here are a few selections, "clever French things," as *The Ambassadors* calls the remnants of Chad's supper: in "The Modern Warning" (1888), "once she had spoken in this sense she abounded and overflowed"; in *The Ambassadors,* Strether "abounded in the sense of his appeal to the ladies"; in *The Wings of the Dove,* Kate Croy "abounded in the sense of her [Milly's] wonder"; in *The Golden Bowl,* Charlotte Stant puts it to Adam Verver—*in Paris!*—that "The Prince may for instance now . . . have made out to his satisfaction that Maggie may mainly desire to abound in your sense"; a stage direction in *The High Bid* (1907): *"Abounding in his sense."* My favorite is James' jeer in *The American Scene* (1907) about "a great commercial democracy seeking to abound supremely in its own sense and having none to gainsay it."

## 3. *The Reverberator* (1888)

Whatever its flaws as an original performance, by no means remedied in the 1907 revision, by no means extenuated or concealed in the 1907 preface, *The American* was of James' major book-length works the most generative of other works, the most fecund. He rewrote it as a play with a happy ending ("Oh, how it must not be too good and how very bad it must be!" as he effused in his *Notebooks,* entry of 12 May 1889).[17] The mere fact of converting *The American* from an old novel to a new play, the transformation from past to present, from genre to genre, may well have affected the thematic conceptualization of *The Tragic Muse* (see below pp. 124–25). Quite loosely speaking, *The Ambassadors* is *The American* all over again, with much sophistication of personages and situations. Much more literally, *The American* was rewritten as *The Reverberator;* but neither the preface to *The American* nor the preface to the volume containing *The Reverberator* advertises the connection or even alludes to it, obvious as it is, as in Ezra Pound's simplifying designation of *The Reverberator* as *"The American* with the sexes reversed."[18]

The main point of continuity is clear; as Leon Edel puts it, "James returned to the Paris of *The American."*[19] But in the beginning, Paris as the scene of *The Reverberator* was improbable—the germ was an anecdote from Venice—and a *Notebooks* passage of 17 November 1887 shows James resisting it and then succumbing. "It is the highest expression of the note of 'familiarity,' the sinking of *manners,* in so many ways, which the democratization of the world brings with it." But who then, besides himself and some American friends in Venice, would be old-fashioned enough to care? *Voilà,* the French! *And yet:* "I have taken a vow never again to do the French in any such collective way (as in the *American); à peu près* effects of that sort are too cheap, too valueless," too, one might even say, melodramatic. "So I found my solution where, with the help of Heaven, I hope to find many others in work to come; viz., in the idea of the Europeanized American," the idea which had already served so well in the cases of Gilbert Osmond and Serena Merle. After that decision, all went on wheels: "It fits together—it hangs together. I knew I should find something—and now I SEE it. *Cela se passe en France*—it begins in Paris and goes on mainly in Paris."[20]

In rewriting *The American* as *The Reverberator* what was tragically dropped was the baffling complexity of Christopher Newman; happily dropped were all traces of duels, matrimonial homicides, Carmelite incarcerations; what was chiefly retained was what had been indisputably "right" in *The American,* the representational topography of Paris, with the relations of the English and French languages

—in a word, the setting, the very context and definition of the Tourist Fiction. The suitor is now a young man Gaston Probert, legally an American but a lifelong Parisian, closely bound to a Gallomaniac ex-American family (Catholic, too), three sisters who have married French, and one brother dead in the Franco-Prussian War. Gaston also resembles Valentin Bellegarde in being a good-for-nothing young chap with a potential head for business. The female cynosure is not French but American, Francie (Francina, wonderfully) Dosson from Boston, who has just enough brains to know not to want to go home. She offends the Probert family by telling tales to the American journalist George Flack, of *The Reverberator,* and the marriage is nearly prevented, but finally Gaston, rallied by his friend Charles Waterlow, an American Impressionist painter who paints Parisian but thinks native, decides to act like a man instead, defies his family, loses his inheritance (Francie has enough), and marries the girl. " 'Well,' said Waterlow, 'you will at least have got rid of your family.' "21

Thus the male lead is both French and American and bilingual all the way, whereas cosmopolitan Francophonic citizenship was a goal toward which Newman was obligated to aspire. Gaston is no American tourist trying to make his way into a French family—he *is* French and now he wants to be an American (like Mr. Brooke of "Travelling Companions" and other young James protagonists anxious to recuperate their lapsed nationalism) more than he wants his next dinner. The Dosson family, on the other hand, if they want anything at all, other than to be out of the United States, want contact with the American Colony (which even Newman was smart enough to avoid). Except for the husbands of the Probert girls, everyone is one way or another an American in Paris, with the happy tonality of that situation. Even the all-American journalist is happy to be on assignment in Paris; "it's ever fresh," he unforgivably says. Even rich agreeable mindless Mr. Dosson is so happy to be in Paris (because his Daisy Miller-like daughters wish it) that he seldom stirs from the courtyard of the Hôtel de l'Univers et de Cheltenham (an invented name; how pronounced in French?) The Proberts are happy to be in Paris for easy access to the Pope but mainly for its being, *by definition,* better than the United States, as proved by their having a natural affinity to it. "When Waterlow asked what made them so exceptionally ticklish he [Gaston] could only say that they just happened to be so"; "ticklish" was in the New York Edition revised to read "of so exceptionally fine a fibre." Everyone agrees that Paris is *le centre du monde,* as surely the Tourist Reader also agreed. No longer need vraisemblance compensate for melodramatic grimness but all is loveliness and laughter. Perhaps in large part it is loveliness and laughter because of Henry James' changed relations with Paris. *The American* is his only major work of French fiction actually written on location, at a time when he was finding the prospect of indefinite Parisian residence less wonderful than he had bargained for. It seems nearly unarguable that certain unpleasant aspects of James' Parisian experience were infiltrating the text of *The American* in disruptive and even relatively uncontrollable ways, and especially that they rubbed off on the characterization of Christopher Newman: there was, I think, on James' part, a frustration at living in Paris, a sadness at the thought of being compelled to leave it, a sense of self-satire at having been so naive as to have fancied it his permanent home. His residence in London long since established, he comes back to fictive Parisian expatriation in a more cheerful frame of mind, the Proberts, the Dossons, and Charles Waterlow presenting three different kinds of American idiocy vis-à-vis "the capital of civilisation"[22]—all laughable because all by the author escaped.

Inexplicably, the Louvre is "river-moated"; otherwise, the Seine, and everything else, is where it belongs, and basically accords with the sense of the Tourist Reader. The city of *The Reverberator* thus obligingly runs from the Bois de Boulogne on the west to Notre Dame at the other end; it clings to the river both south and north; the basic arrondissements are the 1er, 2ème, 4ème, 8ème, and 9ème, except for the painter way out by himself in the 17ème on Avenue Villiers. The Proberts live Seine-side Right and Left Bank, the Dossons lodge at an imaginary hotel on or near the Rue de la Paix. The American Colony ("a little kingdom of the blest") is carefully located "from the Rue Scribe to the far end of Chaillot," somehow pertaining to the Avenue Gabriel, the Rue de Marignan (both 8ème), "and the wide vistas which radiate from the Arch of Triumph [so Englished] and are always changing their names," author insuring his credit with posterity. The Dosson girls shop at the Bon Marché, Flack recommends a visit to the Louvre, they all sit interminably in the Tuileries or on the Champs Elysées, they dine at "the admirable establishment of M. Durand, in the Place de la Madeleine." The only departure from Paris Centre is to Saint-Germain-en-Laye, the suburban setting of "Madame de Mauves," James' chief triumph in French-oriented fiction prior to *The American,* where the personages partake of dinner at the Pavilion Henri Quatre (James ever fond of French names involving "Henri") and of the view, "the curving Seine and the far-spreading city." That we are really and truly in Paris, and not just reading about some romantic spot, is established by frequent reference to buildings, monuments, pleasure places, street names, the latter the most frequent and the most efficacious. Thrice we have the "as they say here" formula, all lanced at Francie by Flack, "the *chronique intime,* as they say here," "the *grand monde,* as they call it here," "I'm a *travailleur,* as they say here." As ever, the formula suggests a modicum of acquaintance with a plenitude of alienation. Our really and truly being in Paris is also established— and embellished—by the steady but discreet infusion of verbal tidbits culled from the French language, most of them evident and easy, many of them touristical, as *porte cochère, table d'hôte,* and, best, *zalon,* so mispronounced by a German waiter "in an intention of English." The more legitimist Proberts spell *roi* and *foi* in the old-fashioned way, *roy* and *foy*.

Who speaks what is worked out with the same care as in *The American* but with a lighter touch. Francie Dosson's progress in French is not the all-serious progress of Christopher Newman; she is, after all, the Daisy Miller type. "She had an unformed voice and very little knowledge," revised to read in the New York Edition "a weak pipe of a voice and inconceivabilities of ignorance." For the most part, she is gently let down and off. In the view of her father, "was not her French so good that he could not understand it?" And her lover alleges "We shall make her speak French; she has a capital disposition for it; her French is already almost as good as her English," to which his father remarks "That oughtn't to be difficult." (But to his sister, the same lover retorts "her English is quite as good as yours. You don't even know how bad yours is.") How good Francie's French is we may suspect from such a brief glimpse as this: "'J'espère bien!' said Francie, who was getting on famously with her French"; either that, or Henry James is getting on famously with his sarcasm.

Francie and Suzanne (Susan, really), Madame de Brécourt, are said to be "chattering" but we have no way of knowing in which language—all the Proberts speak English as well as French, the French husbands least well. Text tells us that "in proportion as the Proberts became majestic they had recourse to French." It is why they removed to Paris in the first place. "They had affinities with a society of conversation; they liked general talk and old high *salons.*" There is a residue of inherent comedy in the notion that good talk is conducted only in French by basically French persons; if it were so, how would it fare with this novel so evidently written in English? As usual, the mythical sleight-of-hand is that much of this novel is written in French. When alone and agitated, or accusing Francie of her sins, the Proberts appear to speak French rather than English: text so indicates by throwing in more than the usual quota of French words and phrases. The Probert girls' husbands have their ins and outs with English. Of the horrible article in *The Reverberator,* Suzanne says to Francie, "Margot is reading it to her husband; he can't read English." (But her very own husband manages to murmur to our lovely Francie, in English, "You are charming, mademoiselle— charming, charming!"). The Proberts' control of language is recurrently subject to whimsy, as "Mr. Probert was particular in this: he could bear French noise but he could not bear American"—it is Mr. Probert's most American trait. Gaston Probert's English is an issue because it involves his "real" nationality: "he pronounced the American language," as James calls it, "as if it had been French," or so it seems to Francie, that expert. Fortunately, there is no attempt to reproduce on the printed page the tonalities of American spoken as if French. The most charming foreign language passage of *The Reverberator* nicely suggests the low key in which linguistic difficulties are treated throughout. It is Delia pushing Mr. Dosson out of the Hôtel de l'Univers et de Cheltenham to go buy a copy of the offending scandal sheet: "On the boulevard, at the very first of those kiosks you come to. That old woman has it—the one who speaks English —she always has it." Every Tourist Reader knows *her.*

III.

# The Portrait of a Lady (1881)
# and Other Italianate Fictions

In his dictated projections for *The Ivory Tower,* James delightfully speaks of his having a "place-scheme" in analogy with his "time-scheme," and, indeed, the multiple places of a James fiction, especially a novel, often constitute seriatim a kind of *progrès d'effet,* virtually a narrative of their own. For *The Portrait of a Lady,* it would be, very roughly, and with extra goings back and forth, Albany-Gardencourt-London-Paris-Florence-Rome-Gardencourt-London-[Rome]. About one third of the novel takes place in England, two thirds in Italy, preponderantly Rome. Other places are experienced en route, none more so than Paris. The structural function of Paris for *The Portrait of a Lady,* so utterly different from its function for *The American* or *The Reverberator,* is that of the waist, the narrowed point, of an hourglass, through which personages and behaviors pass on their way south. The waist is in chapter 20, it is chiefly the American Colony of Paris, and it is not the romantic but the contemptuous view of what is most contemptible about France, in the view of the American *raffiné*, the presence in it, particularly at Paris, of too many of the wrong kind of Americans.

Yet it is also notable how many things French manage somehow to make their presence felt in these allegedly non-French textual parts! As in *The Tragic Muse* good dull Mr. Carteret will live at Beauclere, so here Madame Merle's name is French and also Lord Warburton's (Molyneux). Gilbert and Amy Osmond (Countess Gemini) are the second-generation deracinated offspring of a woman known to her time as "the American Corinne," where reference is to the novel of that title by Madame de Staël, that is to say, they are an American novelist's representation of an American conception of a French conception of Italy somewhat out of style. Henrietta Stackpole's frustrated inability to get at "the inner life" of Europe parallels James' ongoing problems with persons too exclusively "continental" and not friends of Turgenev. Madame Merle is *par excellence* American fatuity abroad, as particularly in her remark, "I don't pretend to be learned . . . but I think I know my Europe."[1] Even in Albany, Isabel Archer is felt by her brother-in-law to be "written in a foreign tongue." In Rome she reads Ampère (doubtless Jean-Jacques Ampère, *Histoire romaine à Rome),* an author lengthily reviewed by James in 1875 in an essay recently (1878) collected in *French Poets and Novelists.*

So, too, there is much more of the French language than you would ever expect from an English-Italian setting. As always, France and French are with Henry James both an actual place and tongue and an imputable a transportable a literary-linguistic communicational exchange mode. Well-spoken persons in Jamesian fictions fall to French from time to time regardless of where they are, and not because they must but because they want to, just as James did (e.g., in his *Notebooks)* and just as he presumed his readership did (e.g., in his personal correspondence). Neither he nor the readership was nearly so up in Italian, however, nor had any near intention of being, and therefore the represented personages of *The Portrait of a Lady* expediently forego the pleasures and privileges of that language, even while residing in Italy, and even on occasions when we can hardly imagine them speaking anything else. Most of the Italian in *The Portrait of a Lady*—and there is little enough of it—comes from narrative authority, it refers to places or things, it is easy and obvious —*signori, portone, piazzetta,* and so on. It may be remembered that Mrs. Touchett proposes to show Isabel four European countries, two of her own choice (we know perfectly what Mrs. Touchett's two are) and "the opportunity of perfecting herself in French, which she already knows very well." Nothing is said about her perfecting herself in Italian, yet Mrs. Touchett lives in Florence and Isabel will live in Rome.

In chapter 22, "this picturesque little group," international, polyglot, interdenominational, Osmond, Pansy, two nuns (one French, one Italian), and, later, Madame Merle, makes a partial exception to the absence of Italian in *The Portrait of a Lady*—partial in that Italian is said to be spoken but no word of it appears on the printed page. First Osmond and Pansy are speaking Italian, reported as English. Then the elder nun, who is French, and who knows no other language, even though she lives in Rome, breaks in, "speaking in French," text says, most of her discourse reported as English, a few words in French, not these: "But we have sisters of other countries —English, German, Irish. They all speak their own tongue," no German or Irish given, all English except for a few tonal Gallicisms sprinkled about. For *The Portrait of a Lady* foreign languages, including Italian, are no problem, they simply don't exist except in reference, and if exoticism is desired a bit of French is run in. As a result, this text and most other Italian performances from the same desk exude an air of French-and-English-speaking Americans out of their own country and curiously positioned vis-à-vis a linguistic environment almost completely irrelevant to themselves and they to it. Alternatively we may say that this text and most other Italian performances from the same desk exude an air as of France—thanks to her superior language, literature, and prestige—displacing Italy in the American mind even when that American mind is or thinks it is on Italian ground. In Rome, as in or near Boston (e.g., in *The Europeans, The Bostonians*), the American mind is English-speaking plus a smatter of French. At least it is so in the works of Henry James.

In the early the England part of *The Portrait of a Lady* we find little or no French but it tends to arrive with Madame Merle and then there is more of it with Ned Rosier as Isabel goes through Paris on her way to points south. For the rest of *The Portrait of a Lady* it is notable how much of this French is aimed at Isabel. Isabel, who affects to speak little French herself, is quite pelted with French. But sooner or later almost everyone gets in a word or phrase of simple and basic French, Tourist French, such morsels as *bonne, protégé, parti, de confiance* ("as they said in Paris"), *bibelots,* et seq. According to that favorite French phrase of *The American* (and everywhere else in Henry James) Isabel abounds in Ralph's sense, Henrietta in Isabel's irony. Madame Merle drops the phrase *"du bout des doigts"* and Isabel's reflex responds: "She is a Frenchwoman . . . she says that as if she were French." Learning that Madame Merle is in fact American, Isabel performs the appropriate second reflex, finding "much stimulus to conjecture in the fact that an American should so strongly resemble a foreign woman." Neither woman seems to recognize an ironic allusion to Racine in Madame Merle's casual remark *"je viens de loin" ("Mon mal vient de plus loin," Phèdre* 1.3). Rosier and Pansy ask questions about how do you say it in—well, English! The best bilingual passage is a vexed meditation by Rosier on the phrase *jeune fille:* "She [Pansy] was such a perfect *jeune fille;* and one couldn't make of a *jeune fille* the inquiry necessary for throwing light on such a point [how much does she like him?]. A *jeune fille* was what Rosier had always dreamed of—a *jeune fille* who should yet not be French. . . . An American *jeune fille;* what would be better than that? She would be frank and gay, and yet would not have walked alone, nor have received letters from men, nor have been taken to the theatre to see the comedy of manners," not even at the Comédie Française.

In addition to *The Portrait of a Lady,* there are three novels and nine tales which may reasonably be counted as "Italianate." The other novels are *Roderick Hudson* (1875), *The Wings of the Dove* (1902), and *The Golden Bowl* (1904). From the titles it is easily recalled how they are not all Italian in the same way; from the dates of publication it is easily remarked that two of these four major performances are early and two are late. The Italian tales range in date of publication from 1870 to 1889–90—they neither come earliest nor latest in the Jamesian œuvre—but they are preponderantly rather early, seven of the nine belonging to the 1870s, five of the nine to 1874 or earlier. In the serial order of James' 112 extant published tales, as established by their sequence in the 12-volume Leon Edel edition, they are numbers 15, 17, 20, 22, 24, 32, 36, 49, and 55. The best-known of them are "Daisy Miller" (1878) and "The Aspern Papers" (1888).

In the four Italian novels, all but *The Golden Bowl* have more French than Italian, even though in each instance Italy, for reason of setting or major personage, is allegedly an important consideration, a presumptively important linguistic cause, and France not. The tales are more bafflingly mixed in their linguistic proportions. Of the nine, four have more Italian than French, four have more French than Italian, and one ("Travelling Companions") has Italian and French in approximately equal measure. There is more Italian than French in "The Last of the Valerii" (but it has little of either), in "Adina" (Italian over French by about 3-to-1), in "The Diary of a Man of Fifty" (Italian over French by better than 2-to-1), and in "The Aspern Papers" (Italian over French by about 3-to-1). There is more French than Italian in "At Isella" and in "The Madonna of the Future" by about 2-to-1, in "The Solution" by about 3-to-1, and in "Daisy Miller" by about 4-to-1. The conspicuity of French domination in "Daisy Miller" suggests a possible distinction of types: a tale may be regarded as either Italian ("Adina") or as international ("Daisy Miller"). If the tale is Italian, the Italian language, in small gobbets, is welcomed as local color. If the tale is international, the Tourist Writer and the Tourist Reader are naturally most at home with French as their preferred second language.

*Ecco!* there are piquancies everywhere (among the talk of *scudi* and *forestieri*) in Lesser James, for example in "The Madonna of the Future" (1873) confrontation between "I summoned my best Italian" and "he broke out into that fantastic French of which Italians are so insistently lavish";[2] for example, the Misses Bordereau of "The Aspern Papers," Americans of French name and derivation, long since permanently resident in Venice; but from a cultural-linguistic point of view the most interesting of these Italian short things is probably "At Isella" (1871). Even less integrated than *The American,* it is, in turn, half travel sketch and half *mélodrame;* simultaneously, the travel sketch half is "international," French being its alternative language, and the second half is "Italian"—just barely across the border into Italy, the text appropriately performs its shift of language from French to Italian. French being the favored second language of the first or Swiss half is still more peculiar in view of its being German-speaking Switzerland, a fact not cited but instead we are told of its being "Catholic" Switzerland and all about a French priest (the reasons for his nationality are undisclosed) and the tourist-pro-tagonist reads in his Bædeker about *"Albergo di San Gothardo, vaste et sombre auberge Italienne"* so that we know he (an American traveler) is using a *French* Bædeker and the Saint Gothard road reminds him of "an old steel plate in a French book that I used to look at as a child" and at Realp he notes "a very affable maid-servant, who spoke excellent lowland French" and at the Hospice the tourist guest and the monkish hosts discuss Alexander Dumas rather than Manzoni and there finally past the Dogana it is Italy Herself! Now we hear our first Italian word: " 'Nothing to declare—*niente?*' . . . *'Niente'* seemed to me delicious; I would have told a fib for the sake of repeating the word." With *the* woman, the *Signora* (call her Italy), the national language comes explicitly into question:

> "Do you understand Italian?" she asked.
>
> I had come to Italy with an ear quite unattuned, of course, to the spoken tongue; but the mellow cadence of the Signora's voice rang in upon my senses like music. "I understand *you*," I said.
>
> She looked at me gravely. . . . "Are you English?" she abruptly asked.
>
> "English is my tongue."

Even so, French influence continues as she shrugs her shoulders "more gracefully than any woman I ever saw, unless it be Mlle Madeleine Brohan of the Théâtre Français." Then for all-American reasons we are back in Italy and Italian: " 'I don't know how it is that I'm talking Italian at such a rate. Somehow the words come to me. I know it only from books. I have never talked it.' 'You speak as well,' the Signora graciously affirmed," like Christopher Newman affirming M. Nioche's English, "as if you had lived six months in the country." To her, "an incorporate image of her native land," the American explains: "I have come on a pilgrimage. . . . To under-stand what I mean, you must have lived, as I have lived, in a land beyond the seas, barren of romance and grace. . . . Italy, for us dull strangers, is a magic word. We cross ourselves when we pronounce it." Later still, she bursts into sobs and "I suddenly lost my Italian. 'Dearest lady,' I cried in my mother tongue, 'forgive me that I have troubled you.' "

*Roderick Hudson* is predictably in the polyglot stream, or, to shift metaphors, it represents a superimposed view of Francophilia *on top of* Americanism Abroad *on top of* hapless passive all-receptive Italy. At least eight personages, plus narrative voice, manage some Italian; the same personages, plus narrative voice, manage some French; perhaps twice as much French as Italian; Christina Light and narrative voice together speak about half the Italian and about half the French. Enough so that it is quite the rare and delightful note of vraisemblance when Miss Blanchard incidentally denominates "this very city of Rome where we sit talking nineteenth century English."[3] Except for the Cavaliere and Assunta, there are no Italians of novelistic consequence, and these two are connected to the expatriating Americans the Light ladies rather than to any fellow Italians. Rowland Mallet and Roderick Hudson, who have and who pick up languages with ease, proceed to Rome via Paris. There is talk of the Louvre and of "the theatre" (Mademoiselle Delaporte is named) and of Honoré de Balzac (James' first Balzac essay coinciding in date of publication with the last serialized episode of *Roderick Hudson,* December 1875) and of Mrs. Browning (thrown in for good measure?) and of George Sand and of (at Geneva) Jean-Jacques (Rousseau), while back at Northhampton Massachusetts Mary Garland of an evening reads out loud *Corinne* to Mrs. Hudson and in the same township "On the base [of Roderick's first statue] was scratched the Greek word $\Delta\iota\psi\alpha$, Thirst." How *drôle!*

Cavaliere speaks with "a strong Italian accent"—thus we know it is not Italian he is speaking but English or French. Christina's English has, conversely, "a vague foreign accent," obviously from either her Italian or her French. Madame Grandoni thinks her to possess "three or four languages" and to have read "several hundred French novels." Mrs. Light claims for her daughter a knowledge of French, Italian, German, and English (as in *The Princess Casamassima;* these are also the four languages of Miriam Rooth in *The Tragic Muse)* "better than most natives" and happily adds that the director of the Paris opera wanted her (for his ballet). " 'Oh, not quite,' said the Prince, in English." It is not much of a speech in English but there is little evidence, assurance of the author aside, that the Americans do any better in Italian. Mary Garland arrives in Rome apt in Italian, her aptitude not very aptly accounted for, and is soon said to be having a "long colloquy" with the French chambermaid, probably not in Italian and not in English either. "I have imagined," Roderick offers to Rowland, that "she [Christina] wishes me well, as they say here"; the phrase is of course *vuole bene;* we are not informed how he picked it up. Christina tells her poodle to say to people *"buon giorno a Lei"* and *"tanti complimenti"* and from one or another additional mouth we have a grand imbroglio of *consequenza, Dio buono!, Santo Dio!, Perchè,* and Madonna, signorina, padrona, the principles of italicization being uncertain. We have *chic* and chic, both ways, along with a general shower of touristical French *(hôtel-pension)* and worldly elegant French, even when reference is ultimately sacral *(à la grâce de Dieu).*

"I want to go straight to London"[4] (from Switzerland), Milly Theale says to Susan Shepherd Stringham years later in *The Wings of the Dove* (1902), and so they go, avoiding France, avoiding Paris, where, it is felt, the dead and gone Theale men had already wasted too much of their substance. But when Milly wants help establishing herself in Venezia, "The great Eugenio . . . crossed from Paris," thus proving that Paris can't be all bad, thus also reminding us that French is still the international language of rich arrangements. Wisps of French things cling to the text in odd places: the Condrip children have "grown near the rose," a French phrase favored by James in *The American* and thereafter; Kate Croy is susceptible to "the religion of foreign things," as developed in Merton Densher, who has been to Biarritz; at Florian, in Venice, Lord Mark is seen reading the *Figaro;* the destructive violence of the French Revolution analogically attaches itself as always in James to the destruction of beautiful women. Perhaps *The Ambassadors* was still on his mind.

References to Italy are far more immediate, practical, topographic, Venetian, limited. Pedestrian Densher who has no money for gondolas ("he humbly—as in Venice it *is* humble—walked away") conducts us to Rialto, Bridge of Sighs, Grand Canal, Piazza San Marco (most, most descriptively rendered!) where "the Molo . . . the old columns of the Saint Theodore and of the Lion were the frame of a door wide open to the storm." We will no longer, if we have been properly attentive to Jamesian practice, expect a flood of Italian, not even from wicked Eugenio (all the other personages being Anglo-American), who "by a profundity, a true deviltry of resource . . . always met the latter's [Densher's] Italian with English and his English with Italian." We shall rest content with our *quartiere* and *traghetto* and *poco bene* and *tanto bello,* reflecting that were we ourselves there in person we might do no better nor very differently. Not so with our French! French is another story and ever the same. There is more of it than of Italian, for no reason except that Henry James and the Tourist Reader are once more conspiring in its ubiquity, 60 percent, say, coming to us direct from narrative authority, the remaining 40 percent from scattered Francophiliac Anglophonic mouths. Every one knows French! Kate uses it on her father, Milly in writing and viva voce on Susan Shepherd Stringham, on Lord Mark (elsewise such a booby), then on Lord Aldershaw, Densher on Kate, Milly on Sir Luke Strett, Aunt Maud on Densher, Kate on Densher. They say things like *n'en parlons plus, à bientôt, beaux yeux, ces dames, tête-à-tête.* Whether in London or Italy, French goes along at the same rate. What it means is: "these people you are reading about are not limited to the tongue of their native land but may express themselves in an alternative *langue* a 'foreign language' even if (as you see) it is seldom for more than a word or two at a time and those words not exactly unusual."

*The Golden Bowl* is the only major James novel where French is not the second language but the third. Italian is the second language, especially in the first half—Prince Amerigo and His Friends, Including His Wife And Father-in-Law—he, they, and narrative voice happily chatter away in English, with intrusions of Italian, decidedly at the expense of their French. As usual, linguistic capacities are carefully specified. The Prince adores all things English and American, especially funds; he marries into an American family; his English is perfect, "either for lip or for ear," as text has it; he practices "American," as text also has it, in order properly to converse with Adam Verver, imputed master of that language. Prince's affair with Charlotte Stant is allegedly abetted by her perfection in Italian, superfluous though it be, his English being perfect. Charlotte has a "strange sense for tongues," Prince especially feeling in her "a perfect felicity in the use of Italian." It comes natural to an expatriate girl who has grown up in Florence, her parents "from the great country," i.e., the United States, "themselves already of a corrupt generation, demoralised falsified polyglot," strong terms, while she and Maggie furthermore have been getting to know each other at a convent school in Paris, doubtless at the same time perfecting their French.

Prince and Charlotte regularly speak English, facilitating narrative transcription and reader response. They speak Italian on occasions choice, choice not only for themselves but for that prurient party the Tourist Reader, as in the shop when first encountering the golden bowl, on the assumption, mistaken, that the shopman knows no Italian. Charlotte's Italian enables one of the novel's finest dialogic triumphs, Prince on the terrace at Matcham calling up to Charlotte in Italian (rendered in English), "Come down quickly!" to which Charlotte sails down her amorous answer from a high window, *"Vengo, vengo!"* It is what might be called an adulterous bilingual cosmopolitan consummation, for whether or not we know Italian we will surely know what she means. In the opening pages of the novel Prince recalls for us how he even thinks in English, "familiar with the tongue from his earliest years," how he speaks to himself in English (as Henry James apparently spoke to himself in French, e.g., in the *Notebooks*). Maggie his intended tells him he speaks English too well (her meaning not clear) to which he answers that when he speaks worse he speaks French (his meaning not clear), "to say nothing of his evident feeling that the idiom [French] supposed a cleverness she [Maggie] was not a person to rise to." For *The Golden Bowl* misunderstandings are among other things quite polyglot.

Significantly or not, the first Italian word in *The Golden Bowl* is "galantuomo" and the last is "cara." In between we enjoy an easy romp with such spotty wonders as *cinquecento, sposi* (the key word is often repeated), *Speriamo, forestieri,* per Bacco, per Dio, Santissima Vergine, and other interpolations of similar provenance. It is simple Italian, basic Italian, well suited to the Tourist Reader of modest parts. The French of *The Golden Bowl* is quite different. We have heard Prince tell Maggie that when he speaks worse it is French. Now he telegraphs Charlotte his congratulations on her engagement to his father-in-law: " '*A la guerre comme à la guerre then*'—it had been couched in the French tongue," and the rest of the telegram is given in English but in italics as if it were really in French and only translated. (That is why the word *then* is in italics.) Most French in *The Golden Bowl* is properly in italics, whether it emanates from Prince, Fanny Assingham, or narrative authority, the three principal users. This French shows a far more sophisticated vocabulary than the Italian word list, a vocabulary more adventurous in idiomatic usage, more indifferent to the Tourist Reader (or, alternatively, assuming from the Tourist Reader more attainment, more effort, and, if not, more shame), perhaps even a bit defiant. How many readers will know all this French? If they do not, they will have the option of looking it up or doing without. More or less in narrative order, and more or less exhaustively, we have:

*crême de volaille*
*bassecour*
*bêtises*
*morceau de musée*
*disponible*
*de part et d'autre*
*tableau-vivant*
*revendeuse*
*doyenne*
*Est-elle toujours aussi belle?*
*pâte tendre*
*chinoiseries*
*par exemple*
*petites entrées*
*meuble*
*cabotinage*
*en très-haut lieu*
*retentissement*
*point de repère*
*maîtresse de maison*
*bousculade*
*il n'y avait pas à dire*
*bons amis*
*engrenage*
*les situations nettes*
*situation nette*
*Si bien*
*tout bêtement*
*portée*
*louche (" 'Louche,' love?"*—Colonel Bob to Fanny)

*Cela s'est vu*
*blasés*
*Voilà*
*revanche*
*les grands seigneurs*
*vieux Saxe*
*baroque* (given as French)
*émigré*
*petits fours*
*Le compte y est*

The final French phrase may, like the beginning and closing words of Italian, by some readers be taken for "significant." For others the word *émigré* will perhaps stick out, as leading, once more, to France and French, and to the French Revolution, the ambivalent dark side of France, prison, violence, guillotine, the Terror (yet also Art!), all this applied to Maggie Verver and her husband. Certain details of the shop *di antiquario* chime in (rather more in tone with *The Ambassadors* than with *The Golden Bowl*): "things consular, Napoleonic, temples, obelisks, arches, tinily re-embodied, completed the discreet cluster." On the brighter side, Paris is for Adam Verver and everyone he knows something special if vague, "Paris being always for Mr. Verver in any stress of sympathy a suggestion that rose of itself to the lips," and to other lips as well, we think, as James lays in the accustomed morsels from his rich budget of Parisian impression, "charming in itself," "smothered in flowers," "strange appearances in the air," "the general exotic accent and presence," "the superior, the supreme, the inexorably enveloping Parisian medium," all comically rebounding on the Tourist Reader or, more accurately, on people Tourist Reader knows quite well but would gladly not know at all: "preparatory, for gathered barbarians, to the due amputation or extraction of excrescences and redundancies of barbarism," as in dentistry. Adam Verver stores his art treasures in Paris, among other places. Fannie Assingham has once met the Prince there. The Prince's people pause in Paris en route to London. Once Maggie and her father were delayed in Paris on their way to Italy. Many years earlier, he and his first wife, Maggie's mother, had found their account, then so young and innocent, in the Rue de la Paix and "the Boulevards." At Fawns we notice "the last salmon-coloured French periodical." In

London we find the Prince reading the *Figaro* as James males have been doing time out of mind.

"Why I should find it a pleasure, in France, to imagine myself in Italy, is more than I can say; the illusion has never lasted long enough to be analysed," James rather idly asks himself in *A Little Tour in France* (1884).[5] The better question would be as to the opposite illusion (lifelong), why it was (and still is?) a pleasure, in novels and tales ostensibly located in Italy, to imagine yourself speaking and hearing, not Italian, but French? The France of the French language, and thus of letters, of arts and civilization, is by no means limited to such geographical areas as are known to the makers of linguistic atlases. Like fine wines, France and French travel. You the Tourist Reader may not only go *to* them but you may take them *with* you— to any place at all; so that now we, later readers of the Tourist Reader, find ourselves tempted to say that consequently these "Italian" works are "really" about France, after all, only a pardonable exaggeration. (The reverse will not hold. James' fictions set in France contain few traces of Italy.) Indeed, in the pages of Henry James it is difficult to escape France and French, the exception proving that rule being the English Period (which we will come to in due course). It may also be said that personages who dislike the French regularly find themselves objects of considerable disapprobation, as Olive Chancellor of *The Bostonians* and Lady Agnes of *The Tragic Muse*. Even *in* Italy, James' Americans and English are disjunct from background in ways that Christopher Newman was not (only James' narrative practice was) and it is partly because they have imported not only themselves but a goodly bit of their superficial Frenchness. The visual scene is recognizably Italian. There are Italians lounging about. They are said to be speaking Italian. But you hear very little Italian spoken (often, next to none) and, on the other hand, if you listen carefully you hear—French! It is like being abroad in two countries at once, one for beauty, one for brains, you presumptively bringing no overplus of either but only your lack and your desire and your infinite capacity for appropriation and transport.

# France Englished:
# *The Princess Casamassima* (1886)

> There is nothing in all history which, to borrow a term
> from the painters, "composes" better than the opposi-
> tion, from 1600 to 1800, of the audacity of the game
> and the certainty of the reckoning. We all know the
> idiom which speaks of such reckonings as "paying the
> piper." The piper here is the People. (1875 review of
> *Correspondence Inédite de la Comtesse de Sabran et du Che-
> valier de Boufflers)*[1]

## 1. The English Fond

France Englished might just as well be England Frenched, a minor
witticism either way, only a gentle invitation to pay closer attention
to the textual passions of Henry James. His book title is also a joke,
the very words of it being Christina Light's title, imported from
*Roderick Hudson* (1875), and only a Neapolitan title, at that. Recently
critical comment starts with the critical findings of Mark Seltzer in
*Henry James and the Art of Power,* findings only partial, however, for
their restriction to English actualities.[2] Given all the Franco-American critical-theoretical hubbub of about the same time concerning
Poe's "Purloined Letter," one might also recall that Poe's police-
detective-criminal-political tales are French in setting and characteri-

zation, Parisian, in fact, for it was felt to be at Paris, rather than at London, that professional surveillance—the word itself is French—originated. Its mucky post-Revolution originations are abundantly displayed and documented by Balzac, "Quatrième Parti.—La dernière incarnation de Vautrin" in *Splendeurs et Misères des Courtisanes* (1839–47), a title somehow omitted in Adeline R. Tintner, *The Book World of Henry James,* despite six handsome chapters investigating Balzac and James.[3] The Garnier edition (Introduction notes et choix de variantes par Antoine Adam) has, among its bibliographical headings, "Sont à consulter pour le monde de la police," with items dating back to 1815, and "Sont à consulter pour le monde des prisons et des bagnes," with items dating back to 1825, and in one case, 1725. By the Englishing of France, or the Frenching of England, I have in mind matters more comprehensive than police or prisons, however; I have in mind the ways in which *The Princess Casamassima* approaches to one another the two conflicted cultures, on the one hand by means of representations ostensibly English yet as Frenchified as possible, and, on the other hand, by means of French incursions into the text, nominally English; as we shall see, that text also inscribes Italian and German incursions as well, and text has its reasons.

There is less French here than there will be in *The Tragic Muse.* *The Princess Casamassima* further differs from that performance (and from *The American, The Reverberator, What Maisie Knew,* and *The Ambassadors)* in so little of its action taking place in France. For *The Princess Casamassima* the functions of France and French are almost—but not completely—severed from geography, even if wonderful terrifying France is always potentially visible across La Manche. France in *The Princess Casamassima* is disjoined from specific place only to be expanded in *personnages*—in Eustache and Madame Poupin, in Florentine Vivier, in Florentine's father, in Hyacinth himself. France floats freely, as it were, to be picked up—wherever and by whomsoever. France is exportable importable culture, thought, literature, tone, image, suggestion, language, the question of our speech. France is also power, politics, society, "the world." The main topic of *The Princess Casamassima* is thus, appropriately, signification, voiced and scriptural, even unto handwriting and enunciation—representationally focused in London but internationally understood. " 'We have never been abroad,' said Hyacinth, candidly. . . . 'Oh, well, there's a lot of nonsense talked about that!' Captain Sholto replied."[4]

Inscription quite literal and material, not metaphorical and ideal, is several times interpolated as a primary topic of the text. Hyacinth is said to have "the Princess' note in his pocket, with the day and hour as clear as her magnificent handwriting could make them." Later, he in turn "had written a note to Millicent, in a hand even more beautiful than usual—his penmanship was very minute, but at the same time wonderfully free and fair." It is the worst kind of mistake and missed opportunity to read *The Princess Casamassima* only as a frustrated frustrating exposé of something going on below the surface: what is going on is, precisely, the surface, the linguistic surface, the text, on frequent and revelatory occasion conceived as narrative representation of prior written and spoken behaviors. We are told about the final fatal note to Schinkel in terms of handwriting even more than of substance: "The three lines in question were signed D. H., and the letter was addressed in the same hand. Schinkel professed that he already knew the writing; it was that of Diedrich Hoffendahl. 'Good, good,' he said." What the three lines say, precisely, we shall never know; how Schinkel pronounces his one given word we must try to imagine.

As with actual prior writing (by hand), so with actual prior voice, as textually represented; once again the Princess and Hyacinth ("a youth on whom nothing was lost," the phrase repeated from "The Art of Fiction," 1884) are singled out for special attention. "The Princess's voice was low and rather deep, and her tone very quick; her manner of speaking was altogether new to her listener, for whom the *pronunciation of her words and the very punctuation of her sentences* were a kind of revelation of 'society' " (emphasis added). She makes "him feel how little *he,* in comparison, expressed himself like a person who had the habit of conversation; he seemed to himself to stammer and emit common sounds." Quite to the contrary, what she says to *him* is "You haven't a vulgar intonation . . . you do and say everything exactly in the right way." We shall soon come to those, English and other, whose intonations are not so commended, whose not saying everything "in the right way" leads to doubts concerning their doing everything in the right way. And we must constantly ask ourselves what can possibly be meant by such language as "vulgar," "common," and "the right way."

Numerous allusions to tone of voice are aggregated toward the end of the text. Christina Light speaks "in a tone which would have made the fortune of an actress if an actress could have caught it." Paul Muniment speaks to her "in a tone which might have implied that the discussion was idle," to which tone (ambiguous term!) her response is "You have the most extraordinary tone." Tone of voice also disappears from the text of *The Princess Casamassima*—so we are apprised—its disappearance variously attributed to inattention, inarticulation, or silence. Of inattention: Hyacinth "perceived that she [Princess] scarcely measured a word he said to her or a word that she herself uttered." Of inarticulation: discovering his corpse "a strange low cry came from her lips." Of silence eloquent, ambiguous, or downright ominous: "a dozen objects around him which seemed as much a part of herself as if they had been folds of her dress or even tones of her voice." As we regard Hyacinth and Captain Godfrey Sholto, mutually *regardant,* we note that "what these two pairs of eyes said to each other requires perhaps no definite mention"—not merely eyes but two pairs, four in all. There is also in the text occasional attention to the difference between voiced and scripted signifiers; their relation is sometimes bilingually confusing: " 'Is that your name—M. Paul?' . . . 'Oh, bless you, no; that's only her Frenchified way of putting it. My name *is* Paul, though.' " Written, English Paul *is* French Paul—spoken, it is not.

As for political background, what's first to notice are a couple of broadly inclusive antithetical ambivalences. In *The Princess Casamassima* England is the passive and France the active principle (I do *not* mean female and male). England has neither her art nor her revolution whereas France is notoriously both creator and destroyer of civilization. In a 17 October 1882 letter to Grace Norton, James laconically observes that "France has preserved the physiognomy of the past much less than England and than Italy."[5] More than a decade earlier he had written to the same correspondent (16 July 1871) of "the murderous Irish riot in New York. . . . For a few hours it was really quite Parisian."[6] Violent French destruction of material artworks is a major and recurrent theme of *A Little Tour in France* (1884) but so is the well-nigh heavenly delight of the French language in the Anglophonic ear. As art and violence lie at or near the center of *The Princess Casamassima,* so *A Little Tour in France* is its indispensable preparation and guidebook. Recoiling from "the red radicalism of France, the revolutions, the barricades, the sinister passion for theories," James concludes that "it is a terrible pattern of man," the French pattern, while at the same time he insists that that same French pattern is notable and admirable for "a *netteté*"—there is naturally no English word which will serve for what he wants to say—"a faculty of exposition, such as the English gentleman is rarely either blessed or cursed with."[7]

Precisely to the point and in fewest words (with considerable *netteté*, in fact): "The blast of the great Revolution blew down most of the statues in France." James' notice of public destruction is recurrent ("public destruction" *veut dire* destruction in public by the public of property which either is or might be public, if not dynamited or set fire to):

> It is hardly too much to say that wherever one goes in certain parts of France, one encounters two great historic facts: one is the Revolution; the other is the German invasion. The traces of the Revolution remain in a hundred scars and bruises and mutilations, but the visible marks of the war of 1870 have passed away.

> Wherever one goes, in France, one meets, looking backward a little, the spectre of the great Revolution; and one meets it always in the shape of the destruction of something beautiful and precious.

> . . . the fine old porch—completely despoiled at the Revolution— of the principal church . . .

Reading "certain radical newspapers" at Lyons, "I wondered . . . whether I was losing all my radicalism; and then I wondered whether, after all, I had any to lose. . . . I failed to settle the question, any more than I made up my mind as to the probable future of the militant democracy, or the ultimate form of *a civilization which should have blown up everything else*" (emphasis added). On the other hand, "At Toulouse there was the strongest temptation to speak to people, simply for the entertainment of hearing them reply with that curious, that fascinating accent of the Languedoc, which appears to abound in final consonants, and leads the Toulousains to say *bien-g* and *maison-g,* like Englishmen learning French." A portress in the same city has "a speaking eye" and her "talk was all in *n*'s, *g*'s, and *d*'s, and in mute *e*'s strongly accented, as *autré, théâtré* . . ." What could be better than *that?* Only the French language even more generally listened to and loved. At Le Mans "my ear was soothed by the fine shades of

French enunciation, by the detached syllables of that perfect tongue.
. . . I felt a charm, a kind of sympathy, a sense of the completeness
of French life."

Thus from the Franco-American listening post which backs up
narrative authority in *The Princess Casamassima,* most if not all native
speakers of English, inasmuch as they *are* English, emit sounds both
common and variously distasteful. (It will be remembered that the
Princess is in her origins one-fourth English, one-fourth American,
and one-half Italian, while Hyacinth is half-French.) In the interests
of a more democratically equable speech, I deliberately mix the
noises of different social classes in the citations which follow—why
not, if each and every mode of speech is bad and the whole structure
of class discrimination by means of speech markers even worse?
Beginning, then, at random, with "The very way Rose Muniment
sounded the word 'intellect' . . . she pronounced it as if she were
distributing prizes for a high degree of it." Butler-talk is represented
by the announcement of Hyacinth "in a loud, colourless tone," and
by such information as that "she was on a visit to a 'juke.' " Miss
Marchant, visitor to Medley, has "a handsome, inanimate face . . . a
beautiful voice, and the occasional command of a few short words.
She asked Hyacinth with what pack he hunted." Paul Muniment
speaks "with a provincial accent, which Hyacinth believed to be that
of Lancashire." Princess, who is a great noticer, "had already perceived that he pronounced amiable 'emiable,' " text supplying two
scriptural variants to indicate one voiced deviation from standard
pronunciation; Princess also notices, "as she had noticed before, that
he pronounced 'weary' *weery."* Lady Aurora, exemplifying to Hyacinth "that 'best breeding' which he had seen alluded to in novels
portraying the aristocracy" utters herself in "almost incoherent speech,"
that is to say "pantingly, with strange [by no means signifying
"foreign"] intonations." Specifically, and quite unacceptably, she
"sounded the letter *r* peculiarly" (in the New York Edition "She
sounded the letter *r* as a *w"*). At the Sun and Moon "here" becomes
" *'Ere,* 'ere?' "★ At Crookenden's party one old lady refers to the

---

★The wonderful pub name is possibly from *Hamlet,* by far James' favorite source of Shakespeare
allusion, here and elsewhere (first line of first speech by Player Queen in Act 3, scene 2). Or it is only a
personal locution: in a letter to his father from Rome, 19 January 1873, James romanticizes "days and
nights wondrous with sun and moon" *(Henry James Letters,* 1:329); in chapter 3 of *The Bostonians,* Basil
Ransom alleges " 'old truths—as old as the sun and moon.' "

"tremendously musical house," dropping her *h,* as Hyacinth never does. Millicent Henning, "daughter of London," figures for him "the sociable, humorous, ignorant chatter of the masses," while "her beauty [physical] glorified even her accent." She says *shime* for shame, *Plice* for Place, *abear* for bear, *'ands* for hands. (She would surely say *Jimes* for *James.*) Her cockney intonations, with her desire to rise, generate some of the novel's finest moments, as " 'I don't know how I *'ave* pitched on my things,' she remarked, presenting her magnificence." In conversational exchange:

> "Might one know the name of the lady who sent you?"
> [Captain Sholto:] "The Princess Casamassima."
> "Laws!" cried Millicent Henning.

She means "Lord!" but is too polite (and too devout) to say so. Hyacinth is by contrast the smoothest of the smooth: even when asking for change in a Mayfair bar, "his request [was] very civilly enunciated."

Semantic horrors (obnoxious as to sense) and oddities of diction are textually separable from phonemic horrors (obnoxious as to sound), even as issuing from the mouths of the same speakers, but these semantic and dictional horrors equally demarcate social classes and are recognized by textual authority with distaste both for the system of demarcation and for the social varieties of English-abuse (in the American ear). When Hyacinth writes Princess from Venice that on return he won't "hold the same language" we are tempted to translate "language" as "opinions," which is part of what he means—but it is not what he says. In Paris seated at Tortoni's, ears full of *good French,* real and imagined, he had remembered Millicent's "vulgar tricks of speech," "her detestable habit of saying, 'Aye, that's where it is' " (several other specimens are given, none to a twentieth-century taste so very dreadful—how far is the quoted phrase from *voilà?*): "These phrases had fallen upon his ear many a time before, but now they seemed almost unpardonable enough to quarrel about." Hyacinth is, "in the language of the circle in which she moved, her fancy," from whom she desires "to enjoy what she called a high-class treat." In extenuation of her semantic and phonemic malfeasances it must be said that she is a notable mixture of "bad grammar and good health" ("part of the familiar human sound of his little world") with a refreshing "freedom from the sophistries of civilization" as displayed by the more "civilized" *personnages* of *The Princess Casamassima*. It may also be said of her that in addition to a good heart and a beautiful body she has a good mind, perceptive and judicious. Hyacinth and Captain Sholto have it all over her in cultural sophistication but she "has" Captain Sholto and Hyacinth. She revels in her inability to "interpret" the spoken wisdom of the latter, "inexpressible" as it no doubt is.

"I like to know all sorts of people," the Princess says, her first cited words in the text that carries her title, not her name. The Princess also likes to speak in all sorts of ways, as in her solution to the barmaid problem (after the revolution): "Oh, drown her in a barrel of beer!" Actress and ventriloquist, she has no established speech habits but adjusts them to context, to situation, to auditor. As she addresses a string of banalities to Lady Aurora, we see (hear) her switch roles as she switches pronouns, while brilliantly maintaining her syntactic parallelism: "that's where you English are strong, in braving ridicule. They have to do it so often, haven't they?" Millicent Henning denounces Princess "for a bold-faced foreigner," and so she is. (But so, for that matter, is Henry James.) Aside from mispronunciation, Lady Aurora herself always speaks correctly, formally, simplistically, and reductively, in the best British way, parodically considered. " 'Oh, it's so pleasant knowing a few foreigners!' Lady Aurora exclaimed, with a spasm of expression. 'They are often so very fresh.' " On the same occasion, "Lady Aurora remarked that there were many delightful books in French" (Hyacinth later finds them denoting "a limited acquaintance with French literature and even a certain puerility of taste").

Political talk, so much more publicly repercussional than the pleasantries of social life, is naturally amenable to a far more dangerous consequence of verbal and intellectual corruption, especially as envy, spite, hatred, mendacity, and mindlessness for its own sake are by an irrelevant irresponsible leveling populism surreptitiously substituted for awareness, compassion, analysis, aspiration, and cure. Talk tells, in *The Princess Casamassima;* prose style tells the tale. Who can question the truth of James' narrative voice when it veers around to sound like this:

They [the men] came oftener [to the Sun and Moon], this second winter, for the season was terribly hard; and as in that lower world one walked [as James years later was to recall walking London] with one's ear nearer the ground, the deep perpetual groan of London misery seemed to swell and swell and form the whole undertone of life. The filthy air came into the place in the damp coats of silent men, and hung there till it was brewed to a nauseous warmth, and ugly, serious faces squared themselves through it, and strong-smelling pipes contributed their element in a fierce, dogged manner which appeared to say that it now had to stand for everything—for bread and meat and beer, for shoes and blankets and the poor things at the pawnbroker's and the smokeless chimney at home. Hyacinth's colleagues seemed to him wiser then, and more permeated with intentions boding ill to the satisfied classes . . .

We may well think Hyacinth not far wrong in that conviction. But text also tells tales of verbal-intellectual chicane proceeding from the same persons yet according to quite different motives and in quite opposite directions, the "loud, contradictory, vain, unpractical babble" of dissent for the sake of self-love. Paul Muniment, more ruthless than the babblers, and possibly more perspicuous, is "naturally intolerant of [Sun and Moon] palaver," "imbecility," "ignorance," "vanity," this forever "thumping the table and repeating over some inane phrase" in "a kind of eternal dirty intellectual fog" not to be confused with the climate of London or the smoke of pipes. Earlier, Rose Muniment has told Hyacinth, "You say that just like a man that my brother described to me . . . you use almost the same words that he did," and Hyacinth is naively shocked at Paul "casting ridicule upon those who spoke in the name of the down-trodden." Dead metaphors make for dead ideas or none, or worse than none, they make for cant. Among other features, the text of *The Princess Casamassima* incorporates a veritable florilegium of radical-liberal cant; as, for example:

> "Don't you belong to the party of action?" said Hyacinth, solemnly.
> "Look [Listen] at the way he has picked up all the silly bits of

catchwords!" Paul cried, laughing, to his sister [an outspoken conservative]. "You must have got that precious phrase out of the newspapers, out of some drivelling leader."

Most of the time, not all, Hyacinth is in fact a perfect little *précieux* in comparison with his linguistic milieu, including such of it as is furnished by that Princess who, "He has perceived, long before . . . had no desire for vain phrases" ("after all, he had a French heredity, and it was not so easy for him to make unadorned speeches"), and who, yet, is quite capable of such a statement as "we take a great interest in the people," her statement promptly contradicted by Madame Grandoni (she too got up from Rome and from *Roderick Hudson*), not for the language, but for the imputed sentiment. As an Italian-speaking German, Madame Grandoni is not equipped for sensitive response to the niceties of English usage (or their lack). As an English-speaking Francophiliac, Hyacinth is a natural-born skeptic about provincial English lexical-political differentiations. Lady Aurora has just referred to the people of the upper classes when " 'We don't call them the people,' observed Hyacinth, reflecting the next instant that his remark was a little primitive." Even with emphasis added—italics for force, not for French—cant remains cant, as when Princess declares that she wants "to know the *people,*" and even in that best of tongues—Eustache Poupin responding to a Sun and Moon loudmouth, *"Vous insultez le peuple—vous insultez le peuple!"*—cant remains cant. Anastatius Vetch refers to Poupin as "that poor, infatuated phrase-monger" and recalls the Poupin theory that Columbus was French. Hyacinth "knew their vocabulary"—the Poupins', female and male—"by heart, and could have said everything, in the same words, that on any given occasion M. Poupin was likely to say." Radical-liberal politicized types talk badly indeed, in *The Princess Casamassima,* on purpose to be false, as when Poupin ridiculously declares that if he must suffer he trusts it may be for suffering humanity but also for France, thus halving his international and national duplicity. Hyacinth lowers himself to the Princess' lowest (that is, most self-deceived) wish when he tells her the aristocracy can't all be "a bad lot (he used that expression because she had let him know [wonderful phrase!] that she liked him to speak in the manner of the people [another wonderful phrase]." Not all cant is political, of course. According to an adjustable formula variously useful for Mrs. Bread in *The American,* Madame Merle in *The Portrait of a Lady,* Verena Tarrant in *The Bostonians,* and to be used again for Mrs. Temperly in the tale of that name the year after *The Princess Casamassima,* Christina Light is "the most remarkable woman in Europe." It is at least likely that in 1886 she is the most remarkably written about.

England is the setting of which James writes and the setting within which he mostly wrote, not, however, quite as an "English writer" but to a very considerable extent as at least a partial Francophile and to an even greater extent as a resident American national wielding a shared native tongue—not yet to insist on other tongues—with a proficiency well beyond the scope of most local users. James is the colonizer and the colonized both, returned to the point of origin, and in that sense, rather than as a realist-novelist-qua-*policier* he is the secret agent of the linguistically shining text. S. Gorley Putt accurately and justly observes that "Henry James was by no means unmoved by the revolting selfishness he saw in the behavior of the London rich" ("those critics who consider Henry James to have been a temperamental Tory are very far indeed from the truth"), but Putt also reminds us that James "was, after all, an American citizen, and could properly show his political colours in no more active fashion than, say, his membership of the Reform Club." Thus James' "attack was to be launched on the front where he was at once strongest and most sensitive: the moral-aesthetic front."[8] Let us say rather the textual front and add, to such words as "strongest" and "most sensitive," the word *safest*. For these extra- and intra-textual reasons, England, specifically London, as the primary represented site of *The Princess Casamassima,* bears, as who should say, a charmed life, if not exactly a pretty one. Only in two chapters do we escape to the continent, whereupon we are promptly extradited (as it were) back to London, "the richest expression of the life of man," as it is said, but by no manner of means the *only* expression of the life of man— brought back to tread "greasy pavements" and inhale the "smoke-seasoned fog" of the "great city," which is also an "immeasurable breathing monster," Paris and Venice having loomed and then "shimmered away into reminiscence and picture."

In certain other respects England has in *The Princess Casamassima* rather a bad press, though not so devastatingly bad a press as it is going to get in *The Tragic Muse*. We have already stumbled onto or over some of these respects. Here are a few, carefully chosen others. There is generally to this superbly and toploftically toned text a certain *Hamlet* ambience, a sense of insanity not so much counting where all else is mad. Madame Grandoni gratuitously informs Prince Casamassima that "here everything is forgiven. That a person should be singular is all they want," an outsider's observation subsequently much elaborated in chapter 12 ("Eccentricity") of *The Education of Henry Adams*. The English, Madame goes on to say, are (at least) not dirty, "not like our dear Romans," enabling Prince to retort that "They are full of gin; their faces are purple" (James preferred beer and wine). The Princess likewise "appeared, on the whole, to judge the English world severely; to think poorly of its wit, and even worse of its morals. 'You know people oughtn't to be both corrupt and dull,' she said." (Princess is Catholic.) She compares mid-1880 England to the old régime of France "over which the French Revolution passed like a whirlwind," blowing statues down. Throwing herself into lower-middle-class life at Madeira Crescent, "her discoveries in this line diverted her, as all discoveries did, and she pretended to be sounding, in a scientific spirit—that of the social philosopher, the student and critic of manners—the depths of the British Philistia." Philistia is a beautiful British word, not an original importation from New York, but who except our expatriated stylist from overseas would think to precede it by the definite article? The selfsame Madeira Crescent ("mean and meagre and fourth-rate") is by Hyacinth invidiously contrasted with "the high-piled, important look of the Paris perspective." Having read about the goings-on of the affluent idle in "the light literature of his country," Hyacinth readily imagines, as we, following the satiric iridescences of the Jamesian textual performance, imagine with him, Captain Sholto *en vacances* ("in the recreations of his class") "ploughing through northern seas on a yacht or creeping after stags in the Highlands." In real life, Scotland was one of James' favored retreats but you would never guess it from his fictive page. Hyacinth once calls attention to "so many narratives in the air." We have now glanced at perhaps half of them, which are, alas, as nothing until they are brought into contact with another set of narratives emanating from the continent, narratives perhaps even less "emiable." It is their fierce pressure against the English *fond* that gives *The Princess Casamassima* its extraordinarily dialectic, its multilinguistic, its specifically *literary* power.

## 2. Continental Contributions

In the conviction that no account of *The Princess Casamassima* is worth much until it takes right hard hold of its multilinguistic textual facts, I offer a columnar word-and-phrase-list based on the 1886 English edition. The novel is *of course* written in English, we say; we might better say that it is also "written in" French, Italian (plus a bit of Latin), and German. These "foreign languages" are sporadically injected into the predominant discourse with the usual and altogether predictable result of subverting the supposed "authority" of that otherwise unquestioned text. Now that text, together with the English language, and the English way of looking at things as embodied in the English language, is transformed from an absolute to a relative value, now it appears as only one arbitrary code among several. At the same time, the presumed identity of scriptural signifier and conceptual signified is put asunder. Introduction of a second language— and a third? a fourth?—takes us giant strides toward international interlinguistic humility. Alternatively, the disproportionate amount of French may suggest to some observers that we have on our hands a Frenched-English text (reenacting the Norman Conquest) retrogressively interrupted by older Romance languages and then further and impertinently interrupted by a Teutonic language. The political allegories of *The Princess Casamassima* are manifold, but first of all the politics of the text is linguistic. And as all these languages converge on represented fictive London the very idea of language is split off from presumptive geographical connection: "I am not of this country. I speak as one speaks to young men, like you, in other places." Thus Madame Grandoni, an Italian-speaking German, in English, to Hyacinth Robinson, himself half French in parentage and in subsequent linguistic acquisition. The pivotal point of *The Princess Casamassima* is Paul Muniment's announcement to his *confrères* at the Sun and Moon that "Hoffendahl's in London." Two of the three words are English. The name is German. The man is German. (But he is not in Germany.) So is Schinkel German, who informs Hyacinth, pedantically yet much to our present purpose, apropos of the *other* courier: "he spoke to me always in English, but he is not English; he sounded his words like some kind of foreigner. I suppose he is not German, or he would have spoken to me in German. But there are so many, of all countries!" Indeed; see the word list.

Writing to his sister Alice in 1880 (25 April), Henry James explained that at Naples he had "kept away because [Richard] Wagner ["the composer"] speaks no French and I no German, as you are probably aware."[9] He exaggerates, perhaps. Truly, however, the German-language component of *The Princess Casamassima* is modest in vocabulary range—twenty separate words, by informal count—yet no negligible matter for those desiring to cleave close to this curious text. If the vocabulary is modest it is also cunning, cunning and stark, short simple words having mainly to do with truth, beauty, time, power, and God. (It will be noticed that the French and Italian speakers also specialize in secularized petitions to deity.) James' minimalist German vocabulary is furthermore clumped in two places, in the middle (at the "Hoffendahl's in London" pivot) and at the disastrous end, Italian having ceased many pages back, and French even earlier. Other textual proprieties are easily made out, e.g., the spate of highly emotive French poured forth by Florentine Vivier from her prison deathbed (beginning at the fourth entry). Readers of imagination and patience may find much amusement in leisurely inspection of the phrase list; I am meanwhile drawn on to even more pressing considerations.

As in *The American* and other internationalized works by Henry James, there is in *The Princess Casamassima* considerable jollity resulting from wordplay with the bilingual ambiguities of *stranger-étranger* —the confusions of two languages making for at least twice as much entertainment, even while the issue of who speaks what, and where, and what for, continues deadly serious. Relativistic verbal games abound. In objective third-person narration, Paul Muniment, on our first meeting him at the Poupins, is merely a "visitor"—to Hyacinth a "stranger," as Hyacinth is reciprocally a "stranger" to Muniment, i.e., they have not been introduced. Even in innocent contexts, the word *foreign* exudes an ominous, a potentially aggressive or paranoid tone. We hear with some perturbation, however subliminal, that at

| FRENCH | ITALIAN (LATIN) | GERMAN |
|---|---|---|
| cheffonier | | |
| eau-de-cologne | | |
| protégé | | |
| Dieu de Dieu, qu'il est beau! | | |
| Est-il possible, mon Dieu, qu'il soit gentil comme ça? | | |
| Mon pauvre joujou, mon pauvre chéri | | |
| Il ne veut pas s'approcher, il a honte de moi | | |
| Il a honte de moi—il a honte, Dieu le pardonne! | | |
| Ah, quelle infamie! | | |
| Ah, par exemple! | | |
| Il a honte de moi—il a honte de moi! | | |
| Dieu de bonté, quelle horreur! | | |
| protégée | | |
| de rigueur | | |
| banal | | |
| ouvrière | | |
| par exemple! | | |

| FRENCH | ITALIAN (LATIN) | GERMAN |
| --- | --- | --- |
| comme il faut—dans le genre anglais | | |
| bien du mal | | |
| La société lui doit bien cela | | |
| tisane | | |
| intérieur | | |
| cuisine | | |
| pauvre monde | | |
| avènement | | |
| accapareurs, as M. Poupin used to say | | |
| bourgeois (but bourgeois and bourgeoise) | | |
| J'ai la main parisienne | | |
| il n'y a que ça! | | |
| Là-là | | |
| Pardon, pardon | | |
| soyez tranquille! | | |
| Mon ami | | |
| ces messieurs | | |
| Ah ça | | |

un enfant très-doué

mon petit

en v'là des bêtises!

savant

ma bonne

M. Hyacinthe

interne (also interne)

Mon Dieu

obole

Mademoiselle

désagrément

ces dames

M. Paul

Ah bien, voilà du propre

àpropos

demos (Lat.)

Revue des Deux Mondes

cause célèbre

à charge de revanche, as the French say

| FRENCH | ITALIAN (LATIN) | GERMAN |
| --- | --- | --- |
| naïf (but naïf) | | |
| séances | | |
| à quoi m'en tenir | | |
| le premier venu | | |
| fond du sac, as Eustache Poupin called it | | |
| soirée | | |
| en tout bien tout honneur, s'entend | | |
| mise-en-scène | | |
| | già | |
| | Cara signora | |
| | Che vuole? | |
| | Ma che vuole? | |
| | è vero? | |
| | Capisco bene | |
| | basso popolo | |
| | povera gente | |
| | Che vuole? | |
| bibelots | | |
| milieu | | |

à outrance
banal
chic
corvée
en cachette

attendrissement
flair
à fond
défis

Enfin vous voilá ferme!
éprouvé

Santo Dio!
Dio mio, Dio mio!
factotum (Lat.)

modus vivendi (Lat.)

ab ovo (Lat.)

Gott in Himmel!
sehr
Nun
Doch, doch

| FRENCH | ITALIAN (LATIN) | GERMAN |
|---|---|---|
| *C'aurait été d'un bel exemple!* | | |
| *Trop d'arithmétique!—trop d'arithmétique!* | | |
| *Vous insultez le peuple—vous insultez le peuple!* | | |
| *me voici!* | | *Natürlich* |
| parterres | | |
| | *Ecco!* | |
| | *capricciosa* | |
| | what will you have? | |
| | *Vedremo bene* | |
| | *Poverino!* | |
| | risottos | |
| boudoir | polentas | |
| | contadina | |
| *naïveté* | | |
| régime | | |

Lieder

Basta!

Che *vuole?* as Madame Grandoni says

poveretti

Santissima Vergine!

Dio mio

chiaroscuro

Voilà ce que j'aime en Angleterre

parti-pris

bien entendu

Où en êtes-vous

Parbleu

pâtisserie fine

sur les dents

recueillement

intriguée

Jugez donc

en fin de compte

crânerie

veut en venir

| FRENCH | ITALIAN (LATIN) | GERMAN |
|---|---|---|
| succès de jour | | |
| marquise | | |
| entr'acte | | |
| mouchards | | |
| escamoter | | |
| hôtel garni | | |
| des femmes très-chic | | |
| | campo | |
| le fond de ma pensée, as you used to say | | |
| Enfin | | |
| | rococo | |
| mesquin | | |
| tour de force | | |
| | Che forza, che forza! | |
| hébétement | | |
| papier-mâché | | |
| A la bonne heure! | | |
| du train dont elle allait | | |
| | codino | |

Gräfin

"Mr. Fetch," Assunta called it

Chè, chè
cicerone (Lat.)

artisti
Ci vuol' pazienza!
Evidentamente
Aspetta, aspetta!
quel giovane

à toutes jambes

arrière-pensées
au juste
femme du monde
nuance

pose
chez les bourgeois
dépouillée

vie de province
Vous me rendez la vie!
il y a

| FRENCH | ITALIAN (LATIN) | GERMAN |
|---|---|---|
| | *Poverino!* | |
| | *Sicuro* | |
| | *Felicissima notte, signori!* | |
| | *sangue di Dio!* | |
| *allure* | | |
| *éclaircissement* | *gratis* (Lat.) | |
| | *cara mia* | |
| *salon* | | |
| *nous causions justement de vous* | | |
| *nous causions—nous causions!* | | |
| *au point où nous en sommes* | | |
| *liqueur* | | |
| *fine* | | |
| | | *Also* |
| *chartreuse* | | |
| | | *Lieber Gott, you Vrench, you Vrench* |
| *bonhomme* | | |

*grincheux*

*Il me faudrait des conditions très-particulières*

*Qu'est-ce qu'il dit—qu'est-ce qu'il dit, le pauvre chéri?*

*vous vous faites des idées!*

*Calmons-nous, entendons-nous, expliquons-nous!*

*je le constate*

*Il faut être conséquent, nom de Dieu!*

*je ne permets pas ça!*

*idée fixe*

*Comme vous y allez!*

*suivante*

*E andata via, caro signorino*

*E possibilissimo!*

*capisce*

*Erlauben Sie*

*not so? [nicht wahr?]*

*Il vaut du galme*
*[Il faut du calme]*

FRENCH

ITALIAN (LATIN)

*Peccato!*
*povera vecchia*
*Sola, sola*

GERMAN

*es kann sein*
*nicht wahr?*
Das kann sein—das kann sein
*Schön*
Schön, schön

Hoffendahl's Hyacinth sat on a "trunk, a most foreign-looking article," German, we suppose. Trunks are obvious travelers. So are people. Madame Grandoni is first given to the (at the time) unsuspecting reader as "a stout, odd, foreign-looking woman." Her first remark is a reference to herself and the Princess as "strange women" (eccentric, peculiar, bizarre, not English). She says this "with a foreign accent." The Princess tells Hyacinth that her "husband is a foreigner," that is, again, not English, and then she explains, "an Italian." Princess later explains that she too is "really a foreigner, you know." In each of these citations, the words *stranger, foreign, foreigner* —always the same range of English words—refer to a different country or culture. Whatever it is it is not English, it is other, it is outside, it is somewhere else, it is different, it is probably on one or more of these accounts to be suspected. The unaccustomed is by definition the foreign; the foreign is by definition the unaccustomed. At first sight, Prince Casamassima is to Hyacinth "the tall foreign gentleman (he recognized his foreignness at a glance)." Foreign may be chic, if it is a question of Princess breakfasting at noon, "in the foreign fashion . . . as he too was so foreign"—now "foreign" no longer means non-English but unconventional, anything but *banal*— "he might like that better," but foreign may also be at the other extreme internationally conspiratorial or the fear of it. Madame Grandoni fears "that Christina was seriously compromised by her reckless, senseless correspondences—letters arriving from foreign countries." But these countries, whichever they may be (besides Germany), are not one whit more "foreign" to "England" than Christina and Madame Grandoni.

Most of the time "foreignness" is defined, recognized, and textually represented as voiced signification coming from beyond whatever linguistic state of perfection is for any particular time and place assumed to be "normal." You can tell these foreigners by their mispronunciations, which are (of course) quite different from the intra-linguistic mispronunciations of a Millicent Henning or a Lady Aurora. Unless they are special cases (Hyacinth, Princess) Anglophones are as ever inept at the foreign languages. Captain Sholto has (thinks he has) "a little French and Italian (he exaggerated these latter quantities)"; but Christina "had seen him in foreign counties," i.e., out of England, "she had seen him in Italy, and she was bound to say he understood nothing about those people." The Muniments are likewise language-bound. Paul Muniment and the men at Crookenden's always refer to Poupin as "Puppin." So does Rosy: "The Puppins are the charming foreigners I have told you about" (leading to Lady Aurora's inanities about foreigners being "fresh").

Foreign folk in England must almost of necessity speak some English. Being thus by definition bilingual, and in many instances more than that, what else they speak is somewhat at the discretion of narrative control. Madame Grandoni, who *is* German, speaks no German but Italian and English instead. Her inclusive statement about the German character is given in English: "I am not false. It is not our German nature." Germanized English in the text of *The Princess Casamassima* goes by default to Schinkel, who also has most of the real German phrases. And this Germanized English, most of which comes near the end of the novel, is just as wonderful as the true German tidbits—best of all, no doubt, to most ears, when Schinkel says to Hyacinth "I lofe you." ("Self-loaf" is his favorite phrase.) As text wishes, Schinkel expresses himself (in "honeyed words") according to class and exilic status both, i.e., in German and English, in Germanized English idiom, *and* in cockney: "*Also,* my dear Robinson, have you passed your Sunday well—have you had an 'appy day?" How skillfully he manages his elision—*an* rather than *a* before *'appy!* Schinkel's idiomatic constructions regularly veer off from English into German speech habits, as, plus mispronunciation (to Puppin-Poupin): "*Lieber Gott,* you Vrench, you Vrench, how well you manage! What would you have more?" (Another chartreuse.) Schinkel equally mispronounces Poupin's French: " '*Il vaut du galme—il vaut du galme:'* that was the German's version of the Frenchman's words; and Hyacinth repeated them over to himself several times, almost with the same accent. They had a certain soothing effect," perhaps because his own French is so far superior. Schinkel and Christina Light the Princess Casamassima reenact (re-speak) an important passage in *The American:*

> "You know me by my bad English." . . .
> "Your English is remarkably good—I wish I spoke German as well. Only just a hint of an accent, and evidently an excellent vocabulary."

Flattering hypocritical Princess is wrong on every count, except perhaps for her desire to speak German better (so she could the better conspire). Schinkel's Germanisms, her linguistic hypocrisy, the German language, all come together brilliantly in the closing pages, which are littered with false statements of various sorts, "I have called him myself, but he will not say" and "It's a pity you haven't got some room," contrasted with the linguistic decency of the (English) cabdriver "who said, 'Thank you, my lady,' " to the Princess Casamassima, "with expression, and drove off."

This "separation of language" (said of Francophonic Florentine Vivier vis-à-vis her then Anglophonic son) is a nice phrase for the novel entire—(three pages later "she had become quite inarticulate"), the Tower of Babel horizontalized, as it were. According to that configuration, French speakers are laid as low as the rest, for it is humanity as a whole here suffering frustrated communication. "And will she speak French?" Pinny inquires of Mrs. Bowerbank, in connection with the proposed visit to Florentine Vivier, and is rewarded by sentimental platitude: "Oh, a child will understand its own mother, whatever she speaks." The pathetic-farcical bilingual disjunctions of the actual visit are easily recovered from the phrase list, for example:

> Florentine murmured, in words no one present was in a position to understand—
> "*Dieu de Dieu, qu'il est beau!*"
> "She won't speak nothing but French since she has been so bad —you can't get a natural word out of her," Mrs. Bowerbank said.

The reader who overhears is in a better position than Mrs. Bowerbank to understand but in order to do so must shift from the primary to the secondary language and back again, encompassing as well the social assumptions involved in the (English) connection of sickness ("so bad") and "French" together with the "natural" definition of what constitutes "a natural word," i.e., a word in *my* language.

" 'I am suffering extremely, but we must all suffer, so long as the social question is so abominably, so iniquitously neglected,' Poupin remarked, speaking French" and opening chapter 7. It is the usual Jamesian sleight-of-hand (tongue). The text (narrative authority) alleges, assures us, that the language in question is French, and so the fact of the French language is thematized, but the *statement* of that fact is in English as is even the alleged French; in other words, we are given represented translation of an alleged French statement. The whole scene proceeds in similar fashion, French words and phrases scattered here and there for vraisemblance, most often reported as quotations from a putative prior discourse: *"accapareurs,* as M. Poupin used to say" (but who "says" "M." and how shall we pronounce it?), " *'J'ai la main parisienne,'* M. Poupin would reply modestly," as if he said it all the time. Immediately before the statement about the Parisian hand, Poupin is quoted as saying "What will you have?" and perhaps what we should hear is *"Que voulez-vous?"* (or *"Che vuole?"*). Paul Muniment follows as best he can ("Hyacinth immediately perceived that there was nothing French about *him"*), as back and forth the conversation is said to go in two languages, "M. Poupin had spoken French, which he always preferred to do, the insular tongue being an immense tribulation," among several others, "but his visitor [stranger to the French tongue though native to England] spoke English." The Poupins understand an English comedy—*the* English comedy of *The Princess Casamassima*—no more than Christopher Newman understands the opera at which he assists in Paris (which happens to be written in Italian, not French); "Poupin's humanitary zeal was as unlimited as his English vocabulary was the reverse." Poupin *is* France, one aspect of it, permanently abroad, for political and novelistic reasons, however complex, permanently adrift between conflicted language (and literary) systems. " 'But you have no right to act for the people when you have ceased to believe in the people. *Il faut être conséquent, nom de Dieu!'* Poupin went on." As *The Princess Casamassima* points out, again and again, nobody knows what the referent of "the people" *is.* It might even be said that nobody wants to know. Political discussion breaks down at the same time that—and to the degree that—language ravels away into strings of disjunctive equivalents. " *'Pardon, pardon,* I resist!' cried Eustache Poupin, glaring . . . and Madame [his mate] repeated that they resisted—she believed well that they resisted!" Their eloquence wants to say something else.

Despite the ambivalently privileged position of French—a topic at which we shall soon arrive—some of the best verbal pyrotechnics in *The Princess Casamassima* are attributed to speakers of Italian, perhaps because there are so many of them (as is seldom noticed)—Princess,

Prince, Madame Grandoni, the incomparable Assunta (she, too, "up from" *Roderick Hudson* and utterly unaffected by her stay in England); even Hyacinth writes home from Venice that he is "studying Italian" with the aid of "the works of Leopardi and a second-hand dictionary." Princess Casamassima has with her at Medley a chef with whom she speaks Italian: "Hyacinth understood [it] sufficiently," even before Venice, "to perceive that she addressed her cook in the second person singular, as if he had been a feudal retainer. He remembered that was the way the three Musketeers spoke to their lackeys." Christina is nothing if not intercultural, she who thinks Lady Aurora "as good in her way as St. Francis of Assisi." Madame Grandoni hears her "by the hour together improvising on the piano revolutionary battle-songs and pæans," we are dying to know in what language. It is conjectured that when the Prince her husband shall cut off her supplies she will disdain a suit for separate maintenance, "she would be more likely to waive her right and support herself by lessons in music and the foreign tongues." (" 'And do you think that *il y va* of my neck—I mean that it's in danger?' she translated, eagerly. 'Oh, I understand your French,' " says Paul Muniment, whether he does or not.) "Excuse me if I ask impertinent questions," the Princess rambles on and on, "we speak that way—rather, you know—in Rome, where I have spent a large part of my life," and we notice that she is in equal command of her interpolated English idiom.

Rolling through English ruralism Madame Grandoni wakes from a doze "to greet the scenery with comfortable polyglot ejaculations." Madame Grandoni greatly desires precise control of her utterance: "what do you call it in English?—steady." She also moves with comparative ease among her languages, " 'Good-morning, good-morning. I hope you are well,' said Madame Grandoni [to Hyacinth in English], with quick friendliness, but turning her back upon him at the same time, to ask of the Prince in Italian, as she extended her hand, 'And do you not leave London soon—in a day or two?' " Text gives her Italian question in English translation. She is said to communicate with the Prince "in Italian, which she evidently spoke with facility, through with a strong gutteral [stereotypical German] accent." She is glimpsed reading "a French book, in a pink cover." Christina claims to have "ever so many foreign ones, in paper."

Of all the confused, frustrated, mispeaking personages in *The*

*Princess Casamassima*, the Prince is perhaps most complex in his representative ineptitude, so typical of us all, even those of us lacking his aristocratic-barbarian background: "He had much of the aspect which, in late-coming members of long-descended races, we qualify to-day as effete; but his speech might have been the speech of some deep-chested fighting ancestor." (He is conversing with Madame Grandoni in "Italian.") Prince has perpetual difficulty pronouncing certain English sounds. *Sholto* comes out *Cholto*. He can barely manage Chiffinch Street ("pronouncing the word with difficulty"). He comments on his troubles, naturally blaming the foreigners among whom he finds himself: "I tried to ask the cabman who brought me back to explain to me what it is called; but I couldn't make him understand. They have heavy minds." So they do but that truth is obscured by linguistic confusion. To Madame Grandoni: "And does she associate with no people of good?" To Hyacinth: "you know very well the Princess." To Madame Grandoni, Hyacinth being present, "in a rapid aside, in Italian, 'Isn't it the bookbinder?' '*Sicuro,*' said the old lady. . . . 'Please introduce me to the gentleman,' he added, in English." Except for *sicuro* every word of it is in English but we are to imagine ourselves hearing Italian. In a desperate scene, Prince and Hyacinth attempt to approach each other from their opposed directions:

> His [Prince's] English was far from perfect, but his errors were mainly errors of pronunciation, and Hyacinth was struck with his effort to express himself very distinctly . . . it was a sign of training [family, class, nationality] to explain adequately, in a foreign tongue . . . he heard him carefully put one word after the other . . . Hyacinth reflected that at a pinch he could have encountered him in his own tongue; during his stay at Venice he had picked up an Italian vocabulary.

Leaving England, heading south toward Italy, Prince meets in Paris Madame Grandoni fleeing in the same direction, and writes his threats to his wife in a letter addressed to her new lover Paul Muniment *in French*. " 'He addresses you that way, in plain terms?' 'I can't call them very plain, because the letter is written in French, and I naturally have had a certain difficulty in making it out, in spite of my persevering study of the tongue and the fine example set me by poor

Robinson.' " In all which dire and devious goings-on magnificent Assunta is said always to take "a sympathetic, talkative, Italian interest," even if she calls Mr. Vetch "Mr. Fetch." Assunta speaks with her whole body, not just her mouth, "the Princess's Roman tirewoman indulged in a subtle, suggestive, indefinable play of expression, to which her hands and shoulders contributed, as well as her lips and eyebrows." Or she speaks no word at all but waves "her forefinger in front of her nose, in a manner both mysterious and expressive." Perhaps expression is in the long run more important than communication, which seems always to fail, reason and virtue being at bottom more important than language, in which they are supposed to be embodied.

"It's an accident," Madame Grandoni says of her being not Italian but German, "the world is full of accidents." Accidents and causes alike are smothered in talk:

"Ah, my dear friend, *nous causions justement de vous,*" Eustache remarked. . . .
"Oh, *nous causions—nous causions!*" his wife exclaimed. . . .
"A cat may look at a king, as your English proverb says," added Schinkel, jocosely. . . .
"I just came in to wish you good-night," said Hyacinth.

The predominant and official setting of *The Princess Casamassima* is London. The personages who inhabit the setting come from all over Europe. The action(s) real or imagined are international. The text is English with multilingual extensions. The novel is not a political tract but a sad and satiric representation of human folly, human sinfulness, human suffering, human limit, human complicity. It is not designed to excite you to action, *of one kind or another,* or to induce in you political attitudes, for or against this or that. It is designed to make you think. " 'It used to be so pretty when she spoke English—and so very amusing,' Miss Pynsent ventured to announce, with a feeble attempt to brighten up the scene. 'I suppose she has forgotten it all.' " Florentine Vivier meanwhile continues the only way she can: " *'Mon pauvre joujou, mon pauvre chéri,'* the prisoner went on, in her tender, tragic whisper," went on in French, for French is what she knows, and French is what she is, regardless of where she finds herself at the hour of her death.

## 3. Spécialités de la Maison

Secretly and silently—the matter is not once alluded to by James, but I shall come to it—what goes on in *The Princess Casamassima* is once again the attachment of French Literature to Henry James, by Henry James, through naturalistic intentional emulation, prose stylistics, and other maneuvers. Matters openly talked about are somewhat different and may be suggested by five mock titles *par exemple!* France Chic, France Heaven and Hell, Hyacinth Robinson the Split of a Split, Exilic Poupin *Ambassadeur*, Truly Paris At Last and Evermore.

*France Chic.* This set of textual motifs commences early with "The cheffonier (as Amanda was always careful to call it)"—in the New York Edition carefully changed to "cheffoneer" in quotation marks —with mention of "a portrait of the Empress of the French," also Pinnie's, "taken from an illustrated newspaper and framed and glazed in the manner of 1853." It is kept alive with the recurrent formula (but less often recurring than in *The American*) of "as they say": in the phrase list *"à charge de revanche,* as the French say" (Hyacinth to Mr. Vetch) but not in the phrase list (as containing no French words), "to give myself the change, as the French say" (Captain Sholto to Hyacinth) and "that part of the public for which a penny is not, as the French say, an affair" (narrative voice). Mr. Vetch has long ago been to Boulogne and Paris. Hyacinth likes to imagine himself reading the *Revue des Deux Mondes,* which at Medley the Princess actually provides him, recommending a story of M. Octave Feuillet (this causes him to see her "as a sudden incarnation of the heroine"). Hyacinth balks not at being "whistled for by a princess"—such as she is, only our old friend, poor, dear Christina Light—because it brings him into parallel with "the heroes of several French novels in which he had found a thrilling interest." His bodily gestures are disparagingly referred to by Millicent Henning as "those beastly little French shrugs." From time to Time, Paul Muniment jeers at his French affectations. Hyacinth looks French, he has read Michelet and Carlyle, he has learned French easily, and he speaks it well, including "the accent." Once he endites to Madame Poupin "a respectful letter, which he composed with some trouble, though much elation, in the French tongue, peculiarly favourable, as he believed, to little courtesies of this kind." Doubtless his letter is all he supposes it to be, but France in *The Princess Casamassima* exhibits qualities hardly to be encompassed in the notion of epistolary etiquette.

*France Heaven and Hell.* This title is simply an alternative designation of France as creator-destroyer, France Matrix of Arms and Arts *(gloire)*, of democratic politics, of careers open to talents, of painters and architects and poets and playwrights and actresses and *par excellence* tellers of tales (and historians and critics), France who also blows down her own, as well as her neighbors', statues. As Paul Muniment tries to explain to Lady Aurora, " 'The principal conclusion that Mr. Robinson sees his way to . . . is that your father ought to have his head chopped off and carried on a pike.' 'Ah, yes,' " she says, "the French Revolution." If Heaven is the very sound of the French language, the mere thought of it in the mind of the non-French speaker, Hell is the same French language inciting to periodic violence, for surely it was not English nor German nor Italian that inflamed the French populace to the desecration of shrines. Paul Muniment esteems Hoffendahl's "attempt"—evidently four simultaneous assassinations "in four Continental cities at once"—"because it had shaken, more than anything—except, of course, the Commune—had shaken it since the French Revolution, the rotten fabric of the actual social order." (The word *actual* is here given by narrative authority in the French rather than in the English sense—as "present," not "real.") Sorting out the components of that oddly structured sentence, we find ourselves descending in the order of time as well as in the order of magnitude through stages from the Revolution to the Commune to Hoffendahl. A certain degeneration is implied.

Virtually all views of France and French in *The Princess Casamassima* are bifurcated along the lines of the creation-destruction ambivalence; that bifurcation is then magnified by imaginative projections the most highly romantic. Princess says to Hyacinth: "Because you think it's all a mistake? . . . Perhaps it is; but if it is, it's a magnificent one." The Princess has no proper antecedent for her "it" but we guess at a magnificent, if undefined, overthrow. She speaks French a lot, as she did in *Roderick Hudson*, "she could borrow that convenience, for certain shades of meaning." Thus she suggests to Hyacinth "the idea of the *vie de province,* as he had read about it in French works." French is the salon, "the cultivation, the facility, of talk." The French-speaking Christina is perhaps her Anglo-American half. She also dislikes the French people, her reasons never specified. We may surmise that they stem from her Italian half, the result of French pro-Papal activity during the days of Risorgimento. (Despite her Catholicity, Princess should have adored the Risorgimento —so colorful, so disruptive. Muniment reminds her that her dislike of the French is "awkward, if you're a socialist. You are likely to meet them.") Imaginative projection is best observed in Hyacinth's views of Millicent Henning: "Having the history of the French revolution at his fingers' ends," and she having "laid her inconsequent admirer under a peculiar spell," he easily sees her "(if there should ever be barricades in the streets of London), with a red cap of liberty on her head and her white throat bared so that she should be able to shout the louder the Marseillaise of that hour, whatever it might be." Later, Hyacinth imagines "her primitive, half-childish, half-plebeian impulse of destruction, the instinct of pulling down what was above her, the reckless energy that would, precisely, make her so effective in revolutionary scenes." The young woman is in fact Church-of-England conservative. Her destructive instincts are simply Hyacinth's projection of his sense of French politics upon her natural energy. Is it too obvious to point out that in works by Henry James, the idea of "revolution" almost always suggests the French Revolution, not the American Revolution, much less any Glorious or other English Revolution?

*Hyacinth Robinson the Split of a Split.* It may or may not be tedious, but it is surely repetitious how often we are told or reminded of Hyacinth Robinson's divided heritage, the French plebeian mother (herself "a daughter of the wild French people"), the presumed English aristocratic father. His mother's father is even more splendid than she, even if all poor Pinnie can recall is how orphaned "Florentine had once mentioned that in her extreme childhood her father had fallen, in the blood-stained streets of Paris, on a barricade, with his gun in his hand," which would have been during what is generally known as the February Revolution in 1848. Hyacinth's father, on the other hand, would appear to be all English aristocracy, "though a poor specimen," especially in comparison with his partner staid and uninteresting. "There was no peace for him [Hyacinth] between the two currents that flowed in his nature, the blood of his passionate, plebeian mother and that of his long-descended, supercivilised sire." As Hyacinth is so obviously divided between the French Revolution and the love of art (architecture, it would seem, more than anything else, i.e., *buildings,* preferably not to be dynamited) it is tempting to expand the hereditary split into a totalizing thematic division or simple allegory. But France and England do not in *The Princess Casamassima* confront each other in precisely that way, no stretch of the imagination converting England into a major or central generatrix of the aesthetic idea—France is that—but only at best a decent conservator. But then Hyacinth's half-France is further split, split a second time, according to the novel's French-as-creator-and-destroyer ambivalence, so that he ends, if one may put it a bit ridiculously (the proportions are so inexact), as representing one-quarter revolution, one-quarter art, and one-half conservation of art. He does not write books but binds them. And indeed all the English in *The Princess Casamassima* are conservators, in their various ways, rather than inaugurators. Amanda Pynsent makes ladies' garments in outmoded styles (once imported from Paris, no doubt). Millicent Henning models the latest fashions (from we know where). Anastatius Vetch plays other people's music in a theater orchestra. Captain Sholto nonchalantly works at spending an inherited affluence. Lady Aurora busies herself distributing her family's superfluous leisure time and extra money. It must also be noted that Hyacinth enjoys neither of the two real benefits of his French heritage—the French language and the trip to Paris—through his mother. The first is his own acquisition, the second a gift from Pinnie and Mr. Vetch. Princess commiserates Hyacinth on the early loss of his mother, "because French mothers are usually so much to their sons," at least in the folklore. The sentiment seems inclusive and imprecise.

At their first meeting, Princess, after getting off her *à quoi m'en tenir* (twice), suddenly says, "in a totally different tone"—always this attention to tones of voice—"Excuse me, I have an idea you speak French," to which Hyacinth murmurs back, in what tone we scarcely dare imagine, "I have some little acquaintance with it. . . . I have French blood in my veins." In fact, Hyacinth has learned French, as well as socialism (of a mixed French and international cast) from

Poupin, who naturally regards the poor young man (who "had never been to Paris" and who knows nothing about it save as the Poupin *intérieur* "gave rather a vivid idea of that city," possibly misleading) as "one of themselves," *c'est-à-dire* "a child, as it were, of France, an offshoot of the sacred race." Hyacinth has previously been one year at an "Academy" which boasts "an 'instructor in the foreign languages.'" Despite his not knowing if he is more English or more French, or even which he might prefer, he prides himself on possession of the Gallic tongue. At the Muniments, he offers to help Paul with *his* French: "'I feel the advantage of knowing it,' Hyacinth remarked, finely," in English. Moments later, Muniment derides his knowledge of French. Hyacinth amusingly threatens to "say something very neat and sharp . . . just the sort of thing they say so much in French." Rosy Muniment irresistibly joins in. "Oh, do say something of that kind; we should enjoy it so much!" A working knowledge of French among the working classes of the London poor would appear to be a dispensable luxury and an ironic irrelevance. "I don't know it for nothing," Hyacinth has just said, but what he knows it for, what good it ever does him, fails to appear. If it served to salve his tawdry end we are not informed. The close of the text is drenched in German.

*Exilic Poupin Ambassadeur.* "Exilic" and *"Ambassadeur"* propose in two different languages two distinctly different situations with a common denominator, two types of long-term residence in a country not one's own—not necessarily, however, the Magic Land of Elsewhere—in one or another sort of representing role. Poupin is, or fancies himself to be, exiled for political reasons; he compensates the penalty in several ways, among them by serving as France's unappointed spokesman to and for *The Princess Casamassima*. Poupin's contribution to the novel is clearly structural, despite all the textual ridicule, a prime function of thematized France Englished or England Frenched. In James' tale of two or more cities he is also half of that neat reciprocating pair of prime geographical displacements and interpenetrations which is composed of Poupin's perpetuating presence in London and Hyacinth's brief but intense visit to Paris. This pair of notations signifies one grand historical whole, which may be suggested by some such historian's phrase as "the movement(s) of the people(s,)" French, English, Italians, Germans, and others by implication.

Comparison and contrast are the inherent fictive modes of the international literary performance. At Crookenden's bookbinding establishment, where, naturally enough, "wages and beer were the main objects of consideration," along with the material beautification of printed gatherings, we no sooner hear how "the British workman, when animated by the spirit of mirth, has rather a heavy hand," which mirthful hand sits heavily on the youthful spirits of our sensibilitarian protagonist, than we are met by the deliberately countervailing dignity of "foreign" Poupin in support of Hyacinth's defensive tactics: " '*Enfin vous voilà ferme!*' (the Frenchman himself, terribly *éprouvé* at the beginning, had always bristled with firmness and opposed to insular grossness a refined dignity)." In all such formulations, cunningly designed for the titillation of a sophisticated Anglo-American readership, the grossness of the readership's linguistic compatriots is a given, always to be denigrated in relation to continental graces, normally French. Continental graces reveal their manifold aspects through many a turn and counterturn. To the perfervid conversational atmosphere of the Sun and Moon, close air packed with platitudinous pseudo-question "And what the plague [euphemism] am I to do with seventeen shillings—with seventeen shillings?" and "ribald reply" (not quoted), enter Poupin speaking awkward English or flawless French, the language of liberty, equality, fraternity, the arts, advanced and advancing political and social theory, elegance, and the cultural assumptions generally of the civilized center *(centre)*, to announce, as if he alone were privy to the priceless information (not verified) "that in the east of London, that night, there were forty thousand men out of work. He looked round the circle with his dilated foreign eye" which fixes the comrades, all male, as "to make each man responsible for hearing him."

The fictions within the Poupin fiction are, first, that Poupin is in fact what he maybe once was and still pretends to be, and, second (which is also James' fiction), that English-speaking people desire to hear about nothing so much as their total and hopeless inferiority to all things French (*ceteris paribus* the message being propounded at length by *The Princess Casamassima*, to be continued at even greater length in *The Tragic Muse*). Juxtaposition of one set of facts or presuppositions with an alien set of probabilities ironically and comically deflates the international romanticism originating in the same juxtapositions (nationalism, language, class). It may or may not ever have been true, Poupin's plight; it is not true now; it is nevertheless (or *therefore?*) a wonderful fiction making for a wonderful celebrity (in certain circles): "He owed his position at the 'Sun and Moon' to the brilliancy with which he represented the political exile," now defined by narrative authority as "the magnanimous immaculate citizen wrenched out of bed at dead of night, torn from his hearthstone, his loved ones and his profession, and hurried across the frontier with only the coat on his back." Was it so? or did we only read about it, perhaps in Balzac? No matter; it works. "Poupin had performed in this character now for many years, but he had never lost the bloom of the outraged proscript." He owes his bloom also to the good-natured tolerance of his English mates, who overlook his "want of tact in his calling upon them to sympathise with him for being one of themselves," i.e., a resident of insupportable England. "He imposed himself by the eloquence of his assumption that if one were not in the beautiful France [a nice idiomatic Frenchism] one was nowhere worth speaking of, and ended by producing an impression that that country had an almost supernatural charm," which happens to be the same French charm purveyed to the willing readership by Henry James from at least as early as "Madame de Mauves" to as late as *The Ambassadors* and even beyond. Realistic Paul Muniment, now standing in for the more skeptical reader, reminds Hyacinth that "Poupin would be very sorry if he should be enabled to go home again (as he might, from one week to the other, the Republic being so indulgent and the amnesty to the Communards constantly extended), for over there he couldn't be a refugee."

Poupin is especially valuable for simultaneously representing to the text of *The Princess Casamassima* the conflicted claims of cosmopolitan internationalism, clearly the personal preference of Henry James, and the rampant constituent nationalisms of the later-middle nineteenth century. Potentially torn apart by that division, the Jamesian text appears to cry out for a "world-center" amicably to compose its hostile groupings, and in 1886 that center can only be the capital of the world, Paris. No one was likely to think it London, where James mostly lived, much less the New York he hailed from. Yet after his year in Paris James himself seldom found it easy to think any such folly: the New Yorker-resident-in-London was clearly and predictably if sporadically annoyed at and resentful of French presumptions of supremacy, largely left over from Napoleonic days. Poupin still lives in those days. Intellectually, culturally, politically, Poupin is alleged to structure the whole world, with all its various and variable destinies, according to a simple cartographic metaphor, almost certainly unexamined, propounded in the name of the human race, projecting the layout of streets around the Arc de Triomphe, as well as the major Haussmannic thoroughfares, around the entire planet and for all future time:

> he believed that the day was to come when all the nations of the earth would abolish their frontiers and armies and custom-houses, and embrace on both cheeks, and cover the globe with boulevards, radiating from Paris, where the human family would sit, in groups, at little tables, according to affinities, drinking coffee (not tea, *par exemple!*) . . .

And yet in a shorter stretch of time, the cartographical model Poupin has in mind is among the "creations of the arch-fiend of December," and so we are yielded one more dilemma, "he was gratified as a Parisian and a patriot but he was disconcerted as a lover of liberty; it cost him a pang to admit that anything in the sacred city was defective, yet he saw still less his way to concede that it could owe any charm to the perjured monster of the second Empire, or even to the hypocritical, mendacious republicanism of the régime before which the sacred Commune had gone down in blood and fire." But Poupin is also capable of saying to Hyacinth, in his best patriotic rhetoric, given by the text in English translation, "Speak to me . . . of my Paris; *she* is always divine," even if, from one point of view or another, she is not.

*Paris At Last and Evermore.* "These are the principal things I think of; though if you could rake in one or two big generalising glimpses or fragments (even of the Arc de Triomphe say) there are one or two other places—as second volume of *Princess Casamassima,* where suchlike might come in," referring of course, to the New York Edition ("Memoranda to A. L. Coburn For the Paris Subjects").[10] Paris *pièce de résistance* (no other phrase will quite do) finally appears at chapters

29–30, in a total of 47, and for that little spell we are back as if in such a typical Tourist Fiction as *The American*. Christopher Newman had first flashed upon the eager eye of the Tourist Reader on "a brilliant day in May, in the year 1868," at the Louvre—in fact June 1876 in the pages of the *Atlantic Monthly*—Bädeker (so spelled) at hand, presumably (for James, not Newman) the fourth edition of 1874, "remodelled and augmented." Now (*The Princess Casamassima* "ran" in the *Atlantic Monthly* from September 1885 through October 1886, at which time it must have been a joy to be alive) Hyacinth Robinson, without mention of guidebook, is visibly reposed "beside a little table in front of Tortoni's," Boulevard des Italiens 22, "the most dandified café in Paris," worn out with sightseeing and other thrills—he must have heard a great deal of *French*. More than a century later, I have available to antiquarian researches, nostalgic services, and a sense of the Tourist Reader *then,* an 1888 Bædeker, an 1883 and an 1888 Galignani, straddling the year of the fictive visit.

Hyacinth looks east, to where Boulevard des Italiens changes its name to Boulevard Montmartre, at the Variétés theater, "which blazed through intermediate lights [gas, still] and through the thin foliage of trees not favoured by the asphalt." He will not this night be in the theater to see Chaumont, "the *succès du jour.*" Like Isabel Archer sitting up late to review her life (and *The Portrait of a Lady* to that point), he will sit and *think*—remember, ask questions, put two and two together. It is a brilliant stroke of construction in this novel about talk and talkers that the hero should be represented as at last in Paris exchanging not one word with another living soul. Unlike Isabel Archer, however, he is far from alone, there "on the boulevard, as he watched the interminable successions" of pedestrians, as if they were the generations of humanity. In *The American,* Christopher Newman had undergone a world of trouble from an irrelevant class-conscious Anglo-French family. At Tortoni's, proletarian Anglo-French Robinson happily consumes a *marquise,* pineapple ice in champagne, about which he heard a gentleman speak the night before at the Comédie Française, an expensive "decoction." Everybody at a Tortoni table, he is sure, must be a celebrity suitable to tourist romanticism as derived from French Literature (of the earlier nineteenth century and not earlier):

He knew about Tortoni's from his study of the French novel, and as he sat there he had a vague sense of fraternising with Balzac and Alfred de Musset; there were echoes and reminiscences of their works in the air, confounding themselves with the indefinable exhalations, the strange composite odour, half agreeable, half impure, of the boulevard. "Splendid Paris, charming Paris"—that refrain, the fragment of an invocation, a beginning without an end, hummed itself perpetually in Hyacinth's ears; the only articulate words that got themselves uttered in the hymn of praise which his imagination had been offering to the French capital from the first hour of his stay.

This is a particularly striking instance of what I mean by the attachment of literatures: Henry James, an American writer, of the very best, conspicuously surpassing and superseding previous American aspirants (Emerson, Hawthorne, Lowell, et al.), easily keeping abreast or ahead of contemporary American competitors (Howells, Mark Twain, the provincial local colorists), thus constituting himself as the new American Literature; writing a novel predominantly in the English language and set in England (but partly peopled by strange types, James being one of them, "foreigners"), generally following the social-satiric tradition of Dickens and Thackeray, thus constituting himself as a resplendent item, by no means the least, in the English literary tradition; and then, as I have been pointing out, soaking that English tradition, by way of the French language and the many French things which the English text refers to, in the French literary tradition as well, not to mention the aestheticizing, the formalizing, the stylizing of inherited Anglo-American traditions with the aims and methods of French realism-naturalism, thus also constituting himself as an integral participant in French Literature, *confrère* of Balzac, de Musset, *et les autres;* so that we finally come to realize how it is not only the silly Poupin who projects international amity and dominion around the globe, emanating from Paris *centre* like boulevards, but someone else as well, someone not imagined but real, and needing only to be recognized. Indeed there is a James letter of 9 August 1901 to Morton Fullerton comically reproducing this whole international picturation: "with *me* (born under *our* stars, not to say stripes), perched here in my little Cinque Port [Rye], over against the coast of France, reaching out to the capital of capitals, the Paris of Parises, where you, in strange, high, lighted chambers, with boulevards at your feet, and the glory thereof, and chancelleries in your ears and Europe, in short, in your hand," and the rest of the world by implication.[11] The attachment of literatures, especially the French, often appears to me in the form of a fable. Once upon a time there was born in New York a small squid who at maturity found himself all out and alone in the great worldwide ocean called Literature and who liked his independence well enough but also felt the need of some socialization and as he swam around and pondered these things he encountered various enormous fishes named Greek Literature and Spanish Literature and Latin Literature and German Literature and Chinese Literature but none of them seemed quite right not even English Literature to whom he said in passing "I'll be back" and finally he met up with a fish named French Literature, approached, and, with a limber tentacle and powerful suction cup, he attached himself, for ever and a day, to that smoothest of all glistening flanks.

In the Jamesian text, a ghost is the projection of a missing personage, most often but not always in memory, a personage dead or otherwise unavailable for present association. And what in the vast Jamesian *œuvre* can be thought more brilliant than the created ghost of Hyacinth's grandfather, the father of Florentine Vivier, whom Hyacinth has never in this life seen—he has only seen his mother, to remember, but the once—long since dead in the bloody events of 1848, but long since imagined, at London, by his lonely alienated grandson, as "the revolutionary watch-maker who had known the ecstasy of the barricade and had paid for it with his life," as Henry James may well have imagined himself as likewise now paying while equally winning the whole world of literature, the grandfather possessing, all imaginably, "many of the most attractive traits of the French character," yet also "reckless, and a little cracked, and probably immoral," like nothing so much, in short, as *The Princess Casamassima*? Best of all, the grandfather speaks, under "the influence of a gaiety which even political madness could never quench," the best of French, "the French tongue of an earlier time, delightful and sociable in accent and phrase, exempt from the commonness of modern slang. This vague yet vivid personage," this literary ghost, "became Hyacinth's constant companion"—and now we know why Bædeker has been neglected—"he roamed about with Florentine's boy," and we with them in this brief two-chapter revivification of the archetypical Tourist Fiction.

With grandfather guide, Hyacinth visits museums, gardens, churches—"(the republican martyr was very good-natured about this)"—passages, arcades, avenues, bridges, quays, Tortoni's, the usual attractions: "Our young man took almost the same sort of satisfaction in the Louvre as if he had erected it." His overall impression is that of *The Princess Casamassima* entire and is in that respect literary: "All Paris struck him as tremendously artistic and decorative; he felt as if hitherto he had lived in a dusky, frowsy, Philistine world. . . . It seemed to him that Paris *expressed herself,* and did it in the *grand style,* while London remained vague and blurred, *inarticulate,* blunt and dim" (emphasis added). Hyacinth naturally fails to look up Poupin's "democratic friends, ardent votaries of the social question," who live in the Batignolles and the Fauberg Saint-Antoine, even though he stays in a *hôtel garni* in the Rue Jacob, as recommended by *les Poupins.* His greatest touristic satisfaction comes from discovering the whereabouts of the barricade where his grandfather died: "he at last satisfied himself (but I am unable to trace the process of the induction) that it had bristled across the Rue Saint-Honoré, very near to the church of Saint-Roch."

Everyone except Crookenden (who recommends "two or three days of alcoholic torpor" on English soil) has wanted Hyacinth to see Paris, and of course the Tourist Reader has been restrained only with the greatest difficulty, solaced with minor sops of French tossed in his or her direction from time to time, anything to allay the gluttonous craving—so unanimously, indeed, as "to place his journey to Paris in a light almost ridiculous." The Poupins, of course, are enthusiasts, as ever, and so is or was Pinny, who leaves him money for the trip in her will, and according to Mr. Vetch, "had a particular wish that you should go to Paris," perhaps in belated remorse for her slighting of Florentine in favor of her aristocratic seducer, and Paul Muniment, even. At Tortoni's, Hyacinth thinks of them all, he reviews the previous text of *The Princess Casamassima,* as it were, while wondering how long he may sit at a table without ordering another *marquise.* The Variétés discharges its crowd to the pavement and to the terrace of the café, gentlemen with ladies ("he knew already how to characterize the type—*des femmes très-chic"*). Then, almost in the tonality of *The Ambassadors,* still more than a decade and a half in the unknown future, "The nightly emanation of Paris," the informal unplanned *son et lumière* of 1886, "seemed to rise more richly, to float and hang in the air, to mingle with the *universal light* and the *many-voiced sound"* (emphasis added), simply the civilized center of the beautiful and the true and the good, however idealized. Hyacinth walks "home," back to his nameless hotel on the other side of the Seine, the text tracing his route from the congestions of populace to the condition of finding himself "almost isolated." Rue Royale leads him to Pont de la Concorde, and there we lose him. Not, however, until we have looked, with him, at the Place de la Concorde, between the Tuileries (gardens) and the Champs Elysées and meditated the meaning of its changes of name from the Place Louis Quinze to the Place de la Révolution to its present, and perhaps permanent, name. Bædeker estimates "upwards of 2800 persons" beheaded there in the Revolution. Guide James, perhaps noting that in 1886 Paris had gone some time without a popular devastation (and would go much longer), is after something more inclusive. His Hyacinth "sees" (visualizes) the guillotine, the tumbrils, the victims, but much more than that he "sees" (comprehends, intellectually) that, "strangely, what was most present was not its turpitude and horror, but its magnificent energy," almost as if the Revolution had been written by Honoré de Balzac. Before and after his trip, Hyacinth talks with various people about Paris—Anastatius Vetch desires to know if the Rue Mogador be the same in 1886 as in 1840: "the old man," we are further informed, "had thought his letters clever. He only wished that he had made them cleverer still; he had no doubt of his ability to have done so." It is the voice of Henry James ventriloquizing, perpetually revisiting and revising his very own word, now in the middle way between *The American* and *The Ambassadors.* Some, myself in certain moods among them, will wish him to have lingered there even longer, as if to say, with Milly Theale in *The Wings of the Dove,* as she looks at the picture which prefigures her death, "I shall never be better than this."

# V.

# Paris As Golden Meter:
## *The Tragic Muse* (1890)

### 1. *The Great and Damning Charge*

We shall arrive at that phrase in due course and after certain
clarifications—for example, of the term "international novel" ("tale,"
"fiction," "theme," or whatever), as variously and perhaps misleadingly used by various Jamesians: some seem to require an American
protagonist, even though other nations are available, any two of
them constituting internationality.* Henry James being an American

---

*In the New York Edition prefaces to *The Spoils of Poynton,* and to the *Lady Barbarina* and *Daisy
Miller* volumes, James lends himself, quite maddeningly, to the dubious notion that internationality
presumes the American presence vis-à-vis Europe—especially obscure his naming *The Princess Casamassima* and *The Tragic Muse* as works in which international interest is negligible. These references
may be found in the Library of America edition of *French Writers, Other European Writers, The Prefaces
to the New York Edition* (New York, 1984), pp. 1149, 1208, 1280–81.

automatically gives us one nation and what he writes about often gives us a whole lot more. But what he writes about—nationally—he sometimes misstates, as, on 3 March 1888 to Thomas Bailey Aldrich of *The Tragic Muse:* "the scene will be in London, like the *Princess*—though in a very different *monde*."[1] Well! the *Princess,* as we have seen, is sufficiently a tangle of conflicting national languages and cultures, mainly four (five if you count the author's American-ism separately). *The Tragic Muse* can even less be said to be "in" London, one third of the novel being so conspicuously "in" Paris. *The Tragic Muse* is rather more like a literary war between the two nations, written by an American onlooker, his national animus concealed or suppressed, his French preferences quite in the open. It may well be called an international novel and, in significant senses, French.

A further complication is that composition of *The Tragic Muse* was coterminous with such events as *The Diary of Alice James,* that fervent pro-Irish England-hater; the beginning of another (not the first but the most determined) attempt to write for the stage; and the latest revisiting of *The American* (following hard upon its previous return, in 1888, as *The Reverberator*), that chancing to be the novel-to-play James was tinkering while *The Tragic Muse* accomplished its lengthy course through seventeen issues of the *Atlantic Monthly*. And *The Tragic Muse* is *about* theater and drama: but it is not exactly a prelude to the dramatic years, for James was already deeply into *The American* again while also writing the new novel concerning, among other things, plays and players. The play he was working on was itself a revision of an international novel of some years back, so that international comparisons and temporal throwbacks were surely alive in the mind of the bifurcating author, even if the nations in question appear to have shifted about: in 1876–77 he was living in Paris and writing against, but also "into," France, as it were—now in England.

As for Alice James, if she was less than the source she fancied herself she was doubtless a sounding board. When her diary was published, H. (as she calls him) was scandalized at how his own careless conversation had been carefully included. In the view of Alice, inspiration ran in the opposite direction: "H., by the way, has embedded in his pages many pearls fallen from my lips, which he steals in the most unblushing way, saying, simply, that he knew they had been said by the family, so it did not matter" (17 June 1891).[2] However it may turn out with respect to who owed what to whom, it is easy to conjecture H. amused, refreshed, and sustained by the viva voce equivalent of such sprightly Alice-isms as "oh! the coarse possibilities of the British fibre!" (29 July 1890) or "gloating over foxes torn to pieces by a pack of hounds" (17 February 1890). In the same entry as the last remark we find Alice "stifled by the all pervasive sense of pharasaism in the British constitution of things. . . . I asked H. once how it struck him . . . he said that he didn't think it could be exaggerated." At least we may believe Alice helped keep H. up to the mark, and that her fiercely loyal, vicarious, invalidic participating interest in the joint fortunes of *The Tragic Muse* and the staged version of *The American* served to remind the brother how curiously these two works were come to be connected, for *The American* was not only, now, a play (with a happy ending), but it had been, more than a decade ago, a singularly important novel for its author, representing the issues of literary nationalism and literary internationalism, the personal life (where he was living, Paris) and the literary life (what he wrote about, Americans in Paris), and only the action and the setting disjunct. Recast and revived, the play, representing the novel, belonged to two different literary genres and to two different historical periods.

Opening night for *The American* was 3 January 1891 at Southport. Alice James' diary for 7 January promptly and obligingly asks, rhetorically, "can you wonder at the maddening irritation with which the critic fills the artist soul? . . . H. replies, 'No, but one is so inadequate for it, and would have to be a Frenchman to hate them enough, and to express the irony, scorn and contempt with which one ought to be filled!' H., with his impervious mildness, certainly *is* inadequate to the subject." Perhaps his subtlety escaped her. It has escaped others. Of James' personal letters in the years 1875–1881, Percy Lubbock judiciously remarks the "caustic reflections on the minds and manners of the English" and that "it should here be pointed out that his correspondence was the only outlet open to these irrepressible sentiments."[3]

No, the outlet best open to these irrepressible sentiments was once more that inclusively intertextual fictionalized situation which may be called Henry James' attachment of French Literature, not in every detail but in the general drift of it, the devotion to style, form, execution, language, doing, the *thing done,* the attention to the material, the functional, the practical. The treatment of the English in *The Tragic Muse* is finally to be understood in the light of its being James' most French novel, hence in its range of reference his most aesthetic, aesthetic here meaning anti-Philistine, anti-bourgeois. Granted, these terms were not quite the same to the American in England as to the *confrères* in France—they would need adjustment to local affairs, and a generalized toning down. In his first essay on Balzac, James had years earlier described for the edification of "us English readers" the cruelty of French satire: "Like all French artists and men of letters, Balzac hated the bourgeoisie with an immitigable hatred, and more than most of his class he hated the provincial. . . . Balzac and his comrades hate the bourgeois, in the first place, because the bourgeois hates them, and in the second place, because they are almost always fugitives from the bourgeoisie."[4] Thus for the English reader *The Tragic Muse* may predictably furnish forth some such pleasure as was presumably found by the French in their perusal of *La Chartreuse de Parme,* where they are so systematically insulted through invidious comparison with Italians. As for American readers, who can say what unholy pleasure they derived from this wicked denunciation and ridicule of their old *bête noire,* now hailed into the high court of international Francophiliac aesthetic standards as the very type and reductio ad absurdam of vices hitherto chiefly attributed to the poor Americans, namely the bourgeois, the provincial, the Philistine hatred of art?

*The Tragic Muse* is such a view of English culture as might have been natural to the author had he remained resident in Paris. It is a literary production in the tradition of *épater le bourgeois* and by 1889 what other bourgeois did James know nearly so well? In adopting himself into French Literature, in attaching it to his own œuvre as cradle and context (but never to the risk of not *also* belonging to English Literature and to American Literature, such as it was, as well), James was mainly a devotee of Balzac. What stands out most in his criticism of Balzac is his passion to forgive Balzac everything. James was harder on other French writers, perhaps hardest of all on Flaubert. But now in *The Tragic Muse* James pays tribute to Flaubert by insinuating himself into the Flaubertian tradition, except that as

Flaubert excoriated France from the standpoint of art, James, fusing art and France, even more than in *The Princess Casamassima,* excoriates England from the standpoint of French art, chiefly French dramatic and theatrical art. James' 1893 essay on Flaubert contains a passage essential to the present point (and so we come in the end to the great and damning charge, that fascinating phrase):

> That was the indispensable thing for him in a social, a personal relation, the existence in another mind of a love of literature sufficiently demonstrated to relieve the individual from *the great and damning charge,* the charge perpetually on Flaubert's lips in regard to his contemporaries, the accusation of malignantly hating it. (Emphasis added.)

It is wonderful to watch our Frenchfied (Anglo-) American shrink at the very thought of such a thing! And shrink the more as he sees how the indictment, however paranoid, might make even more sense applied closer and closer to home:

> This universal conspiracy he perceived, in his own country, in every feature of manners, and to a degree which may well make us wonder how high he would have piled the indictment if he had extended the inquiry to the manners of ours. We draw a breath of relief when we think to what speedier suffocation he would have yielded had he been materially acquainted with the great English-speaking peoples.

Flaubert was long since dead. In the 1893 essay and in *The Tragic Muse* James continues to exculpate himself from the great and damning charge—it was, we suspect, the deepest dyed sin he was capable of conceiving. The narrator in "The Death of the Lion" (1894) still broods: "I begin to see deeper into Gustave Flaubert's doleful refrain about the hatred of literature."[5] In his 1888 essay on the Goncourts' *Journal* James had at least glimpsed a different wisdom: "Gautier's defect is that he had veritably but one idea: he never got beyond the superstition that real literary greatness is to bewilder the *bourgeois.* Flaubert sat, intellectually, in the same everlasting twilight."[6] And now, for the time being, someone else likewise so sat.

## 2. *Retrogressive Structure*

In *The Tragic Muse,* France—Paris—is the setting for approximately one third of the action, mostly the first third—chapters 1–12, 18–21, part of 28—the other two thirds taking place in England. The French third coming first, all the rest is virtually by default rendered anticlimactic and wistfully reversionary. The novel is so constructed as paradoxically to come apart as it advances; to run downhill as it runs along; to turn backward against its proper progress. It is because the last two thirds are in England, it is England which is the cause of retroaction. The personages are perpetually referring themselves and each other back to their situation in a prior and better world and a better place and a better time. To a really astonishing degree, the text of *The Tragic Muse* is flavored with, and structured by, memories of Paris on the part of persons not *in* Paris. Paris is the Magic Land of Elsewhere. And earlier. Paris is Once Upon A Time.

The first third of the novel establishes as bastions of value never to be overthrown in this world France a geographic space and French the language in it; within them, as pinpointed particulars, the city of Paris (to be strolled around) and the Théâtre Français. It is like a nation of four estates, equal and interchangeable. France, French, Paris, the Français are supplied the reader in copious, in overwhelming, in nearly relentless detail—they shall serve to indict, transcend, and recompense us for English silliness, muddle, commercialism, Philistinism, the hatred of art and of literature. In some ways, *The Tragic Muse* is like a secularized-aestheticized version of the Gospel According to St. John: "In him was life; and the life was the light of men. And the light shineth in the darkness; and the darkness apprehended it not" (1:4–5—King James Version). Readers must not be scandalized when Miriam says to her mother, of Madame Carré: "She's founded on a rock."[7] Apostolic Christianity would seem to reenact itself at the Théâtre Français. Or is it only a Jamesian phrase? In the stage and novelized versions of *The Other House* we find the line "Your friend there has his feet on the rock!"[8] Or is it a family phrase, as in Henry James, Senior, "the house of your peace is built upon a rock"?[9]

Another phrase useful, nay indispensable, for *The Tragic Muse* turns up in James' *Notebooks* apropos of that novel: "my impression of Bartet, in her *loge,* the other day in Paris." In another *Notebooks* entry of about the same time, James is talking to himself in the voice of Julia Dallow talking to Nick Dormer: "I adore you. Only you must promise me—you are slippery and I must have some pledges. *What did you mean that night in Paris?"* (emphasis added).[10] So to the text direct and to the retrogressive structure; it is the first instance of backward reference and it falls in chapter 15:

> "What did you mean that night in Paris?"
> "That night?"
> "When you came to the hotel with me . . ."

And so forth. The same scene in which Miriam says Madame Carré is founded on a rock represents Nick remembering what Gabriel Nash said about Mrs. Rooth "at the exhibition in Paris," Mrs. Rooth remembering that Miriam had reminded Biddy Dormer "of something that had passed between them in Paris," Mrs. Rooth telling Miriam (so that Nick may overhear) what Miriam had told Mrs. Rooth about Peter Sherringham's state of soul "that night we went to the foyer of the Français." The last major event in *The Tragic Muse* is Miriam's triumph as Juliet, a part which she had recited in Paris. Miriam Rooth is the primary personage of the novel redemptive for England, but her art is half an import: the play is Shakespeare, the execution is brought from across the channel.

Miriam to Peter—innocently? a structural revelation all the same —"Your being where I shall never see you is not a thing I shall enjoy; I know that from the separation of these last months—after our beautiful life in Paris, the best thing that ever happened to me or that ever will." (In the same speech she calls Peter *mon bon,* which is what James, in a good mood, called himself—*Notebooks,* passim.) Or is she in Paris still, the quasi-Jewish girl "of the incorruptible faith: she had been saturated to good purpose with the great spirit of Madame Carré," like a secularized reflection of the Blessed Virgin? Miriam-Peter conversations are punctuated by backward allusion to the earlier time, the other place: "You told me moreover in Paris, more than once," and "our dear, sweet days last summer in Paris, I shall never forget." It is as if summer would never come again. None of the characters ever seems to forget what was said and done, there, then; and in case of need, someone else is quick to point it out.

"We know you, we know you; we saw you in Paris" is the thematic and structural statement of the novel, perpetually catapulting the bewildered reader backward one or two hundred pages into a prior state of affairs, with which the present state of affairs is being contrasted, invidiously, as usual. The center of gravity is always displaced after a doubling: it is now but it is also then, or then is the cause of now, or then is the measure of now, or then is the obliteration of now, so much the more wonderful it all once was! Social occasions seem to be mostly prior, at Paris, last summer. "I have an idea I wasn't nice to you that day in Paris," Miriam says to Biddy, Biddy of course knowing what day she means. It is as if conversation worth recalling, worth going into again, had taken place only in the enchanted quartiers. Even memories non-enchanting are assigned the same origins: "Nick added a remark to the effect that Mrs. Dallow would remember to have had the pleasure of meeting Miss Rooth the year before—in Paris, that day, at her brother Peter's," each item carefully specified and in series. "You met him [Gabriel Nash] in Paris and didn't like him" he further reminds Julia, having already prompted her about Miriam, "Don't you remember her that day at Peter's, in Paris?" It is as if people hardly existed out of Paris or at any other time.

A reminds B that she met C in Paris. B remembers. Then B forgets. A reminds B again. Or B reminds herself, sometimes more than once, sometimes superfluously: "I saw her [Miriam]—perhaps you remember—in your rooms [Peter's] in Paris [naturally]." Who can tell how many times the reader had been told this or the like? It is the text talking to itself, as one might say, reminding itself, confirming itself, establishing itself, structuring itself, always in reverse order to what is going on, which is exactly the point: precious little is going on. It *went on,* earlier in the text, earlier in fictive time, and in a foreign setting. The personages of the fable, the fable itself, exist primarily in what they saw and heard and said and did in Paris and in their subsequent rememberings and comments upon the same.

Characters encountered in London now but encountered in Paris first are glimpsed through a kind of superimposition of time and place, narrative and setting, two actions and two place-times represented as merged. Nick recalls Nash, whom he has not seen since Paris, he remembers their walk, their talk, Notre Dame at night. And so they talk now: " 'Don't you remember our talk in Paris?' . . . 'That's what has come on since we met in Paris.' . . . 'I think you saw her in Paris.' . . . 'Do you remember the Tragic Muse?' . . . . 'That girl in Paris' . . . 'Oh, Peter's girl: of course I remember her.' . . . 'She tells me something was said about it that day at Madame Carré's.' " Miriam likewise remembers Nick (next chapter): "I remembered our meeting in Paris and the kind things you said to me." That much not sufficing, "she repeated to Nick that she hadn't forgotten his friendly attitude in Paris." Does Nick remember *her* in Paris (another new chapter and how little has changed)? Indeed, "He remembered her loudness, her violence in Paris, at Peter Sherringham's, her wild wails, the first time, at Madame Carré's." Miriam in her turn remembers and repeats what Mademoiselle Voisin said to her at the Théâtre Français, "I'm acting for *you* tonight."

Nick "heard Nash say something about the honour of having met Mrs. Dallow in Paris." People are always hearing some one say something like that. Recognition and recall, the backward glance, the reminder, the dating of significance to the former occasion, the placing of significance in France, in Paris, these textual markers are not incidental but thematic and formal, they structure and shape the narrative space, in a way they *are* the narrative space, its bones and musculature. Peter "became acutely conscious [in London] of what Julia had said to him in Paris." It is obviously in Paris that persons get off their best remarks; if these remarks are nothing very spectacular, at least they are listened to and remembered. Remarks made in the past continue to direct present actions and states of mind, even though the same characters are now in England with rights of free speech and quite at liberty to express themselves. Paris brought out the best in them as England does not. Persons who do not desire to remember must be nudged: Nick "endeavoured to give his mother a notion of who this young lady [Miriam] was and to remind her of the occasion, in Paris, when they had all seen her together." Lady Agnes, who is pure English, has already "remembered how they had met him [Nash] in Paris," and, even though Nash is English, "how he had frightened her," Lady Agnes being susceptible to flutters when abroad.

## 3. Walking Tours of Paris

" 'You enjoy Paris—you are happy here?' . . . 'Oh, yes, it's very nice.' " British speech habits flatten out "the general sharp contagion of Paris." Still Biddy Dormer, who says Paris is very nice, likes "the curious people, the coming and going of Paris." Her brother Nick Dormer assures their impossible English mother that "everything is amusing here" ("What nonsense Paris makes one talk!"). Nick "was fonder of Paris than most of his countrymen, though not so fond, perhaps, as some other captivated aliens," presumably certain wandering Americans. It is not only at, and because of, the Salon that the Dormer family wear collectively "an expression, [which] was after all a kind of tribute to the state of exhaustion, of bewilderment, to which the genius of France is still capable of reducing the proud": much comedy derives from the antithetical natures of the English and the French, in despite of their geographical proximity. The Dormers are more particularly of "that tweed-and-waterproof class with which, on the recurrent occasions when the English turn out for a holiday . . . Paris besprinkles itself at a night's notice." We notice who is active, who passive, in this sprinkling action. The English are not, however, vis-à-vis one another, hopelessly and altogether without wit. Lady Agnes protesting that the "things" in the Salon are "too odious, too wicked" (because French), Parisianized Peter Sherringham replies, " 'Ah' . . . laughing, 'that's what people fall into, if they live abroad. The French oughtn't to live abroad,' " i.e., in Paris.

*The Tragic Muse* appropriately begins at but outside the Salon des Artistes Français, so designated since 1881, at the Palais de l'Industrie, Champs Elysées, south side, demolished in 1897 but on the same site as the present Grand Palais and Petit Palais. In honor of Nick Dormer, who will chuck politics in favor of portrait painting, the Salon is one of two French institutions furnishing French ammunition and major scenes to *The Tragic Muse;* the other, the Comédie Française, in honor of Miriam Rooth, heroinic aspirant to high achievement in the drama, will soon, and greatly, overshadow it. Indeed, James has little to say about the Salon except that it is art and is French and is therefore doubly obnoxious to the more obnoxious type of English.

In a later passage the text recurs to the Palais de l'Industrie, how it "glittered in the light of the long days," but it is only an item in a list. "And where are we to go?" Lady Agnes wants to know (still in the gardens of the Palais de l'Industrie), "I hate eating out-of-doors." In the course of reading *The Tragic Muse* we come to a number of eating and drinking establishments, few of them named, some of them inarguably out-of-doors. Peter and Julia Dallow join the Dormers for dinner at an unidentified and largely undescribed restaurant which Julia thinks of as a "pot-house," the same Julia who at dinner says, ever memorably, *"Merci, pas de vin."*

In Paris, as later in London, everyone is situated in entirely predictable places easily identifiable by a readership British or American. Peter Sherringham has his rooms, his "little corner at the [British] Embassy" (Rue du Faubourg-St. Honoré 39). Madame Carré is perhaps furthest from the tourist and hotel area, in the huitième on Rue de Constantinople, somewhere between Parc Monceau and the Gare St.-Lazare, *à l'entresol* (like Maria Gostrey). Miriam and her mother, out of funds, also have a dwelling slightly odd in location, at the Hotel de la Garonne—not given in Bædeker for 1888, conceivably never existing, and nonetheless most precisely described as "in a small, unrenovated street, in which the cobble-stones of old Paris still flourished, lying between the Avenue de l'Opéra and the Place de la Bourse. Sherringham had occasionally passed through this dim by-way, but he had never noticed the tall, stale *maison meublée,* whose aspect, that of a third-rate provincial inn, was an illustration of Mrs. Rooth's shrunken standard." The hotel is off the beaten tourist track but not far off: it is easy to walk Miriam home. Later the Rooth women add a small apartment, no street given, no arrondissement, small balcony, terrible furniture, a view of roofs, chimneys, tiles, tubes, and, coming up to the balcony, "the great hum of Paris," a sound James almost never fails to note. Others, in Paris more briefly, put up at hotels, Julia at the Hôtel de Hollande, Rue de la Paix 20. The Dormers' hotel, not named, is "up" the Rue de Rivoli, i.e., east of the Rue de la Paix, "near the Palais Royal," therefore near the Théâtre Français. The usual desire for a look at a "real" *French* interior (so disappointingly like any other) is hopefully answered by the brief exact account of Madame de Carré's "small beflounced drawing-room," where the Tourist Reader is free to wander about with Gabriel Nash "looking at the votive offerings which converted the little panelled box, decorated in sallow white and gold, into a theatrical museum," not quite a temple but almost, full of presents, portraits, wreaths, diadems, letters, trophies, tributes, relics, which are yet "hardly more striking than the confession of something missed . . . like a reference to clappings which, in the nature of things, could now only be present as a silence," a nice little foretaste of presence-absence thematics in *The Ambassadors*. Peter's rooms are apparently of little or no interest; and little or nothing is said of them.

Glamour of place, romanticism of setting, is chiefly engendered and sustained in the text of *The Tragic Muse* by represented walks about Paris as indulged by the English personages—the French do not walk about Paris in quite the same way. In chapter 5 the Dormers have come from the Palais de l'Industrie into the Champs Elysées, perhaps a little east and north of where they were: we find them at the Place de la Concorde, where the "friendly [and painterly] glance" of Nick "covered the great square, the opposite [left] bank of the Seine, the steep blue roofs of the quay, the bright immensity of Paris," and of the Place de la Concorde itself "the grand composition." As is customary with these Parisian observations in the Jamesian fiction, we learn something, not always tumultuous, about the position, behavior, temper, prospects, of the personage who observes; we also, in our role as Tourist Reader, learn something—often, much—about what it is that is *being* observed, Paris, that is, a fixed entity preexisting the fiction and continuing after, and outside of, its perusal, but not as Paris exists *in* the fiction, represented *in* the text, the ascertainable outside (Paris) fetched and lodged *within* the experience of reading—a double exposure.

The Dormer women (one nice outnumbered by two dreadful) proceed to their hotel, enter, leave, wander (Lady Agnes "joylessly") in the Palais Royal (grounds), the Rue de Richelieu, "and emerged upon the Boulevard," doubtless the juncture of Boulevard des Italiens and Boulevard Montmartre where Hyacinth Robinson sat at Tortoni consuming his *marquise* and lost in thought. Nick and Peter walk off in a different direction, Nick "demonstrative and lyrical," as befits the visitor, Peter *blasé,* as befits the old hand. Listing Nick's touristical enthusiasms naturally enables James to make a list for the reader at the same time, while he also, as usual, indicates, as precisely as he wishes, the location (setting, circumstances, situation, context, milieu, ambience) where action is alleged to be "taking place" in the simultaneous illustration of "character." Nick's "express enjoyment of Paris" is constituted by "the shop-windows on the quays, the old books on the parapet, the gaiety of the river, the grandeur of the Louvre, all the amusing tints and tones." There is a certain inclusive generality to the descriptive style: one may not always know if Nick and Peter were physically present at each and all of the denoted places or merely viewed them from a distance. The young men are too absorbed in conversation to notice exact detail and narrative looseness suits their represented mood.

*The Ambassadors* is among other things conspicuous for long lonely walks of Paris taken by Strether. In *The Tragic Muse* the topography of the city is registered and enjoyed (or not) by couples. We have just seen Nick and Peter going about. Now Nick invites Julia to wander through Paris on his arm. They come out of the restaurant (not named) to the boulevard (this time the Boulevard des Capucines); to sidewalk cafes; to "a profusion of light and a pervasion of sound," two of the more common observations about late-nineteenth-century Paris made by "strangers," as if all other large cities were in comparison dark and silent (mindless and inexpressive); to "that night-aspect of Paris which represents it as a huge market for sensations," now re-represented. Dominating the scene and their vision of it is a building flamboyantly thematic: "opposite the Café Durand the Madeleine rose theatrical, a high clever *décor,* before the foot-lights of the Rue Royale." They think they might take a drive in the Bois de Boulogne (west) or they might walk to the Place de la Bastille (east). In fact, they do neither but sit at Durand, which was at Place de la Madeleine 2; where, it is safe to assume, many Tourist Readers of *The Tragic Muse* had themselves sat or firmly intended to sit soon. A century later, Durand long gone, we must read differently—as I have several times had occasion to suggest, we can always read the original readers. Finally Nick and Julia walk back to Julia's hotel, according to textual directions "along the boulevard [Madeleine, then Capucines], on the right hand [southern] side, to the Rue de la Paix." Not a false step in the stroll and not a Tourist Reader who may not determine within a meter or two just where Nick and Julia are. But they are hardly an ideal couple for Paris walks: "All she had said on the way was that she was very tired of Paris."

The best walking tour of Paris is taken by Nick and Gabriel Nash. By previous arrangement, they meet at a café, name not given, "on the corner of the Place de l'Opéra," from which spot, in the heart of Anglo-American tourist-land, they set forth in quest of the *"quartiers sérieux,"* "down" (southward) along the Rue de la Paix to the Rue de Rivoli, across it, past the gilded railing of the Tuileries (gardens), into gorgeous local-color prose, descriptive, topographical, historic:

> The beauty of the night—the only defect of which was that the immense illumination of Paris kept it from being quite night enough, made it a sort of bedizened, rejuvenated day—gave a charm to the quieter streets, drew our friends away to the right [south], to the river and the bridges, the older, duskier city. The pale ghost of the palace that had died by fire [the Tuileries, during the Commune] hung over them awhile, and, by the passage now open at all times across the garden of the Tuileries they came out upon the Seine.

However aesthetic the prose, however "organically" necessary to the narrative it encloses and conveys, however total the incarnational subsumption of "meaning" (achieved intention) by "image" (the sequence of sentences conceived as in and of itself the basic narration), there is still leeway for the offering or confirmation of factual data the most utilitarian, e.g., "the passage now open at all times." Apparently, it had not always been, and James like a good Bædeker provides the latest correct up-to-date information, as, the reader may remember, he pretended to do in the opening sentences of *The American.* The palace that died by fire is of course the one that Strether will so wistfully remember.

Nick and Nash "came out upon the Seine," came out, that is, from point to point of the processive narration as well as from point to point of its topographical placing, came out to space different from just before, to space which opens into "balmy night, the time for talk, the amusement of Paris, the memory of young confabulations." At the Ile de la Cité our wandering English are overwhelmed by a second wave of alienating-romanticism-deliberately-sought-in-vain-and-now-chanced-upon-by-accident. They were discussing "the beautiful," *et voilà!:*

"Ah, the beautiful—there it stands, over there!" said Nick Dormer. . . . "Notre Dame *is* solid; Notre Dame *is* wise; on Notre Dame the distracted mind can rest. Come over and look at her!"

You would think Notre Dame (the building) was the thought of God. As if to steer back from the ideal to materiality, the text tells where they (we) are, and how arrived, plus new tips on Parisian sightseeing:

> They had come abreast of the low island from which the great cathedral, disengaged to-day from her old contacts and adhesions, rises high and fair, with her front of beauty and her majestic mass, darkened at that hour, or at least simplified, under the stars.

Then, now that past or future Tourist Reader is once more *au courant* about light conditions (gaslight turned down or off at night), back to the ostensive narrative—the young people of England "experiencing" in France—and we return to the proper tense of narrative, past tense:

> Our young men . . . crossed the wide, short bridge which made them face towards the monuments of old Paris—the Palais de Justice, the Conciergerie, the holy chapel of Saint Louis [normally known as Sainte Chapelle]. They came out before the church [Notre Dame], which looks down on a square where the past, once so thick in the very heart of Paris, has been made rather a blank, pervaded, however, by the everlasting freshness of the great cathedral-face.

The blank is the clearing to the west of Notre Dame, resulting in the enlarged Place du Parvis, another example of James noting changes in the visitable cityscape. As always, it is a moot question whether James is working from maps and guidebooks or from memory only. Like everyone else, he probably had in his possession a variety of guidebooks which he used for a while and got rid of as he no longer found them necessary.

Notre Dame as a visual monument dominates the Parisian scene of *The Tragic Muse* on its sensuously perceptible rather than its currently functioning side—no one goes to *holy* mass there, they look at the *architectural* mass, the façade, the shape, the form, that which composes to the eye for contemplation and revery:

> They walked around Notre Dame, pausing, criticizing, admiring and discussing; mingling the grave with the gay and paradox with contemplation. Behind and at the sides the huge dusky vessel of the church seemed to dip into the Seine, or rise out of it, floating expansively—a ship of stone, with its flying buttresses thrown forth like an array of mighty oars. Nick Dormer lingered near it with joy, with a certain soothing content; as if it had been the temple of a faith so dear to him that there was peace and security in its precinct.

The "faith" (not exactly Catholic) is the same as that of which the Comédie Française is sanctified as a chapel of the present, Notre Dame being rather of the past, yet even as the past it throws light, or darkness, or contrast—whatever is meant by "distinction"—over the rest of Paris, the "smartnesses," the order, the symmetry, the handsomeness, "the extravagance of gaslight, the perpetual click on the neat bridges." On the Right Bank again, Nick and Nash find a small café, "a friendly establishment . . . far away from the Grand Hotel." They hear the Seine. It reminds Nick "of the old Paris, of the great Revolution, of Madame Roland, *quoi!*" As James was writing, the beginning of the French Revolution was 100 years or so in the past, the beginnings of Notre Dame more like seven centuries. It seems to be all one past, one old Paris, one old France, Paris and France of the Revolution, Paris and France before the Revolution, Paris and France now, virtually unchanged in basic feeling, however altered in detail. "The streets of Paris at that hour," any hour, and almost any page, "were bright and episodical," full of French, of Parisian "life," exhibited in particular streets and places, associated with particular landmarks and monuments, the emotional colorations which for the moment change the lives of the English *étrangers* who for the best time of their lives encounter them.

The time span for the French third of *The Tragic Muse* is approximately the same as will be used again, even more effectively, in *The Ambassadors*. The Salon is in spring. By chapter 10, "summer was about to begin." In *The Ambassadors* Paris will empty and at the end of the process dump poor Strether back on Woollett; in *The Tragic Muse* summer empties the poor pathetic pitiable English out and back on England, Dormers first, others to follow. Amusements shrink. The Place de la Concorde "became, by a reversal of custom," and standard tourist joke, "explorable with safety" and "a larger, whiter desert than ever." In the deserted city Miriam notices more than ever such signs of Paris as prevision "her own dawn of glory." The Comédie Française "continued imperturbably to dispense examples of style." People who can afford it go to "the charming country that lies in so many directions beyond the Parisian *banlieue"* —present tense again, the tense of travel writing. In chapters 18–21, some of the personages, with the Tourist Reader tagging along, are in Paris again but mostly (chapters 20–21) at the Comédie Française, which is both a new subject and the same subject all over again.

### 4. *The Théâtre Français*

"Above all don't forget I yearn for some outside aspect of the Théâtre-Français, for possible use in *The Tragic Muse;* but something of course of the same transfigured nature; some ingeniously-hit-upon angle of presentment of its rather majestic big square mass and classic colonnade" ("Memoranda to A. L. Coburn For the Paris Subjects").[11] The photograph was perhaps superfluous, the Théâtre Français having since 1890 loomed in the text of *The Tragic Muse* as transfigured, ingeniously presented, and massive to the point that it may well be felt to imperil all other considerations. The Comédie Française *is* Paris (which *is* France), the golden meter of art. The repertory is French, the players play it in French, it is the best French there is, hence the best language available to humanity. By virtue of the French tongue, the Comédie is the focal point of French Literature, French drama, French art, French culture, French civilization. As Gabriel Nash remarks, with his apparent insouciance, "I think the Théâtre Français a greater institution than the House of Commons." He does not say, although he might have, greater than the Chambre des Députés. His point, the novel's point, is double and unfair: art is greater than politics, France is greater than England, just as truth is preferable to mendacity, the intelligent to the stupid; all this bravura resting on personal authority (Henry James'), *comme qui dirait:* "I may say that I know the Comédie Française."[12]

Chapters 20–21 take place *at* the Théâtre Français, slightly before the midpoint of *The Tragic Muse;* they may be said to constitute its pièce de résistance and perhaps even its raison d'être. Let it never be said that they are not led up to! Chapter 4 is full of premonitory first mentions: of the Comédie Française as greater than the House of Commons; of French plays that nice young English girls can't see; of Rachel; mostly of Madame Carré the old French actress (evidently a pupil and follower of Rachel) generally retired but still active. Madame Carré is unmarried, as is the much younger Mademoiselle Voisin. The private affairs of both women are thus by narrative fiat —and by the overall tone taken by the novel toward such matters— ruled off limits, out of the text, and exclusion of these matters is then cited as yet another example of French supremacy, the ability to mind your own business as well as to discriminate the private from the public life. It will not escape the notice of a cunning reader that by virtue of these singular textual maneuvers both actresses are textually viewed as completely apart from any considerations of family, James' *bête noire française* in such previous French performances as *The American* and *The Reverberator* (small rumbles of the storm are still to be heard in *The Ambassadors*). There are many things about the French, against the French, like French marriage customs, which *The Tragic Muse* is carefully constructed to keep out of sight, so that Madame Carré, for example, may be incomparably, and some will even think uncritically, defined as, in the view of the innocent Biddy Dormer: "Is it the famous Honorine Carré, the great celebrity?" She, and we, receive full answer from Peter Sherringham, who has a "permanent stall at the Français": "Honorine in person: the incomparable, the perfect! . . . The first artist of our time, taking her altogether," as how else should the reader take Henry James an authority from New York? Madame Carré "says" things in Peter's rooms ("She and I are old pals") and she is linked not only to French drama but to French fiction, the best. Against drama as a genre Gabriel Nash proposes the merits of *La Cousine Bette,* Peter assumes an invidious contrast against Augier, *Les Lionnes pauvres* (1858) (" 'What an extraordinary discussion! What dreadful authors!' Lady Agnes murmured to her son") and finally furnishes the anticipated line: "She is the Balzac, as one may say, of actresses." Later Miriam and Madame Carré recite, one badly and the other very well, the parts of Clorinde and Célie from *L'Aventurière* (a play in verse of 1848). At dinner, Julia Dallow suggests that Peter should take the Dormer misses to the Théâtre Français: "Even the programme appeared to have been pre-arranged to suit . . . just the thing for the cheek of the young person—'Il ne Faut Jurer de Rien' and 'Mademoiselle de la Seiglière.' "

James' occasional jests at the expense of French frivolity are as nothing compared with his seriousness in engaging on behalf of *The Tragic Muse* "the tradition." Madame Carré (she without a family save as the theater provides) is indirectly descended from none other than "the great *comédienne,* the light of the French stage in the early years of the century, of whose example and instruction Madame Carré had had the inestimable benefit." Surely none other is intended than Elisabeth Félix (1820–58), under whose influence, according to Sainte-Beuve, the Comédie Française was said to have revived. Madame Carré in her roles goes back to Molière (it is, after all, his *maison*): "At the first words she spoke Gabriel Nash exclaimed, endearingly: *'Ah, la voix de Célimène!'* "—reference to *Le Misanthrope* (1666). Reference to Rachel is more pertinent and more frequent. Miriam Rooth is tied to Rachel through her alleged Jewishness and through her passion and talent for acting, and Rachel seems never far from our textual attention: "when Sherringham had cited Mademoiselle Rachel as a great artist whose natural endowment was rich and who had owed her highest triumphs to it, she [Madame Carré] had declared that Rachel was the very instance that proved her point—a talent embodying one or two primary aids, a voice and an eye, but essentially formed by work, unremitting and ferocious work. 'I don't care a straw for your handsome girls,' she said; 'but bring me the one who is ready to drudge the tenth part of the way Rachel drudged, and I'll forgive her her beauty. Of course, *notez bien,* Rachel wasn't a *bête;* that's a gift, if you like.' " Later, Sherringham tells Miriam that she is "of Rachel's tribe," meaning, apparently, Jewish, and Miriam grandly retorts, "I don't care, if I'm of her tribe artistically. I'm of the family of the artists; *je me fiche* of any other!" (Yet "Likely enough," we are still later told, "the Hebraic Mr. Rooth . . . had supplied, in the girl's composition, the aesthetic element, the sense of form.'') After an impassioned rendering of "one of the speeches of Racine's Phaedra,'' Basil Dashwood tells her "You'll be the English Rachel.'' ('' 'Acting in French!' Madame Carré exclaimed. 'I don't believe in an English Rachel.' '') It is the same Madame Carré who magnificently declares: " *'Je ne connais qu'une scène—la nôtre.* . . . I have been informed there is no other.' 'And very correctly,' said Gabriel Nash,'' Henry James obviously agreeing. Peter justifies his calling Miriam by her first name "as one says 'Rachel' of her great predecessor.'' It is hard to tell if the lines of transmission should be read as quasi-familial or quasi-religious, as in a generational procession of female saints or maybe just a sequence of mothers, Madame Carré being to Miriam what Rachel had been to herself. That makes Rachel Miriam Rooth's grandmother, for anyone who is fond of loose analogies.

An extremely strict and demanding grandmother she is, indeed, for the point of all this emphasis on tradition, standards, technique, discipline, is the common Jamesian point about the relation of criticism to creation outside the purlieus of Anglo-Saxondom, that is to say in France. Criticism is what we observe Miriam receive, to her immediate pain but ultimate benefit, from Madame Carré, "her terrible initiatress,'' conceivably drawn from hints supplied by Fanny Kemble and Pauline Viardot,[13] but much more obviously from hints of Henry James in the flesh—remove the wig and he stands revealed. Her (his) criticism is said to be ferocious, analytic, reasonable, clear, cruel, hard, and unEnglish. "It made Sherringham uncomfortable, as he had been made uncomfortable by certain *feuilletons,* reviews of the theatres in the Paris newspapers, which he was committed to thinking important, but of which, when they were very good, he was rather ashamed.'' Actually at the Théâtre Français among the audience where James had himself been assisting off and on for nearly twenty years,[14] Sherringham takes "the serious, the religious view of that establishment—the view of M. Sarcey and of the unregenerate provincial mind.'' M. Sarcey is Francisque Sarcey (1827–99), drama critic for over thirty years to *Le Temps,* a relatively frequent name to be conjured with in the text of Henry James.

Chapters 20–21 of *The Tragic Muse* represent a backstage visit of Miriam, Peter, et al., to the Théâtre Français. As critics and biographers point out, the fictive visit commemorates an actual visit by

James to the *loge* of Julia Bartet, January 1889, she then playing in *L'Ecole des Maris*.[15] Less often placed in the record, and conceivably more provocative of thought, is a 13 February 1870 letter to William James: *"En voilà, de l'Art!* We talk about it and write about it and criticize and dogmatize and analyze to the end of time: but those brave players stand forth and exemplify it and act—create—produce—!" He had seen Molière and Augier "most rarely played," names which figure in *The Tragic Muse*.[16] Never pointed out at all, yet singularly illuminating for a variety of reasons, is the opening sentence of chapter 20: "As many people know, there are not, in the famous Théâtre Français, more than a dozen good seats accessible to ladies" —a point to have kept in mind for your next visit, had it been c. 1890.[17] There once again is the typical style of the Tourist Novel, the modest, the deprecating, the concessionary opening phrase, then the abrupt shift out of past tense as normative for narration into present tense as normative (nearly inescapable) for guidebook prose and of course for the conveyance of information useful in reading *The Tragic Muse* and beyond. In the New York Edition (1908), James appended to the phrase "accessible to ladies" a footnote reading in its entirety "1890."

Finally we penetrate the arcana. Lifelong James was frustrated and annoyed at institutional arrangements—public libraries, the Harvard Yard—which wanted proper penetralia because nobody was kept out, and then he was equally frustrated and annoyed at institutional arrangements—especially convents—literally impenetrable to the male laity in quest. For *The Tragic Muse* the penetrated arcanum is the *foyer des artistes* (with approaches and surroundings, *banlieux*) of the Comédie Française. "What!" some readers will say, "no more than that?" But "Ah," others will murmur soft and low, "I am at last 'in on' something, said to be the greatest of its kind!" A third group of readers, taking no sides, may prefer to scan the apparently pedestrian scene for a subtler signification. These might notice the withheld name of the play of the evening, "six months old, a large, serious, successful comedy, by the most distinguished of authors," present company excepted, "with a thesis, a chorus, embodied in one character, a *scène à faire* and a part full of opportunities for Mademoiselle Voisin." Then they might notice the nominative attributes of Mademoiselle, who "is," in order, success, triumph, accomplishment, and, adjectivally, "the hard, brilliant realization of what I [Peter] want to avert for you [Miriam]." Seldom was prose less definite yet we may safely infer a certain limited indecency as either the penalty or the reward of aesthetic discipline, plus a certain chill of inhumanity, perhaps best represented, in James' representation, and therefore most to notice, by Gérôme's representation "of the pale Rachel." In a bit of Milly Theale-ism ahead of its time and assigned to a different national ambience, Peter looks at Miriam looking at "the vivid image of the dead actress." Upon this and other paradoxical images and behaviors, reversibly "the cold portrait of Rachel looked down." Even so, there remains a disparity between the prose—"a sense of majesty in the place," "the tone of an institution, a temple," "covered with pictures and relics," and what the prose sometimes stoops to specify: " 'That's Dunoyer's first under-skirt,' she said to her mother."

Revising *The Tragic Muse* around 1908 for the New York Edition, James left these key chapters virtually intact, even though he must surely have known that, in the words of a near contemporary celebrant, "This historical playhouse at Paris, the 'First Theatre in the World,' as it was often termed . . . was destroyed by fire on the afternoon of March 8, 1900, but has since been rebuilt on the same site."[18] James' prose survived the blaze untouched, as was predictable, given how deeply drenched was that prose in the language of traditional civilities and how traditional itself was the *maison de Molière* (unlike certain other French monuments). "La Comédie-Française a l'honneur d'être, après l'Académie française, la seule institution de l'ancien régime qui ait mérité de lui survivre"—so writes Emile Augier, Un des Quarante, in a brief article on "La Comédie-Française."[19]

## 5. The French Language As Fictive Texture

The most cursory glance at *The Tragic Muse* reveals two simple facts about its French-English linguistic relations: there is more French than in any other novel by Henry James, and the proportion of French coming from the author's pen—the narrative authority, what I alternatively call narrative voice—is the lowest, that is to say, conversely, the proportion of French in the mouths of the personages represented is the highest (between two-to-one and three-to-one). Everyone in the novel knows French—one minor personage (Mademoiselle Voisin) appears to know nothing else—even those English persons disrespectfully alluded to in the novel's opening sentence as, in the French view, "inexpressive and speechless." Except for Miriam Rooth, little is made of these linguistic attainments, just enough to establish fictive conditions of perfect communication. Julia Dallow's sister-in-law's children are said to be learning French at Versailles, but there is otherwise no such progress in French or any other language as was concocted for Christopher Newman in *The American*. If the personages have had their lessons in French, and Madame Carré hers in English, it was long ago and the pains of instruction are swallowed up now in a grand air of cosmopolite proficiency.

Abroad, Nick Dormer reads only French papers; as he says to Julia, "The local [English] papers,—ah, the thought of them makes me want to stay in Paris." His cousin Peter Sherringham has "a rare knack with foreign tongues," convenient for himself as a diplomat, convenient for James as a novelist of French-talking Englishers for at least a third of the narrative out of their element. Mrs. Rooth speaks "excellent French," as suits the parent of so linguistically talented a child; mother reads French with equal ease, including "the earlier productions of M. Eugène Sue" and "the once-fashionable compositions of Madame Sophie Gay" ("which she was ready to peruse once more if she could get nothing fresher"). Madame Carré evidently knows English, perhaps imperfectly; she prefers to speak French to approximately the degree which the text will permit her, just this side of unintelligibility; she uses a French prose version of *King John* (Shakespeare). Conversations pass with commendable sprightliness from one language to another. Basil Dashwood tells Madame Carré "in very pretty French that he was tremendously excited about Miss Rooth," the pretty French not given but we are to imagine it, and she obviously answers him in French—mainly reported as English but with French liberally strewn around the printed page—yet a few minutes later he is speaking English and Madame Carré is still quite clearly part of the conversation. One personage of *The Tragic Muse* appears to be monolingual and that is Mademoiselle Voisin in chapter 21. Chapter 21, accordingly, will by the generously-minded and romantically-imaginative reader be supposed to "take place" entirely in French even while it is read, for the sake of convenience, almost entirely in English.

At the other end of the linguistic scale, our tragic muse, like her creator in his youth, has been dragged about Europe for the procurement of tongues. Her Italian, and his, enables Peter Sherringham to enact a dramatic moment by sending her a card backstage in that torchy lingo of the south. Mother claims for Miriam four languages, German now added, the same four used in *The Princess Casamassima* and the same four many years earlier attributed to Christina Light in *Roderick Hudson.* "That's three too many," says Madame Carré. English, French, Italian, German is the order given by mother, which is also the order of frequency for *The Princess Casamassima.* "You oughtn't to be an actress; you ought to be a governess," Madame Carré tells the young dramatic aspirant, a popular joke of the period (a man with too many languages should be a headwaiter). Miriam recites in two languages and she announces her recitational wares in two languages: "I can say 'L'Aventurière' " (Emile Augier, 1820–89). She and Madame Carré in fact recite speeches of Clorinde (one of her lines is quoted in French) and Célie, respectively, from the third act. Miriam ruins Alfred de Musset, *Les Nuits,* given by James simply as "Nights," then, something English being suggested, she ruins Tennyson. The next day she is even more international, from Juliet drinking her potion to short poems by Victor Hugo to "the American lyre" (Longfellow, Lowell, Whittier, Holmes, "and two or three poetesses revealed to Sherringham on this occasion," James revealing a deplorable ignorance of the American lyre or at least a momentary inattention). Miriam's Italian and German aside, her French is *perfect,* an essential thematic consideration—so that practically she may consider the pursuit of a theatrical career in either of the two cities comprising her tale, Paris or London, while somewhat more egregiously her puppeteer may interpolate his continual insistence on French superiority, especially as it is useful for the discomfiture of the British:

> "they [the French; Sherringham opining] are the most particular of all; for their idiom is supersensitive and they are incapable of enduring the *baragouinage* of foreigners, to which we [English]

listen with such complacency. In fact, your French is better than your English—it's more conventional; there are little queernesses and impurities in your English, as if you had lived abroad too much."

Again James seems to skirt a possible autobiographical issue. Like James, too, in deciding to live in England, Miriam decides on the English stage, in preference to the French, partly because in England there will be less competition (more insults to the English) and partly because "we" (now she becomes more English than the English) have America, as the French have not (French Canada is not mentioned). Only a couple of pages earlier, Sherringham was abusing the British stage and British audiences' tolerance for bad British speech, "abominable dialects and individual tricks, any vulgarity flourishes, and on the top of it all the Americans, with every conceivable crudity."

Through the first (Parisian) third of the novel, Miriam (slowly improving) continues to recite short French poems, incomparably wonderful, seldom named. Twice in a paragraph of modest dimensions she asks Sherringham "what do they call her in English" and "what did they call *that* in English?"—in both cases the answer and the joke is that they (the English) call it by a French word or phrase *(fiancée, optique de la scène),* having no very good resource in their own language. Miriam's formulaic question goes back to *The American,* as does so much else in James, for instance the favorite proverb about "the most beautiful girl in the world" being able to "give but what she had," the phrase here credited to Dashwood, a regular mouther of platitudes. Once we have the formula with another language, from Miriam, "tremendous *riguardi,* as we used to say in Italy." Mainly, the formula is French-English, as Peter's notion that Miriam may be "according to the contemporary French phrase, a 'nature,' " or reference to "the monologue, as the distraction that had just been offered was called by the French," or, in nomenclature, "the *cuisine,* as the French called it, the distillery or back-shop of the admired profession" (at the Théâtre Français, it may be needless to point out), or Miriam is to Peter a "new 'distraction,' in the French sense," or he, "an *homme sérieux* (as they said in Paris) rather gave himself away (as they said in America," and so forth, "in the train, as they said in Paris," all the way to *"D'où tombez-vous?* as you affected French people say," Nick Dormer now affecting to take Miriam Rooth for French.

"Nick sometimes took precautions against irritation which were in excess of the danger, as departing travellers, about to whiz through foreign countries, study phrase-books for combinations of words they will never use." No one can complain that the French of *The Tragic Muse* is never used. It is used relentlessly. It is used to the point where we may well call it the texture of the novel, the texture of the text, the subtext of the main text, the second rail. French is an organic an inseparable and maybe even an indispensable element in the overall literary performance of *The Tragic Muse,* a notable conspicuous thematized aspect of style, a distinctive signifying feature, an adjunct of structure and even of substance. Delete the French from *The Tragic Muse* and you would have a different novel, perhaps no novel at all. And not only is there a lot of French in *The Tragic Muse* but it is not always the comparatively easy French of the usual Jamesian display. The Anglophonic reader with no French, or little French, or very bad French—and no dictionary at hand—will encounter grave difficulty reading this novel, will feel excluded, even, perhaps, assaulted: it is a main textural message of *The Tragic Muse* that willful ignorance of French properly defines an indolent mindless uncultivated barbarian provincial Philistine Briton or American. For *The Tragic Muse,* France and French are *art,* the sum of all things good, quite heaven on earth, especially literary art, dramatic art, art expressed in language. The language in which art happens to be best expressed happens to be French, "that perfect tongue," as James called it in *A Little Tour in France.*[20] If you want art, you must know French. If you lack French, you must live without art, if, indeed, you may be said to live at all, and you have no one but yourself to blame. It is a very French way of looking at things and no French person could have put it more conclusively. If you did not know that Henry James was American and *The Tragic Muse* written in English you might suppose yourself reading the English translation of a French novel where a scattering of French words and phrases was retained to give it a flavor.

There is incidentally in *The Tragic Muse* some Latin and some Italian, not enough or difficult enough to strain anyone's learning, and no irremediable loss if entirely missed, as *omnium gatherum, tu quoque, lacunae, Ars celare artem, genius loci, Sic vos non vobis, obiter dictum;* as *impresario, ciceroni, Brava!, Anch'io son pittore!, Pazienza, riguardi, bibite.* The French is another matter, and, for the record, here it is (pp. 150f.), maybe not all—I am deliberately omitting repetitions of words and phrases—but certainly most. If we cannot from a mere word and phrase list know all we would like we can at least keep an eye on one or two things: in the following list an eye is kept on who says what and to whom, whence the reader of imagination may engender at least a partial sense of representation in *The Tragic Muse* as well as of that bilingual text which not only represents but *is.* NV = narrative voice.

Assuming the reasonably acceptable accuracy of my ascriptions and frequency counts, it appears that the linguistic narrative of *The Tragic Muse* consists of the invasion of English dullness and the English text by France and French civilization as referenced and by the French language both as referenced and inscribed. Nearly seventy passages involving French are reserved to narrative voice—all figures are naturally approximate—which is no less invasive than the voices of the personages, after which the frequency of French speaking correlates almost exactly with the degree of threat to British Philistine complacency comprised by the personage who speaks it. Miriam Rooth has 54 passages, rather longer passages on the average than any one else's except perhaps Madame Carré's, Madame Carré has 42, Gabriel Nash and Peter Sherringham about half that many, 22 and 18 respectively, and poor Nick Dormer only 13. Either because of their minor roles in the fabric of the fiction overall or their general inutility as human beings, Lady Agnes, Julia Dallow, Mrs. Rooth, Basil Dashwood, Mademoiselle Dunoyer, and Mademoiselle Voisin speak French fewer than 5 times each. Biddy Dormer (however charming!), Grace Dormer, Charles Carteret, Chaytor, Mrs. Gresham, Mrs. Lendon—these pure English types—speak no French at all. In *The Awkward Age,* James will again have a frequency list but reversed: in that novel the more French you talk the worse you are and the pure in heart do without it. But that is not the valence of France and French in *The Tragic Muse.*

| WORD OR PHRASE | SAID BY | TO | COMMENT |
|---|---|---|---|
| En v'la des abrutis! | The French | Anyone | Conjecturally |
| en grand seigneur | Nick | Biddy et al. | |
| taper fort | Nick | Dormer family | |
| Jamais de la vie! | Nash | Nick | |
| c'est à se tordre! | Nash | Nick | |
| état civil | Nash | Biddy | |
| métier | Nash | Biddy | |
| Mesdames sont seules? | Waiter | Lady Agnes et al. | |
| Non; nous sommes beaucoup! | Lady Agnes | Waiter | |
| carte | NV | | |
| Poulet chasseur, filets mignons, sauce béarnaise | Waiter | Lady Agnes | |
| se fait forte, as they say here | Peter | Dormer family | |
| bœuf braisé | Lady Agnes | Nick | |
| Donnez m'en, s'il vous plaît | Nick | Peter | |
| c'est trop fort! | Nash | Peter et al. | |
| nom de guerre | Nash | Peter et al. | |
| à l'entresol | Nash | Peter et al. | |

| | | | |
|---|---|---|---|
| *jeune Anglaise* | Peter | Nash et al. | Of Miriam |
| *dans le monde* | Peter | Biddy et al. | |
| *ces messieurs* | Nash | Peter et al. | |
| *brocanteur* | Nash | Peter et al. | |
| *j'ai été comme ça* | Nash | Peter | |
| *Vous me rendez des forces* | Nash | Peter | Quoting Madame Carré |
| *feuilletons* | Nash | Peter | |
| *raffinés* | Peter | Nash | |
| *Connu, connu!* | Peter | Nash | |
| *cheval de bataille* | Peter | Nash | |
| *flânerie* | NV | | |
| *voiture de place* | NV | | |
| *premières* | Nick | Peter | |
| *en disponibilité* | Peter | Nick | |
| *dame de comptoir* | NV | | |
| *brusquerie* | NV | | Given as French |
| *cabinet* | NV | | Given as French (a private room) |
| *Merci, pas de vin* | Julia | All | |
| *A tout à l'heure!* | Nick | Julia et al. | |

| WORD OR PHRASE | SAID BY | TO | COMMENT |
| --- | --- | --- | --- |
| cassière | NV | | |
| décor | NV | | |
| Bocks (also bocks) | Julia | Nick | French (also German) |
| madère | Julia | Nick | |
| je me dois bien cela | Julia | Nick | |
| salon (a room) | NV | | But salon (a social group) |
| comédie de salon | NV | | |
| comédienne | NV | | |
| Ah, la voix de Célimène! | Nash | All | Reference to Molière |
| belles dames | NV | | |
| Mais celles-là, c'est une plaisanterie | Mme Carré | Mrs. Rooth | |
| chère madame | Mme Carré | Mrs. Rooth | A phrase often repeated |
| il n'y a que ça. La tête est bien | Mme Carré | Mrs. Rooth | |
| Un beau regard | Mme Carré | Mrs. Rooth | |
| Voyons | Mme Carré | Miriam | |
| répertoire | Mme Carré | Miriam | |
| Je ne connais qu'une scène—la nôtre | Mme Carré | All | A notable Frenchism; ceteris paribus, doctrinal for The Tragic Muse |

| | | | |
|---|---|---|---|
| mademoiselle | Peter | All | |
| en attendant | Mme Carré | Peter | |
| qu'est-ce-que-c'est que ça? | Mme Carré | All | "in the finest manner of modern comedy" |
| Je n'ai joué que ça, madame | Mme Carré | Mrs. Rooth | |
| réplique | Peter | Miriam | |
| Voilà, chère madame | Mme Carré | Mrs. Rooth | |
| Vous ne me fuyez pas, mon enfant, aujourd'hui | Mme Carré | All | Reciting from Augier, "L'Aventurière" |
| Elle est bien belle—ah, ça! | Mme Carré | All | |
| ma fille | Mme Carré | Miriam | |
| d'une légèreté à faire rougir | Mme Carré | Mrs. Rooth | |
| Diable! | Mme Carré | Miriam | |
| tableau-vivant | NV | | |
| notez bien | Mme Carré | Peter | |
| bête | Mme Carré | Peter | |
| bonne | NV | | |
| nuance | Mme Carré | Peter | Given as French |
| mon cher | Mme Carré | Peter | |

| WORD OR PHRASE | SAID BY | TO | COMMENT |
| --- | --- | --- | --- |
| scène anglaise | Mme Carré | Miriam | |
| sont encore a dégager | Mme Carré | Miriam | |
| Mon Dieu, que vous dirais-je? | Mme Carré | Miriam | |
| juste | Mme Carré | Miriam | |
| Ah, la jeunesse! | Mme Carré | Miriam | |
| pensions | NV | | |
| maison meublée | NV | | |
| femmes du monde | NV | | |
| passer par toute la famille! | Miriam | Biddy | |
| petits fours | NV | | |
| banal | Miriam | Peter | |
| quartiers excentriques | NV | Peter | Given as French |
| Je crois bien! | Miriam | Peter | Attributed to Miriam |
| quartiers sérieux | Nick | Nash | |
| C'est là que je vous attends! | Nash | Nick | |
| que diable | Nash | Nick | |
| quoi! | NV | Nick | Attributed to Nick |
| Ecoutez maintenant! | Miriam | All | |

| | Mme Carré | Miriam | |
|---|---|---|---|
| *gros moyens* | | Miriam | Attributed to Miriam |
| *gros public* | NV | | |
| *cuisine*, as the French called it | NV | | |
| *consommation* | Miriam | Peter | Given as English (not in italics) |
| *sous* | Miriam | Peter | |
| *cabinet de lecture* | Miriam | Peter | |
| *comme il faut* | Miriam | Peter | |
| *sirop d'orgeat* | NV | | |
| *baragouinage* | Peter | Miriam | |
| *par excellence* | Peter | Miriam | Given as French |
| *je me fiche* | Miriam | Peter | |
| *fond* | Peter | Miriam | |
| *baignoire* | NV | | |
| *cela s'était vu* | NV | | |
| *protégée* | NV | | Given as French |
| *entr'acte* | NV | | Given as English (not in italics) |
| *en ville* | NV | | |
| *bouquetières* | NV | | |
| *approfondir* | NV | | Attributed to Miriam |

| WORD OR PHRASE | SAID BY | TO | COMMENT |
| --- | --- | --- | --- |
| *à la guerre comme à la guerre!* | Miriam | Peter | See *The Golden Bowl* |
| *cabotine* | Peter | Miriam | |
| *armoire à glace* | NV | | |
| *banlieue* | NV | | |
| *Vous devriez bien nous la laisser* | Mme Carré | Peter | |
| *Mauvais sujet!* | Mme Carré | Peter | |
| *parterres* | NV | | Given as English |
| *en fête* | NV | | |
| *répandue* | NV | | |
| *menus* | NV | | Given as French |
| *pose* | Nick | Julia | Undecidable whether the word is in italics for emphasis or is given as French, an occasional problem in the bilingual James text |
| *coquine* | NV | | |
| *fille de théâtre* | NV | | |
| *Voilà!* | Mrs. Rooth | Peter | |
| *nom de théâtre* | Mrs. Rooth | Peter | |
| *locataire* | NV | | |

| | | | |
|---|---|---|---|
| *femme de chambre* | NV | | |
| *comédie de mœurs* | NV | | |
| *ingénue* | NV | | |
| *une sotte* | Mme Carré | Dashwood | |
| *de plus près que vous, monsieur* | Mme Carré | Dashwood | |
| *On dit que c'est très fort* | Mme Carré | Miriam | |
| *par exemple* | Peter | Mme Carré | |
| *des plus belles choses* | Mme Carré | Dashwood et al. | |
| *Insolente!* | Mme Carré | Miriam | |
| *Vous êtes insupportables* | Mme Carré | Peter | Or Miriam |
| *Malicieuse!* | Mme Carré | Miriam | |
| *de là-bas* | Mme Carré | Miriam | |
| *vous-en-êtes là?* | Mme Carré | Miriam | |
| *Elle est superbe* | Mme Carré | All | Of Miriam? |
| *ma toute-belle* | Mme Carré | Miriam | |
| *chez nous* | Miriam | Mme Carré | |
| *le drame* | Miriam | Mme Carré | |
| *de grands effets de voix* | Mme Carré | Miriam | |
| *Tiens!* | Mme Carré | Peter and Dashwood | |

| WORD OR PHRASE | SAID BY | TO | COMMENT |
|---|---|---|---|
| C'est de beaucoup la plus sage | Mme Carré | Peter and Dashwood | |
| baignoires d'avant-scène | NV | | |
| congé | NV | | |
| foyer des artistes | NV | | |
| scène à faire | NV | | |
| Le geste rare | Miriam | All | |
| demoiselle de magasin | Dashwood | All | |
| hein? | Dashwood | All | |
| ouvreuse | NV | | |
| loge | NV | | Given as French; dressing-room, not seat |
| maison de Molière | Miriam | Peter | The phrase is later Englished |
| sur le point d'entrer au théâtre | NV | | |
| nous sommes mieux que ça! | Dashwood | All | |
| toute honteuse | NV | | |
| Vous allez me trouver bien légère! | Mlle Dunoyer | Peter, et al. | Attributed to Mlle Dunoyer |
| Je vous ai bien observée | Mlle Voisin | Miriam | |

| | | | |
|---|---|---|---|
| Vous savez, c'est une montée | Mlle Voisin | Peter | |
| Comment donc? | Mlle Voisin | Miriam | |
| mon Dieu, mon Dieu! | Miriam | Herself | |
| Voilà, c'est tout! | Mlle Voisin | Miriam and Peter | |
| cabotin | NV | | In the same sentence cabotine |
| à la porte | NV | | Attributed to Mlle Voisin |
| corvées | Miriam | Peter | |
| à ses heures | Peter | Miriam | |
| nous mêlons les genres! | Peter | Miriam | |
| femmes comme il faut | Miriam | Peter | |
| à deux | NV | | Attributed to Mrs. Gresham |
| mise-en-scène | Nick | Julia | |
| "Guenille si l'on veut, ma guenille m'est chère" | Nick | Julia | Quoted as a proverbial saying |
| C'est de l'exquis, du pur exquis | Nash | Nick | |
| remplissage | Nash | Nick | |
| cornets-à-piston | Nash | Nick | |
| Elle a bien tort | Nash | Nick | |
| D'où tombez-vous? | Nash | Nick | |
| femme de théâtre | Miriam | Nick and Nash | |

| WORD OR PHRASE | SAID BY | TO | COMMENT |
| --- | --- | --- | --- |
| chic | Miriam | Nick and Nash | Given as French |
| future | Miriam | Nick and Nash | Given as French (probably) |
| optique de la scène | Miriam | Nick and Nash | |
| bien de choses | Miriam | Nick and Nash | |
| pour cela | Miriam | Nick | |
| veut bien le dire | Miriam | Nick | |
| carte-de-visite | Miriam | Nick | |
| début | NV | | Given as English but with accent mark retained |
| tour de force | NV | | |
| Ah bien, c'est tapé! | Miriam | Nick | |
| soyez tranquille | Nick | Julia | |
| à demi-mot | NV | | |
| conseil de famille | NV | | |
| Cher maître | Miriam | Peter | Also "Dear master" |
| homme sérieux (as they said in Paris) | NV | | |
| grandes espaces | NV | | |
| raison d'être | NV | | |

| | | | |
|---|---|---|---|
| *Pour le mariage, non* | Nash | Peter | As if quoting someone else |
| *d'un mauvais* | NV | | Vaguely attributed to Miriam |
| *sur les dents* | Miriam | Nick | |
| *de cette force* | Miriam | Peter | |
| *crânerie* | NV | | |
| *répétitions générales* | NV | | |
| *première* | NV | | |
| *dénoûement* | NV | | |
| *mon bon* | Miriam | Peter | What James calls himself in his *Notebooks* |
| *exalté* | Miriam | Peter | |
| *devinez un peu quoi!* | Miriam | Peter | |
| *Où le fourrez-vous?* | Miriam | Peter | |
| *comme tout le monde* | Miriam | Peter | |
| *tout au plus* | NV | Nick | |
| *Que voulez-vous* | Peter | Peter | |
| *C'est magnifique, mais ce n'est pas la guerre* | Nick | Peter | |
| *démarche* | NV | | Attributed to Peter |

| WORD OR PHRASE | SAID BY | TO | COMMENT |
|---|---|---|---|
| Si vous saviez comme cela me repose! | Miriam | Peter and Biddy | But reference is to Nick |
| comme de raison | Miriam | Mrs. Rooth | |
| simagrées | Miriam | Nick | |
| parlez-moi de ça | Miriam | Mrs. Rooth | |
| Il s'est bien détaché ces-jours-ci | Miriam | Mrs. Rooth and-or Nick | |
| je n'y suis plus | Miriam | Nick | |
| Merci | Miriam | Nick | |
| je veux bien | Miriam | Mrs. Rooth and-or Nick | |
| Tiens bon, ma fille . . . tenir bon . . . tenu bon! | Miriam | Nick | |
| cela se voit tous les jours | Mrs. Rooth | Miriam | |
| pourtant | Miriam | Peter | |
| Je le vois parbleu bien! | Miriam | Peter | |
| c'est bientôt dit | Miriam | Peter | |
| allez! | Peter | Miriam | |
| tout bonnement | Miriam | Peter | |
| Je vous attendais | Miriam | Peter | |
| tout pur | NV | | Attributed to Grace |

| | | |
|---|---|---|
| confrères | Miriam | Nick |
| à la charge | Miriam | Nick |
| Il en faut comme ça | Nick | Miriam |
| n'en parlons plus | Miriam | Nick |
| mêlée | Miriam | Nick |
| faites la part de ça | Miriam | Nick |
| vous allez me lâcher | Nick | Nash |
| vous allez voir ça | Nash | Nick |
| Cela s'annonce bien | Miriam | Nick |

# VI

# The English Period:
## *What Maisie Knew* (1897)

Lying mainly (and for the present occasion somewhat *perdu*) between *The Tragic Muse* (1890) and *The Ambassadors* (1903), the English Period may be described either as that which includes England
*in* (settings, ambience, assumptions, personages, monolingualism,
and so forth) or as that which excludes France (topography) and
French (language) *out*. There are in this period no Parisian tales but
"Collaboration" (1892) and no Parisian novels at all; only part of one
novel, *What Maisie Knew,* takes place elsewhere in France. With a
few exceptions, the French language recedes or disappears altogether
from the Jamesian text. Readers of such tales as "Owen Wingrave"
(1892), "The Altar of the Dead" (1895), "Covering End" (1898),
"The Great Good Place" (1900), and "The Beast in the Jungle"
(1903) will remember, and correctly, that these tales contain little or

no French. To characterize the period up to and including *The Tragic Muse* as James' *French* Period would be to claim much too much, however—James *has* no French Period in the way that he has an English Period—and still it is important to notice that three of the four major novelistic monuments, all, in fact, but *The Ambassadors,* fall in the years preceding the English Period. These earlier years, which of course involve many American, Italian, and mixed cases as well, are also the years of every French tale but "Collaboration" (1892) and "The Velvet Glove" (1909). By the French tales I mean "A Tragedy of Error" (1864), "Gabrielle de Bergerac" (1869), "The Sweetheart of M. Briseux" (1873), "Madame de Mauves" (1874), "Four Meetings" (1877), "Rose-Agathe" (1878), "The Pension Beaurepas" (1879—set in French-speaking Geneva), "A Bundle of Letters" (1879), "The Siege of London" (1883), and "Mrs. Temperly" (1887). To such of these as are too good to miss we may always return.

In a 30 July 1905 letter to the publisher of his New York Edition, James mentions *The Tragic Muse* (which had been preceded in that edition by *Roderick Hudson, The American, The Portrait of a Lady* in two volumes, and *The Princess Casamassima* in two volumes), as the "book which closes, to my mind, what I should call as regards my novels, my earlier period."[1] The distinction is useful not only for formal experiment but for textual reference: the earlier period has most of the French texts; it is followed by an English period which has nearly no France or French (*What Maisie Knew* being the grand exception to these generalities). During these English years James continues a visitant of Paris; his notebooks and personal correspondence are resplendent as ever with French allusion and French *écriture;* but French *écriture* for the eye and ear of the gaping Anglophonic public is sternly withheld—there will never again be so much of it as in *The Tragic Muse*—and Paris is all but banished as a fictive locale. The new regime is conveniently announced in a 17 May 1890 letter to Howells: "One thing only is clear: that henceforth I must do, or half do, England in fiction—as the place I see most today, and, in a sort of way, know best. I have at last more acquired notions of it, on the whole, than of any other world, and it will serve as well as any other."[2]

*The Spoils of Poynton* (1897) is a perfect initiating instance of France and French exiled, distanced yet not entirely extirpated. The spoils themselves speak in "the tongues of other countries [than England]. . . . It was all France and Italy."[3] But the Mrs. Gereth who collected them is as utterly English as it is possible to imagine. She specifically defines her plight as a maltreated widow by contrast with the luckier lot of a French friend, Madame de Jaume. Fleda Vetch, on our first acquaintance with her, is just back from abroad: "she had lately, in Paris, with several hundred other young women, spent a year at a studio, arming herself for the battle of life by a course with an impressionist painter." In the magnificent concluding chapter her premonitions of disaster take her back to the France-going time, "the old days of going to the Continent, [the surmises] that used to worry her on the way, at night, to the horrid cheap crossings by long sea." It is doubtful if she will ever be frightened again on La Manche. Meanwhile, the action of the novel, with its narrative, is purely English and its language nearly as insular. Former Parisian art student obligingly gives us *morceau de musée* and *bibelot,* the former continental antique hunter adds her *n'en parlons plus,* and narrative authority chimes in with *endimanché, flair* (italicized as if French), *objets d'art, cachet,* and "entrée." Louis Seize furniture is spoken of and Marie Antoinette in the Conciergerie.

"The Turn of the Screw" (1898), with that nice governess *nerveuse* as ostensible narrative authority, is again the sort of tale that in another phase of James' fictional œuvre would have been strewn with French. Governess presumably offers French instruction to her little charges but James is determined to prohibit French from his public text. All we get are *Raison de plus* in the prologue and, from governess direct, naïf, *mot* (a fine pair of words!), and "Though they were not angels, they 'passed,' as the French say," showing how governess could if she would (if she were allowed). "In the Cage" (1898), another English production par excellence, proffers miniscule tidbits of foreign (French) romanticism contrasting the overall depiction of British drear. Captain Everard is from a telegram known by the girl to be at "Hôtel Brighton, Paris" (a real hotel, Rue de Rivoli 218) where it is unlikely she will ever stay. Boulogne—only Boulogne!—is dangled at her as a possible vacation spot but she is taken to Bournemouth instead. She is said to be *blasée* and to be "struck in one of her ha'penny volumes with the translation of a French proverb according to which a door had to be either open or shut." For the general run of fictions in James' English Period, the door of France and French is shut.

Neither can French matters be deemed essential to *The Awkward Age* (1899), despite much talk about talk, and about *jeunes filles* in the salon (both these topics evidently to be conceived by the Anglo-American reader as somehow "French"), not even with indecent French novels lying about or passed around. What is far more entertaining than such predictable topics is the distribution of foreign languages, the one place in all James where speakers appear to have been rank-ordered, from worst to best, according to the frequency of their French usage. (Italian in *The Awkward Age* is equally laughable; returned from a long sojourn in Naples, and with her late husband's Italian niece in tow, the Duchess has at her disposal only *caro mio, cara mia, Caro Signore, Basta,* and *che vuole* in English translation; perhaps she withholds her Italian in the certain knowledge that no one would understand it.) Duchess comes first in the rank-ordering of French fluency, followed by Mrs. Brook, only half as bad (or even less bad than that, her vocabulary is so pitiable). Assorted males constitute a field far back. Except for once quoting her mother, Nanda uses no French. Mr. Longdon uses none. In the social world represented in *The Awkward Age* it is *de rigueur* to flaunt your French but if you desire the respect of the thoughtful reader you had much better not. That is what things are like, in the Jamesian text, during the English Period.

Duchess in her desperate dissociations from anything English forever disports herself along and across the English-French linguistic border, her working word list comprised of such goods as *des femmes bien gracieuses, toutes ces dames; Voilà, ma chère; femmes du monde, comme cette petite, esprit de conduite, Elle se les passe, par exemple, le fond de ma pensée, A tantôt, cousinage, coureur, beau comme le jour, Elle l'a bien voulu, doter, parti, Voyons, Pourquoi faire, rassurez-vous bien, Vous avez bien de l'esprit* (to Mr. Longdon, what nerve!), *en tête, Dieu sait comme elle se coiffe* (referring to that "little brown head" of Mrs. Brook's), *âme de peine, ces messieurs, voyez, savez-vous, Je crois bien, soins.* Duchess is much best when permitted the larger latitude of two languages crisscrossing, as "There you are, with your eternal English false positions! *J'aime, moi, les situations nettes—je n'en comprends pas d'autres"* (echoing Madame Carré of *The Tragic Muse*) or "There you are once more—*vous autres!* If you're shocked at the idea you place *drôlement* your delicacy" or "You're all inconceivable just now. *Je ne peux pourtant pas la mettre à la porte, cette chérie*" (Little Aggie); or "You're the most interesting nation in the world. One never gets to the end of your hatred of the *nuance*. . . . Look at her little black dress [Carrie Donner's] . . . her type, her beauty, her timidity, her wickedness, her notoriety and her *impudeur.*" Sometimes Duchess deigns to translate for the provincial barbarians: " 'You're not, as a race, clever, you're not delicate, you're not sane, but you're capable of extraordinary good looks,' she resumed [has she ever left off?]. *'Vous avez parfois la grande beauté.'* " But what she says about Mrs. Brook says more than it seems to say about James' preclusion of French in the English Period: "If she were French she'd be a *femme d'esprit.*"

Mrs. Brook's own French is, in comparison, banal. " *'Rien de plus facile,'* as mamma says" is relayed by Nanda; the rest of it scarcely bears repeating, *au courant, s'il vous plaît, par exemple, Comment donc?* —things like that. Her longest effort is *"c'est le moindre des choses"* and her most typifying statement *"vous me rendez la vie!"* Her voice is said to have at moments "the most touching tones of any in England," a formula imitated from earlier novels *(The American, The Portrait of a Lady, The Bostonians, The Princess Casamassima).* Mitchy is given four French quotations, Vanderbank one, and three are reserved to narrative voice. Nanda and Mr. Longdon, heroine and hero, youngster and oldster, use—as aforesaid—no French. And yet with "The Tree of Knowledge" (1900) these apparent but hardly deep-seated patriotisms with respect to land and language are once again up-ended. A would-be English sculptor ("the Master") lives in London at Carrara Lodge with a "beautiful accent in Italian" and an Italian servitor whom he has the pleasure of addressing as *tu.* His son goes to Paris to become an artist—one always goes to Paris for *art*— discovers there his want of talent, and is confirmed in his suspicion that his father likewise possesses none. As in *The Tragic Muse* and elsewhere, Paris is the golden meter scornfully held up to English Philistia: "He hadn't 'chucked' Paris . . . Paris had chucked him."

*The Sacred Fount* (1901) represents further English closure as it secretes a few faint French reminiscences and suggestibilities. The painting which appears to be at the heart of interpretation is described in present tense, as actual extra-textual places had been described in James' Tourist Fictions of long ago, and the characters include a Comtesse de Dreuil *(deuil?)*, suspiciously "an American married to a Frenchman" (like the bisexed two-languaged mind of Henry James) but of no other account. Narrator tells us "We all know the French adage about that *plus belle fille du monde* who can give but what she has," that favorite old French adage with James. Nearly all French in *The Sacred Fount* derives from narrator, half to himself, half to others. "What will you have?"—perhaps James' favorite Italian phrase and a great favorite with Madame Grandoni— appears yet again in English translation. James' use of English words with French significations continues as narrator twice proceeds "in the opposite sense," i.e., direction, not meaning. *"Quoi donc?"* Ford Obert, R.A., says to narrator. Many pages later, *"Mon siège est fait,"* narrator replies to Obert in a most Racinian tone. In fact, the allusion is to René Aubert, abbé de Vertot, 1655–1735. The same allusion appears in a c. 4 January 1888 letter to Grace Norton[4] and again in "Louisa Pallant" of the same year. *Quoi donc,* for us, is the tale of how Maisie Farange and Mrs. Wix went to France and lived for a while at Boulogne-sur-Mer.

*What Maisie Knew* (1897) is of course the anomalous standout French landmark of the English period—you could even call it, for James, an interim beachhead. Like *The Tragic Muse* it is two parts England and one part France, France the more powerfully asserted by its geographical marginality: for *What Maisie Knew* France is not Paris, let alone the Comédie Française, but only Boulogne-sur-Mer, where the author had lived and gone to school, his parents having the same economizing motives as Sir Claude. It also makes a difference where in the narrative sequence the French third is located— here, at the end. The effect is something like the movement of a three-act play—"It was as if the whole performance had been given for her—a mite of a half-scared infant in a great dim theatre"—with a strong change of scene in the final act denoting a strong change of context, cultural, topographical, and linguistic, while narrative continues inexorably onward, "with their main agitation transferred thus to France."

The all-English characters get no further than the southern end of the Folkestone-Boulogne traverse, Paris their frustration and loss. Boulogne is France stripped and entirely too connected with home and yet with the foreign charm of inn, dock, railroad station, bench, pier, jetty, church (Catholic), France still in manners, in talk, in cuisine, and mainly in romantic real-life attraction and challenge. It is in this oddly exotized setting that James plays out his final debacles among Maisie, Sir Claude, Mrs. Beale, and Mrs. Wix. Their various responses to French matters are maybe not overwhelmingly constitutive of narrative behavior but they are surely expressive of it. Multiple aspects of English relation and attitude interweave their ironies with the French locale and the French language; the *personnages* are thereby encouraged or compelled to expand and expose themselves toward positions of revelation.

The first two thirds of the novel "take place" in London, except for fleeting reference to places outside the city, such as Brighton, where Miss Overmore changes her name to Mrs. Beale. Later, Sir Claude goes, "quite alone," to Paris, but no one else ever gets to the Magic City of Elsewhere. Sir Claude returns with an appropriately aesthetic gift for his stepdaughter, "a splendid apparatus for painting in water-colours." Earlier he had given Mrs. Wix, presumably for use on Maisie, "the history of France," and it is (again presumably) owing to that volume that in the apartment of "the Countess" she remembers "the famous French lady represented in one of the miniatures," conceivably Madame Récamier, a James favorite. From earliest days Maisie has had a French doll and among the thousands of stories Maisie is said to have been in are "the richest romances of French Elise." The typifying note of all this reference is romance, romance postponed or prevented. When Mrs. Beale determines that she, Maisie, and Sir Claude shall have lessons, courses, attend lectures, "on subjects," and Maisie asks which, it quickly appears that they are to be "All the most important ones. French literature—and sacred history," and thus we discover how far is lip service from learning.

In the long London stretches (chapters 1–19) there has not been one French word but at Folkestone we first hear a light scatter—*table d'hôte, éclairage,* portemonnaie—as the characters "began to look across at France." Boulogne is named. Maisie tells her mother "We're going to France" (equal to the "light of foreign travel"). Thematically it is "a crossing of more spaces than the Channel." The Folkestone interlude, transitional between nations, ends with images of black masts and red lights ostensibly suggesting "happy foreign travel." With chapter 22 the tone of the text abruptly changes from prevision to actuality. The relation between narrative and setting is different. The plot is still an English plot—it certainly stems from an English divorce decree according to English legal procedures and social attitudes (presumptively not quite the same as their French counterparts). The characters are as English as heart could wish. But now there is conspicuous disjunction between these persons and actions and the place where they are enacting, even if the persons are just barely inside France and still 200 km. or so from Paris. They have a foot in the door, almost literally they have established a beachhead, but Maisie, who most richly desires and deserves, will neither strike further inland nor pass the door. For once, James' maps or memories of Paris will be of no use to him. Boulogne is not the meal that satisfies but the taste that maddens.

France-not-quite-France, France-at-any-rate-not-Paris, is in numerous ways contrasted with narrative, as the latter has been picked up and dropped on the beach across the channel. The rampart above the beach is "the spot on which they [Maisie and Mrs. Wix] appeared to have come furthest in the journey that was to separate them from everything objectionable in the past," but the appearance of progress is delusory, textual sarcasm heavy. Perhaps for reasons of ironic contrast, Boulogne is itself noticeably intermittent in this final act of *What Maisie Knew*. First we have a slice of romantic French life and then we have a slice of English domestic woe, alternating, until the end, where there is nothing but English woe ahead, hopefully to be transformed, and France has washed away in the troubled wake of a boat proceeding in the wrong direction.

Surely it is significant how the two great turning points of the French action are given mainly in French (easy French). The first is after Sir Claude's return and his lie to Maisie about not having seen Mrs. Beale. As he and Maisie leave the inn, Sir Claude orders breakfast for Mrs. Wix from the *patronne* (who breaks in "with high swift notes as into a florid duet")—"and it was a charm to hear his easy brilliant French: even his companion's ignorance could measure the perfection of it." Then, quite a lot of it *in French,* the revelation:

> He had evidently ordered something lovely for Mrs. Wix. *"Et bien soigné, n'est-ce pas?"*

*"Soyez tranquille"*—the *patronne* beamed upon him. *"Et pour Madame?"*

*"Madame?"* he echoed—it just pulled him up a little.

*"Rien encore?"*

*"Rien encore.* Come, Maisie." She hurried along with him, but on the way to the cafe he said nothing.

Does Maisie understand? How can she *not?* The entire conversation includes only a few French words, all common and several of them repeated. It is like a beginning lesson in French, not much more advanced then Christopher Newman's opening *"Combien?"* in *The American.*

The second turning point of *What Maisie Knew* is at the *gare,* where Maisie makes her doomed bid for the affections of Sir Claude (and a trip to Paris); when she has failed of both desires there is nothing left for her but retreat to England with Mrs. Wix. Personal anguish even blots out French romanticism: "She saw nothing that she had seen hitherto—no touch in the foreign picture that had at first been always before her." Maisie thinks how nice it would be to "nip" into the train for Paris. Then we have the climax of the novel, again largely in French, including James' transliteration of *prenez* to *prenny* (as in his transliteration of Newman's *expray* for *exprès* in the New York Edition of *The American*):

> Sir Claude turned to a porter. "When does the train go?" [The porter understands English and answers in English, then shifts to French:]
>
> The man looked up at the station-clock. "In two minutes. *Monsieur est placé?"* [Sir Claude now answers in French:]
>
> *"Pas encore."* [The porter continues in French:]
>
> *"Et vos billets?—vous n'avez que le temps."* Then after a look at Maisie [these foreigners!], *"Monsieur veut-il que je les prenne?"* the man said.
>
> Sir Claude turned back to her [now speaking French:] *"Veux-tu bien qu'il en prenne?"*
>
> It was the most extraordinary thing in the world: in the intensity of her excitement she not only by illumination understood all their French, but fell into it with an active perfection. She addressed herself straight to the porter. *"Prenny, prenny. Oh prenny!"*
>
> *"Ah si mademoiselle le veut—!"*

But then the porter cries out again *"Ah vous n'avez plus le temps!"* and Maisie cries out "It's going—it's going!"and Sir Claude says "It's gone!" (as in *Hamlet*).

The pathos of that last passage is further multiplied by comparison with earlier clusters of sentiment for France. Not surprisingly, given her previous exploits of responsive imagination, Maisie is the ideal tourist, France her specialty, "the great ecstasy of a larger impression of life." Like James himself, in his youthful epistolary descriptions of himself, "she recognized, she understood, she adored and took possession; feeling herself attuned to everything and laying her hand, right and left, on what had simply been waiting for her." She has "the instant certitude of a vocation," that of being, although English, in France (out of England). "Her vocation was to see the world," the world for the moment being "the institutions and manners of France."

Maisie is a small-scale model of the classic Jamesian tourist. She adores her French breakfast because it is a *French* breakfast. She revels in superiority to Susan Ash, who is all provincial *English*. The text offers copious detail in support of Maisie's passion, as much, perhaps, as is possible in Boulogne, including the "gaiety" of "the language and the weather." The main impression is simply total: "it appeared to her that no one since the beginning of time could have had such an adventure or, in an hour, so much experience." Her lovely romanticism is parodied in Mrs. Wix's argument for sending home Susan Ash ("that interesting exile") without ado: "She has had an experience that she never dreamed of and that will be an advantage to her through life." Meanwhile, complacently, Maisie and Mrs. Wix solace themselves in their white and gold salon, very French, with their French sofa, their French lamp, and their French clock. (In *The Awkward Age* Tishy Grendon's drawing room is endowed with "delicate French mouldings" on the walls, a "low French chimney" —with "a French fire"—"a copy of a French novel in blue paper," and a "French door.")

Other adjuncts of local color feature seaside topography ("the many-coloured and many-odoured *port"*—italicize an easy cognate and the palpitating Anglophonic Tourist Reader finds new glamour in old smells), the *rues,* the populace, the buildings, everything, in fact, conducive to romance. The château "was a part of the place that could lead Maisie to inquire if it didn't just meet one's idea of the middle ages," as probably developed from the book given Mrs. Wix by Sir Claude. Romance extends even to Mrs. Wix confessing in the sight of "the great dome and the high gilt Virgin" that "for herself she had probably made a fatal mistake early in life in not being a Catholic." Even the insects are said to be "French," therefore more interesting than English insects.

Inevitably, for a James fiction "abroad," there is attention to the glories and difficulties of the French language, as previous quotations will have made plain. Even Mrs. Wix picks up a French word or two —*personnel,* misconstrued, is one of them. Somewhat as in *The Tragic Muse* and other James texts, French life is in *What Maisie Knew* enthusiastically defined as a "social order principally devoted to language," as no one would ever accuse the English or American social orders of being. In its good-natured *brio* the text cheerfully overlooks how in their delight with what little French they command the visitors miss the greater part of uncomprehended French sailing past their ears. Maisie has waited long to show off her French. She translates menus for Mrs. Wix and tells her the French names of things. Then comes Mrs. Beale, who is to Maisie what Maisie had been to Susan Ash and Mrs. Wix. Mrs. Beale's tourist triumph over Maisie represents her total triumph over one who is still learning about the "natural divergence between lovers and little girls": "She too was delighted with foreign manners; but her daughter's opportunities for explaining them to her were unexpectedly forestalled by her own tone of large acquaintance. . . . Continental life was what she had been almost brought up on."

What Maisie goes home to in England we may not know but we may guess a fate not unlike those of the other young English ladies featured by Henry James in his English period (Fleda Vetch, the nameless governess at Bly, the nameless telegraphist of *In the Cage,* Nanda Brookenham)—no love, no marriage, no money, no nothing. Mrs. Beale's savoir-faire is indeed a cold douche to our own young lady, and still she has had her day in France, her impressions imperishably recorded. "We find something eternally fresh and delightful in all first impressions of foreign scenes," James had written so long ago as 1873 in a review of a book in French about Italy, "and we confess that the outpourings of even the most ingenuous tourists always strike in us a sympathetic chord."[5] The ingenuousness of Maisie is second to none in its inscription of that first encounter so dear to the tourist and so central to Tourist Fictions. In *What Maisie*

*Knew* James was also rewriting, as he so often did, an earlier performance, "Four Meetings" (1877), in which the passionate pilgrim was likewise estopped well short of Paris and required to go back.

Often overlooked, the French metamorphoses of Mrs. Wix are almost more remarkable than those of the titular heroine, of whom much was to be anticipated, given her intelligence and her tender years. Mrs. Wix, on the other hand, is in the beginning represented as old, impoverished, ill-favored, badly dressed, uneducated, tasteless, unsophisticated, anaesthetic, Philistine, and Protestant (very low). It is easy enough to see and to say how she is moralistic and frustrated-maternal but it is more to the point to remark how her dead daughter Clara Matilda is the tiny mustard seed, so to speak, which, like Maisie, blooms miraculously when transported to French soil. In England, Mrs. Wix informs our only child, bereft of parents, "She's your little dead sister" (not your dead little sister); in France the trinity of women, young and old, dead and alive, bursts into a series of transcendences.

At the National Gallery, Maisie and Mrs. Wix have looked at pictures of saints and angels, "ugly Madonnas and uglier babies, strange prayers and prostrations," in contrast to what is called "morning church, a place of worship of Mrs. Wix's own choosing, where there was nothing of that sort; no haloes on heads." The habit of gazing at Madonnas, once acquired, is with everything else carried over to France where it comes to an *éblouissement* in repetitive fixation on "the great golden Madonna," "the gold Virgin" atop the Boulogne church. Mrs. Wix runs the risk of conversion, not merely religious, as the text continually proposes portentous changes for her, once out of England: "She had begun in fact to show infinite variety"; she "had risen to a level which might . . . pass almost for sublime"; "She was a newer Mrs. Wix than ever, a Mrs. Wix high and great." At the end of these fairy-tale transformations Mrs. Wix has, as it were, "become" Maisie's "real" mother while Maisie has "become" Clara Matilda, "my lost one," as Mrs. Wix calls her. Clara Matilda has indeed been textually cherished all this while for just such an exchange, in which *What Maisie Knew* achieves its most painful pathos and the concomitant heroism of small persons doing small yet wonderful things. Abroad is sometimes like that, depending on who you are.

# VII.

# *The Ambassadors, Gloire Complète* (1903)

## 1. *Nostalgic Return*

Nostalgia is certainly the word for *The Ambassadors,* so long as it is taken to refer not only to matters represented (the comic pathos of poor old American naif Strether hankering after a lost youth) but also and perhaps even more importantly to matters of representation itself. The nostalgia of *The Ambassadors* is, in another word, literary. *The Ambassadors* is appropriately *what* it is because of *where* it is, chronologically speaking, namely the last major term of Henry James' sequential encounter with the French—in their landscape, history, capital, language, art, literature, culture, customs, habits, civilization, what not—and also because of what immediately preceded it, *c'est-à-dire* the "English Period." After that relatively long lapse of the earlier attention, those many years of nearly total neglect, James returns to Paris, France, with evident intent to make up for arrears, to recompense for past omission, to revisit; not so much to repeat the savage comparativism of *The Tragic Muse* as to re-live, in the hope of clarification and improvement, the problematic murk of *The American*. The return of *The Ambassadors* was also a return to American personages in the very best of non-American settings, the city of Balzac, therefore the city of literature. To that city both fictive (as represented) and real (before, during, and after representation, quite apart from representation, quite indifferent to representation) James now returns *as* French (having attached French Literature and language to his own work in myriad ways), *as* English (having also attached that literature to his own work), and *as* American (by birthright—no attachment required), all three. And Strether's emotions on being in Paris again are, as it happens, almost exactly those of James in his 1902 essay about the re-reading of Balzac; that is to say, James' early and late relations with the Balzac text roughly correspond with Strether's two visits to Paris, the Balzac-James analogy cleverly concealed in the business of Stretcher's penchant for Victor Hugo.

Even before publication of *The American,* James was writing, from Paris, where he then lived, in a 22 November 1875 letter to the New York *Tribune*—a message from *here* or *ici* to *there* or *là*—"no American, certainly, since Americans were, has come to Paris but once, and it is when he returns, hungrily, inevitably, fatally, that his sense of Parisian things becomes supremely acute. . . . Was it really so very good as all that?"[1] This habit of mind, this emphasis on revisiting, went back a long way with James. Sixteen years and four days earlier still on 18 November 1859, at the grand old age of sixteen-and-a-half, he had written home to his friend Thomas Sergeant Perry about "revisiting"—in Paris, precisely—"certain familiar spots."[2] In *The Portrait of a Lady,* Gilbert Osmond, flush with *amore* for Isabel Archer and her recently inherited perquisites, composes "a little sonnet to which he prefixed the title of 'Rome Revisited.' "

Over the years the idea of revisiting recurs in a variety of texts referring to a variety of places, by no means all Paris even if Paris is best because of the well-known joke about all good Americans going to Paris when they die. Among passages suggesting *The Ambassadors* in embryo, that is to say the notion of revisiting, the motif of nostalgic return, we may think of the opening sentences in "The Diary of a Man of Fifty" (1879): "FLORENCE, *April 5th, 1874.* —They told me I should find Italy greatly changed; and in seven and twenty years there is room for changes. But to me everything is so perfectly the same that I seem to be living my youth over again." We may recollect the American Dexter Freers in the London of "Lady Barberina" (1884): "They had not arrived, they had only returned." If it is a conspicuous aspect of Jamesian return that he consciously revised and rewrote himself, lifelong, perhaps it is still another aspect that he probably rewrote himself unconsciously as well, a writer so voluminous being singularly vulnerable to unwitting duplication. Thus the opening sentence of part two of "Osborne's Revenge"—way back in 1868—may be said to portend in the most uncanny way the opening sentence of *The Ambassadors:* "His first inquiry on his arrival, after he had looked up several of his friends and encountered a number of acquaintances, was about Miss Congreve's whereabouts and habits."[3]

The "actual" germ of *The Ambassadors* dates from a *Notebooks* passage of 31 October 1895, where James records and meditates a report by Jonathan Sturges of what Howells said to him in Whistler's garden at Paris. The *"sujet"* immediately shapes up as the confrontation of "Howells" (even as "Howells" begins to change into a fictionalized personage) and "Paris" (even as James begins to fuss about "Paris" being the real right thing). Howells, James thinks, "had scarcely been in Paris, ever, in former days," so that now "it was all new to him: all, all, all"; therefore his evening-of-life exhortation to "live." But from the beginning, James was off-and-on resistant to the idea of Paris: "I don't altogether like the *banal* side of the revelation of Paris—it's so obvious, so usual to make Paris the vision that opens his eyes, makes him feel his mistake. It might be London—it might be Italy. . . . Also, it *may* be Paris." Thinking his way further along but still in the same entry, James returns to the question of place, novelistic setting, propriety of the *where* to the *what:* "I'm afraid it *must* be Paris; if he's an American."[4] On the other hand, more happily (in part), as James had written in a review of Taine's *Notes on Paris* in 1875 (and the situation could hardly be said to have changed much in the meanwhile): "We [American readers] apparently are capable of consuming an inordinate quantity of information, veracious or the reverse, about Paris. . . . Many readers will take much satisfaction in reading in English [translation] what could not possibly with decency have originally been written in English."[5] So late as the 1909 Preface to the New York Edition volumes of *The Ambassadors,* James was still fretting the pros and cons of his particular locale, especially bemoaning platitudinous Paris, "the dreadful little old tradition . . . that people's moral scheme *does* break down in Paris . . . [and] that hundreds and thousands of more or less hypocritical or more or less cynical persons annually visit the place for the sake of the probable catastrophe." On the other hand, where else was Strether so likely to find post-catastrophe Chad? Moreover, as I have been suggesting for several paragraphs, "The *likely* place had the great merit of sparing me preparations."[6]

The most famous passage of *The Ambassadors* portentously describes "Paris" (Paris as text, text as Paris) in terms of an imaginary "huge iridescent object," further hinted to be *perhaps* or *for example* "a jewel brilliant and hard." For *The Ambassadors* as a huge iridescent object, the alleged attributes of the imputed jewel are that (1) "parts were not to be discriminated" (2) "nor differences comfortably marked." The critical claim, translated to more literary language, is that *The Ambassadors* dramatically reverses and transcends and obliterates the divisive dialectic disjunctions of *The American,* achieving instead a flawless unification of (shall we say) narrative and setting, of the *what* and the *where.* We no longer find any grammatical shifts from past tense (the verb form of fiction) to present tense (the verb form of travel writing). *The Ambassadors* is all past, all "history," Strether's, James', ours who read. *The Ambassadors* is all Paris remembered in order that it may be revisited, literally or in the imagination which reflects or recalls or projects or even has read a book.

The famous passage continues and concludes: "It twinkled and trembled and melted together, and what seemed all surface one moment seemed all depth the next." It is that last statement, about surface and depth, that has naturally elicited so much loose talk in the James criticism. My own contribution to loose talk is a suggestion that the endlessly reversible surface-depth dyad is textually, representationally, inscribed in four distinctive and clearly analogous modes: (1) in the text's own frequent and conspicuous elisions and omissions of what another text, even another text by James, might well deem indispensable detail; (2) in Strether's frequent and deliberate omission from consciousness of data presumptively germane to his mission, notably the sexual relations of Madame de Vionnet and Chad, together with the fundamentally unchanged (unimproved) character of Chad; (3) in the hiatus of Strether's past, as textually referenced, so vividly marked by the empty interim between his first time (visit) in Paris ("then") and his second and last time (revisit) to Paris ("now")—what *has* the man been up to all this while?; and (4) in textual emphasis on vacant significantly altered spaces in the Parisian topography, the visible "presence," if one may so speak of them, of those things which are palpably "not there." The fourth mode, more material than the others, subsumes and may even have suggested the others: "The palace [Palais des Tuileries] was gone, Strether remembered the palace; and when he gazed into the irremediable void of its site the historic sense in him might have been freely at play—the play under which in Paris indeed it so often winces like a touched nerve. He filled out spaces with dim symbols of scenes," as surely every visitor to Paris has done (but the native French inhabitants of Paris?), for example, the Place de la Bastille, that grand spatial emptiness full of historical signification. What palace, besides the Tuileries? The palace of art? of history? the memory of life itself? All these things are absences, representations of what used to be—sometimes but not always suggesting what might have been—and is not. We will come back to the palace.

## 2. The Significance of Place

Succinctly Maria Gostrey alludes to Chad Newsome as "his situation here," meaning all manner of situation, e.g., his "relationship" with Marie de Vionnet, but where (!) "situation" is also quite easily to be understood as what I have been calling narrative and "here" as setting, that is to say for the present occasion Paris once more, Paris a referenced extra-textual existing-in-real-life "place," in the English sense of the word. As was clearly evident in the case of *The American*, narrative and setting are always at least potentially disjunct the one from the other in the way they appear in the finalized composition of a fictional work, and, as a consequence, they are readily detachable in the readerly reception and critical contemplation of that work. But the alternative is also possible: narrative and setting are always in one way or another at least potentially integrated—even, at times, to the point of identity, and then we like to say, in the older parlance, that the work has an organic unity, or some such unexamined phrase. Indeed, it will seem automatic to many readers, perhaps to most, that the organic unity of *The Ambassadors* is preferable to the blatantly disjunctive dialectics of *The American,* more normal, more natural, every way "better." Certainly the relations of narrative and setting in the two novels are remarkably different, and despite many superficial resemblances of personage, plot, and place.

But there is another way of regarding these matters, namely the textual or linguistic way. Accordingly, what is chiefly to notice is that the very word "situation" derives from the noun *site,* which in recent theoretical usage has even come to sound like a transitive verb as well (analogous with *situate*). "Situation" thus means not only *what* but *where,* or, in a single reified concept, a *what-where.* Voiced or scripted as a question—"that *what-where* you mention, what *is* it, please? and just *where?"*—the obvious answers are either *here* or *there* (or, in the common locution, "neither here nor there"), as relative to the writer, the reader, or both, these apparently simple words being equally susceptible of rigorously restrictive literal denotation or almost unlimited metaphorical extension. *Here* and *there* may well be the most eloquent words of the Jamesian text (however snubbed by Jamesian criticism), nicely corresponding to the ubiquitous *ici* and *là* of the French language, so expansively expressed in a variety of compounds, e.g., *ceci* and *celà,* this-here and that-there. The most familiar of these compounds are surely those formed with prefatory *voi-* (see, look, pay attention to), from which compounding we have *voici* and *voilà,* the latter increasingly more frequent and often followed by an exclamation mark (further to emphasize the obviousness of it all). So we may understand the otherwise incomprehensible verbal habits of those Jamesian personages, otherwise apparently quite sane, who are forever saying "well, here we are!" or "There you are!" as if they were articulating something vastly important and we wonder what on earth it can possibly be. What it can possibly be is among other things Henry James writing the English language bilingually, as if it were also French (as of course it is), with the concomitant expectation that we read simultaneously or back and forth. The quite typical *clôture* of *The Ambassadors* comes to new life in such a context of understanding, particular, internationalized, interlinguistic: " 'Then there we are!' said Strether." It is like the printer's mark THE END and more. It is the totalized backward-glancing retroaction of narrative-setting.*

Another apparently innocent phrase, this time alluding to Strether, is equally illuminating for topography, fictionally considered: "He had taken a long vague walk." Strether's long vague walks are not only a topic of representation, they are also a principle of narrative construction for *The Ambassadors,* a mode of connecting up its spread of significant locations, but in the confoundments of his romantic excitation Strether is often unmindful where he is and the text suits him to perfection: *The Ambassadors* is the world's great testimony to the art of leaving things out (as of course also to the art of putting things in, without which inclusion the leaving out would have no relevance). It is remarkable how much information is cunningly withheld—e.g., the name and street of Strether's hotel or whether the best-lit of cosmopolitan cities has changed over from gas to electricity (of course it has)—or the information is suggested, by generalized description, by innuendo, by tone, by assumption of what the Tourist Reader "cannot possibly *not* know" (preface to *The American*).

Aside from carefully selected places—the Louvre, not the Invalides, not the Tour Eiffel; Notre Dame, not Sacre Cœur—such public places as buildings, squares, landmarks, quarters, streets, gardens, the indispensably divisive Seine, *The Ambassadors* largely "takes place" in and between the dwellings of its major personages. These dwellings are located according to a familiar pattern and the imaginative nostalgic eye of the Tourist Reader soon masters its typifying shape, roughly the same as for *The American,* an irregular polygon with three apexes on the Right Bank (where the wistful desirous Americans stay) and one on the Left Bank (which secretes the penetralia

---

*The last two paragraphs of Virginia Woolf, *Mrs Dalloway* (1925), obligingly read:

It is Clarissa, he said.
For there she was.

they would be at, the Faubourg Saint-Germain, or, more personally, intimate knowledge of a Claire de Cintré, a Madame de Vionnet, the first of these heroines so pre-Napoleonic, the latter Napoleon Herself).

At or near the western end of the Right Bank side of the novelistic polygon is a point defining the American Colony, for *The Ambassadors* the entresol of Maria Gostrey in the Quartier Marbœuf, just south of the Champs Elysées, about halfway between Etoile and Place de la Concorde. Still on the Right Bank but further to the east, in the vicinity of Place de l'Opéra, is where the visiting Americans put up at hotels, some de luxe, some not. The Pococks' hotel overlooks the Rue de Rivoli. It is not named. Neither is Strether's hotel, nearby, of which we know all that we need, "the small, the admittedly secondary hotel in the bye-street from the Rue de la Paix, in which her solicitude [Maria Gostrey's] for his purse had placed him," rich Mrs. Newsome's carte blanche to her ambassador apparently involving no greater expenditure of funds than of interpretational flexibility. If not the rose, Strether lives near it ("it" being l'Opéra). On occasion, the text is wonderfully precise about distances and directions: Strether and Chad sit at a café in the Avenue de l'Opéra and Strether imagines Maria Gostrey sitting up and listening to him "a mile away," or Strether leaves a café near her entresol and thinks he will "walk round by the Boulevard Malesherbes—rather far round— on his way home." Boulevard Malesherbes, in a wondrous or mystic troisième, is where Chad now lives, "in between" (like Valentin) as to nationality and business habits and so "in between" as to domicile, lives now quite respectably, he who had once gone in search of the best French, or said he did, in the Rue de la Montagne Saint-Geneviève. At Boulevard Malesherbes the air is said to be "violet" and the apartment has a "continuous" balcony. Key social scenes of *The Ambassadors* enact on this balcony or in the closely connected rooms just behind it.

One and only one memorable incident commences between banks, "across," as text has it, meaning across the larger "half" of the Seine, at Notre Dame on the Ile de la Cité—you can no more have a novel of Paris without Notre Dame than you are obliged to furnish that novel with a major ado in the plebeian Bois de Vincennes. All the way across, what text refers to as "over," is the secreted woman.

Text has long since explained usage: " 'Over' was over the river, and over the river was where Madame de Vionnet lived." She lives on Rue de Bellechasse, 7ème ar., street number withheld. Rue de Belle-chasse crosses Rue de l'Université, home of the curious Bellegardes in *The American*. Gloriani's house and garden are also "over," James still having in mind Whistler's garden on the Rue du Bac, and if Madame de Vionnet walked from her house to Notre Dame, as Strether thinks she did, then clearly she could even more easily have walked to Gloriani's party. The Left Bank is not, of course, unfail-ingly aristocratic (in the touristic eye). It is where Chad lived, in his low period, and it is where little Bilham lives now, "at the end of an alley that went out of an old short cobbled street, a street that went in turn out of a new long smooth avenue," designations suitable to any number of alleys, streets, and avenues—the textual indetermi-nacy is precise.

Thus narrative proceeds by means of Strether's long vague walks between these various checkpoints of the situational polygon. None of his walks is particularly exhausting and none, so far as we know, is unpleasant. On the contrary, all, we are sure, are fascinating, whether or not we are told what he sees, hears, smells; we have been there ourselves, in fact or in fancy; we may even remember having read all about it in a novel called *The American*. Strether seldom takes cabs and the Métro never. The Métro was available since 19 July 1900, in plenty of time for him, but *The Ambassadors* does not use it. A 25 November 1881 *Notebooks* passage of autobiographical resumé gratefully acknowledges the year lived in Paris—the year, more or less, of *The American*—as "time by no means misspent. . . . I got a certain familiarity with Paris (added to what I had acquired before) which I shall never lose," and which there was evidently no reason to augment.[7] For all practical purposes, the unspecified "time," as a function of "place," in *The Ambassadors* is roughly the same as it had been in 1876–77. "I can't separate," Strether says to Maria Gostrey, "it's all one." Paris is unchanged, only confirmed by the continuing attachment of French Literature, it being no exaggeration to say that the Paris of *The Ambassadors* is also, *par exemple,* James' (Alphonse) Daudet, described in an 1882 review as "a product of the great French city. He has the nervous tension, the intellectual eagerness, the quick and exaggerated sensibility, the complicated, sophisticated judgment, which the friction, the contagion, the emulation, the whole spectacle, at once exciting and depressing, of our civilization at its highest, produces in susceptible natures."[8] Such is the putative fate of our own hero with the name from Balzac, Lewis Lambert Strether, a sophisticated American bumpkin from Massachusetts temporarily turning into something else, presumptively better. It is entirely a representational consequence of where he is. The narrative and the setting are one. No wonder he can't "separate" them. No more can we. Strether, we may further note, is fifty-five years old (James was more nearly sixty) and was in Europe at twenty-five, i.e., thirty years ago, in the early 1870s, just after the Franco-Prussian War, just before James wrote *The American*. But the equations are only approximate.

The working topography of Paris, the polygonic plan of judiciously spread-out locations at which and between which the narrative develops and displays its myriad sequences, is mainly deposited in Books Second, Third, and Fourth, thereafter to be drawn on like money at Strether's American bankers, most likely Munroe & Co., Rue Scribe 7. Paris waits briefly while we dally down from England, and then in chapter two of Book Second we are *there,* with our usual touristical gusto and one minor concession to realism. As haply befalls the passionate pilgrim of advancing years, Strether is not up to much his first day, and so we have his second day, with memorial fragments of his first. Book Second, chapter two, briskly begins: "Strether called, his second morning in Paris, on the bankers of the Rue Scribe to whom his letter of credit"—Mrs. Newsome's credit, not unlimited, we suppose—"was addressed," with the curious double meaning of "addressed." He had been there the previous day and found no letters. This morning there are plenty. Then (or was it the day before?) he pauses "at the top [north] of the street [Rue Scribe, clearly]," where "he looked up and down the great foreign avenue," not named but doubtless Boulevard Haussmann, the word "foreign" featuring as ever its inherent ambiguities (but far less aggressively than in *The American*). It was presumably during his first Paris day that Strether "gave himself up" to the world's capital with no specific reminiscences, for *us,* save attendance with Waymarsh at the Gymnase, Boulevard Bonne-Nouvelle 38, the eastward extension of Boulevard Haussmann and a good stiff walk from their hotel, "chiefly for comedies," according to Bædeker, the kind of place you go to with Waymarsh, yet too good for Jim Pocock, neither theater being Strether's sort of thing; afterward they partake of watered beer at Café Riche, Boulevard des Italiens 16 (expensive) on the way home.

It is on the second day that Strether performs his Great Walk, the longest, furthest, best documented tour of *The Ambassadors*. Letters in overcoat pocket, he comes "down" (southward bound) Rue de la Paix, passes the Tuileries—the gardens not the palace, "The palace was gone, Strether remembered the palace" (Henry James remembered *The Princess Casamassima*), the palace burned 22–23 May 1871 during the Communard uprising, well in advance of *The American* as actually composed but two to three years after its alleged "time of action," dates of burning which James might have read about once again, had he wished or needed to, in the closing pages of *Le Débâcle* (1892), his favorite Zola—and after passing the Tuileries he then passes the river indeed *and* "on the other side" continues up (southward still) the Rue de Seine making straight for Jardin de Luxembourg, *there* to read letters from "home," another and quite different *there*, text yielding a perpetual superimposition of divergent places.

Strether sits to read, to rest, to meditate (much novelistic exposition) and then he is up and away again to the Latin Quarter, Montagne Sainte-Geneviève (Chad's past, more exposition) *where* "He pulled himself then at last together for his own progress back," yet we do not find him back so soon but rather he is next spotted "under the old arches of the Odéon" enviously ogling used books, "substituting one kind of low-priced *consommation* for another," until finally he arrives on the sidewalk opposite and facing Chad's troisième in the Boulevard Malesherbes to be received *there* by little Bilham in the absence of Chad who is off in Cannes (with whom?) and that very evening, at their modest hotel, Strether tells Waymarsh all about it (Book Third, chapter one). The main point of the perambulation is familiar to every Tourist Reader who has lived abroad extensively: pending return of Maria Gostrey, Chad's is "the only domicile, the only fireside, in the great ironic city, on which he had the shadow of a claim." That domicile will take him in, indeed, it will positively engorge him, and he will issue to the light once more only at the end with no worry on his mind more painful than whether or not Chad is "tired" of his lover, he, Strether, having by that time no lover at all nor prospect of any life at all, erotic or other.

There are exactly three Parisian landmarks which the novel of

Paris can hardly do without, and these are Notre Dame, the Louvre, and the Comédie Française. Two of these three spots loom large in *The American* (the Louvre at the beginning, Notre Dame at the end) and if they loom less large in *The Reverberator* it is because the Dossons don't go to that kind of place and the Proberts don't go any place at all (and still the Louvre is talked about as a good place to visit and Notre Dame as a good place to get married). In *The Ambassadors*, Strether, accompanied by Maria Gostrey, with whom he arranged the visit eons ago (many pages back) in Chester, meets Bilham "in the great gallery of the Louvre"; with that same charmingly feckless young expatriate Strether has previously been to the museum of the Luxembourg, where he has seen works by Gloriani. (The detail of place serves more than one function.) Strether encounters the new allegedly improved Chad at the Comédie Française, scene of so much anguished expostulation in *The Tragic Muse*, at a performance of, well, he knows not what, but "one of the glories of literature," *French* Literature, of course, Molière or Racine, all wasted: "He couldn't when the curtain fell have given the slightest account of what had happened." Chad walks Strether back to his hotel with a stop at a café (on the Avenue de l'Opéra). On the way they pause to take in "the great clear architectural street," almost certainly the Avenue de Opéra, the Boulevard des Capucines being much less distinguished for architectural clarity. As usual, there is precision available to the Tourist Reader who desires to work things out in some detail, while those who prefer to rest on their oars may drift around in such statements as "The strolls over Paris to see something or call somewhere were accordingly inevitable and natural," neither more so nor less so than in Schenectady, where Daisy Miller once walked and visited.

The significance of Notre Dame is developed last, but not least, Notre Dame picturesque over and above any other consideration, Notre Dame so unique so indispensable, for what other modern city, purveyor of comforts and conveniences and pleasures, center of culture and civilization, world capital and tourist attraction, may so readily supply a medieval cathedral right in its midst and on an island as well, a cathedral you can view from afar or walk around or even go into? In Book Seventh, Strether and Madame de Vionnet, met within, walk around Notre Dame on their way to lunch, their first and only date, not counting visits at her flat. We have a long look at Strether inside, and Strether looking at Madame. Strether is a Notre Dame habitué of sorts, he goes there with Waymarsh, with Maria Gostrey, with Chad (their reactions unrecorded), and by himself—the latter instance text calls a "refuge," a "remedy," a "way," a "pilgrimage," an "adventure," touching lots of bases. Among a variety of further matters suggested by Notre Dame for the benefit of *The Ambassadors,* matters tending rather to the secular and social than to the sacred mysteries, are "the great romancer and the great romance," indisputably *Notre-Dame de Paris* (1831), plus sixty-nine additional volumes of Victor Hugo recklessly acquired by Strether in Paris (will they fit in his trunk? will he ever read them?) and the propriety of the Protestant or more generally the non-Catholic tourist using Catholic churches in Europe primarily or altogether for the purposes of sightseeing, a sore point, and eminently discussable, in James fictions of Americans abroad ever since "Travelling Companions" (1870).

For the remainder of *The Ambassadors,* approximately the rest of the second half, Paris fictionalized yet real is scattered far, wide, and thin—*en conséquence, ici,* clumped. Strether goes to Chartres, to Fontainebleau, to Rouen ("with a little handbag and inordinately spent the night"); he returns to Paris. The Pococks arrive in Paris. Strether is to conduct Jim to Théâtre des Variétés, "which Strether was careful to pronounce as Jim pronounced them," Boulevard Montmartre, "excellent for vaudevilles, farces, operettas, and similar lively pieces of essentially Parisian character," as Bædeker believes.[9] Waymarsh and Sarah are to dine at Bignon's, obviously chic, expensive, thence to the circus, perhaps Nouveau Cirque, equestrian and aquatic events, or Cirque d'Eté, Champs Elysées, seating for 3500. Chadwick and Mamie by contrast go to the Français (family-bill) after Taverne Brébant, popular beer establishment, presumed not chic, not expensive. Waymarsh and Sarah Pocock, as relations warm, are early-morning devotees at Marché aux Fleurs, any of three easy locations depending on the day of the week. In Book Eleventh, when not out of town in quest of French ruralism, we still move to and fro among hotels and apartments and in Book Twelfth pretty much the same except that, separately and ensemble, it is fading fast, dwindling out of existence, the novel done, Paris used up, Tourist Romanticism once more consumed in and by the consumption of its very own self, only, of course, to flare up again, soon after return home.

### 3. Parisian Interiors

"We, for our part," young Henry James was writing in his first (1875) Balzac essay, "have always found Balzac's houses and rooms extremely interesting; we often prefer his places to his people."[10] Without necessarily transferring that preference to *The Ambassadors,* we, for our part, may now freely confess and gladly indulge a comparable interest in James' Parisian interiors, for practical purposes defined as those places where Strether may if he likes come in out of the rain. He is variously *à l'intérieur* in public places such as Notre Dame (as dry as it is dark), the Louvre (lots to look at), the Théâtre Français (plenty to listen to even if you don't); in a selection of cafés and restaurants, few of them named (restaurants named are for other people, a delicate bit of Strether-pathos); in his own hotel (complete with Waymarsh) and at the Pococks'; and by way of homes away from home in the shabby Bohemian quarters of little Bilham, in Maria Gostrey's all-receiving entresol, in Chad's romanticized troisième, and best of all—much best—in Madame de Vionnet's very special and secluding environment, paradoxically pure Empire and literary. The inside of Gloriani's house Strether does not seem to attain but other guests are said to pass in and out.

According to virtually lifelong compositional-structural habit, James' domestic environments in *The Ambassadors*—they, rather than the nave and side chapels of Notre Dame, or the halls walls plush-padded divans milk-plashing coin-collecting waiters or domino-playing frequenters of cafés, are presently our chief fascination, the answer to "how will he live" being "where shall we look to find him next?"—appear to be cunningly arranged as conflicted confrontations in dramatic face-off. There are three such conflicted pairs: minimally marginal versus flamboyantly luxurious hotels (Strether's and the Pococks'), under-furnished versus over-furnished "nests" (Bilham's and Gostrey's), newly versus anciently elegant quarters (Chad's and Marie de Vionnet's). Taken together, these three oppositions make a series of false or faulty parallels, doubtless deliberate, for whereas Marie de Vionnet's home is clearly more attractive than Chad's (if at all romantically inclined, we should like to live there), and Maria Gostrey's crowded collectibles clearly preferable to little Bilham's lack of chairs with four legs—even so, these two contrasts are not the same *kind* of contrast—we should be hard put to say which hotel we ought to avoid, both are so dreadful though in different ways.

In *The American* and *The Reverberator* the misbehaving-vulgar American democrat was punished for presumption by European or Europeanized totalitarians in their private dwellings; in *The Ambassadors* the well-meaning-and-not vulgar-at-all American democrat is punished by American democrat-despots in his own hotel, a rather democratic hotel, as who should say, with respect to prices and quality. Sometimes together, mostly not, Strether and Waymarsh pace its little court or Waymarsh looks through the glass of the *salon de lecture* at Strether where he writhes. It is in that same *salon de lecture* that Strether is decimated by Sarah Pocock. The room is more comprehensively described as having "witnessed the wane of his early vivacity of discussion with Waymarsh." Strether regularly dines at his hotel (another minor tragedy, given the chances of Paris). He makes touristical-egalitarian friends with the personnel who work the *salle-à-manger,* which is "sallow and sociable" and indeed "slippery" (so is the staircase; we are not informed with what). Late in the novel he sits there alone remembering the chill of early Paris spring, the chill of his American friends' condemnation, noting the fact of *too much glass* (admitting light but not warmth) as it "expressed the presence of Waymarsh even at times when Waymarsh might have been certain to be round at the bank," procuring his daily supplement of Americanism. Just as he remembers the palace (Tuileries), Strether remembers the meals. He can smell them now. The Pococks' hotel is for its brief flaming hour the obvious antithesis of Strether's. *Its* windows, with balcony (but maybe not a continuous balcony) overlook a famous tourist street, as his do not. We know his room has windows only from his placing on the sill Mrs. Newsome's infamous telegram, held down by his watch. The Pocock rooms are not of course American but Paris-for-the-American trade, "glazed and gilded . . . all red damask, ormolu, mirrors, clocks." In *The Ambassadors'* interiors, the briefer the description the more inconsequential the occupants—and vice versa, Madame de Vionnet receiving not only the highest compliments but the most expansive prose.

Brevity of description equally, but for different reasons, consorts with dwellings comparatively empty of contents. Little Bilham's studio ("his own poor place," as he rightly calls it, narrative authoring elaborating its "overflow of taste and conviction and its lack of nearly all else") richly suits Strether's appetite for "the legend of good-humoured poverty, of mutual accommodation fairly raised to the romantic," that is to say artist life and artist talk, while in fact the studio is "cold and blank" and not especially suggestive of that legend or any other. It houses a "faraway makeshift life, with its jokes and its gaps," jokes not repeated, gaps not specified, and it seems to boast three or four chairs, nondescript, the uncertainty of the number saying all. Little Bilham's studio is immediately preceded by allusion to the Louvre, making for a couple of contrasts: the Louvre is better furnished, the Louvre is public rather than private. Virtually *all* descriptions of interior space in *The Ambassadors* presume or imply an "outside," a street, a boulevard, a place, a museum, a cathedral, a theater, a restaurant, a circus, a park, e.g., the Luxembourg Gardens, furnished with "terraces, alleys, vistas, fountains, little trees in green tubs, little women in white caps and shrill little girls at play." *The Ambassadors* is as full of lists as a poem by Walt Whitman.

The main contrast for Mr. Bilham's rooms is however Maria Gostrey's rooms. Maria Gostrey is an expatriated collector, she collects things, she collects Strether, and sometimes the things and Strether get in each other's way. We hear no word about the structure of her entresol or between-floors, many words about its contents: these bear upon their owner, upon the conversations that occur in their midst, upon Strether's intermittent presence there throughout the narrative, and upon his deletion at the time of denouement. It is at Maria Gostrey's that Strether erroneously believes "he should find the boon with the vision of which he had first mounted Chad's stairs," the romantic troisième regrettably lacking an elevator, the "boon" being simultaneously Paris and home, i.e., Elsewhere and not-Elsewhere somehow coalesced. Like Chad, Maria Gostrey is a genteel scavenger, as Madame de Vionnet is not. The ingredients of her "final nest" she has picked up "in a thousand flights and funny little passionate pounces." Her staying power is prodigious, we think; somehow we know she will never leave but sit tight in her "compact and crowded little chambers." These strike Strether immediately as "almost dusky . . . with accumulations, [which] represented a supreme general adjustment to opportunities and conditions," fine and dandy so far as they go yet vaguely threatening: "Wherever he looked he saw an old ivory or an old brocade, and he scarce knew where to sit for fear of a misappliance," an eccentric word for a most particular malaise. Sitting in *The Ambassadors* is a problem only at Bilham's and Gostrey's, at Madame de Vionnet's Strether sits comfortably enough and at Chad's he positively lounges. But here, "The life of the occupant [!] struck him of a sudden as more charged with possession even than Chad's," as veritably a "temple" to "the lust of the eyes and the pride of life"—these satisfactions which may never be his. Strether's Puritanical aversion proves temporary; on his last visit, the closing scene of the novel, the very same things appear to him in nearly an opposite light, "the place had never before struck him [same phrase] as so sacred to pleasant knowledge, to intimate charm, to antique order, to a neatness that was almost august." Then the telling detail: *"To sit there was . . .* to see life reflected for the time in ideally kept pewter" (emphasis added), reflected also in a string of typifying adjectives, bare, proud, small, old (repeated), substantial, vivid. And still, Strether concludes, rightly, "I'm not . . . in real harmony with what surrounds me. You *are."* It is the distinction between himself a pilgrim and her an expatriate. It is also subsumptively the distinction between *The American* (disjunction of narrative and setting) and *The Ambassadors* (unification of the same). But Strether's narrative, as separable from the total narrative text of *The Ambassadors,* is itself disjunct from the setting of modern Paris. And despite his tribute to antique order he fails to notice that in Maria Gostrey's chambers there is no slightest hint of that historical depth which almost overwhelms him chez Madame de Vionnet. And he also fails to reflect on the fact that even Woollett now has a factory hovering between the second and the third generations of industrializing Newsomes.

Of Chad's rooms, his continuation therein less assured than Maria Gostrey's in Quartier Marbœuf, we are chiefly aware that they are wonderful for the giving of parties small or large and that from the continuous balcony you can flip cigarette butts and burnt matches onto the uncomplaining all-tolerant romantic Paris sidewalks known to the locals as *trottoirs*. Strether is often found on that balcony, over which he is said to "hang." Behind it are three almost equally continuous rooms intercommunicating by wide doors and each of them opening to the balcony. "Oh a charming place," Strether says to Waymarsh, "full of beautiful and valuable things. I never saw such a place." Inside or out, there are always "the haze of tobacco," "music more or less good," "talk more or less polyglot," and "occasions of discussion" (about what?). Either the rooms are enormous or they expand like loaves and fishes; at the party honoring (discomfiting) Sarah Pocock, Strether thinks he "had perhaps seen, on Fourths of July and on dear old domestic Commencements [Harvard], more people assembled, but he had never seen so many in proportion to the space." As the terms of comparison suggest, the festivities are of a sort normally held on large grounds outdoors, and it is a fine example of how in *The Ambassadors* the two basic kinds of space, outer and inner, are so often invited to interchange. Like Maria Gostrey *(ces Américains!)* Chad collects, most recently "a landscape, of no size, but of the French school, as our friend was glad to feel he knew," and more glad still when his "taste" is confirmed by Gloriani, that outsized Italian male feline predator ("The deep human expertness in Gloriani's charming smile—oh the terrible life behind it!"—women, no doubt).

*Au contraire,* the habitat of Marie de Vionnet, the one and only nonpareil of *The Ambassadors,* is French history according to Henry James, an American revenant abroad, French history consisting almost entirely of the Revolution and the First Empire. Strether thinks "The place itself [the building] went further back—that he guessed, and how old Paris continued in a manner to echo there," but Strether hardly hears any such echoes, Strether neither knows nor cares, just as he never cares to reflect by how many years Notre Dame may be said to antedate Napoleon. Madame de Vionnet is *old* (not personally, of course), Madame de Vionnet is *great* (wonderful, not large), and therefore Madame de Vionnet is *Napoleonic*. That is as French as things get in Henry James and about as old. His vaunted sense of the past is for the most part Franco-American, and it takes up the tale not much earlier than the two intertwined revolutions. Anything prior to the French Revolution, the First Empire, might as well be lost in the mists of antiquity. Nor does the text of *The Ambassadors* ever consider the rather obvious fact that the "things" Madame de Vionnet "has," not "gets," can't possibly have been in the family more than two or three generations, for Napoleonic-type objects might have come into a body's possession, even if not vulgarly acquired in the fashion of a Gostrey or a Newsome, so late as 1815. No acquisitor *she,* de Vionnet, unlike Chad and especially Maria, who "rummaged and purchased and picked up and exchanged," just like upstart Americans, "whereas the mistress of the scene before him," him being Strether, "beautifully passive under the spell of transmission—transmission from her father's line, he quite made up his mind," because it is her mother who is English, "had only received, accepted and been quiet." It is a social preference, like another, subject to variety of opinion, subject, much more, to literary interpretation.

What we have in the case of Madame de Vionnet's flat and of the conspectus of tonalities associated with it, is a powerful yet muted recreation of *Princess Casamassima* thematology, the ambivalent maximizing of France as creator and destroyer both, especially as epitomized in the French Revolution, both creation and destruction subsequently spread over Europe, those processes epitomized by the First Empire. Madame de Vionnet is inevitably associated with *les gloires* of French Literature and Art, on the one hand, making her the most wonderful person the world has ever seen, and, on the other hand, with the Violent Needless Destruction of Public Buildings and Monuments (which are also art), making her dangerous. Behind the ambivalence bristles late-nineteenth-century post-Darwinian Energy (the name at which every knee must bend), morally neutral but fertile with events both good and evil. Reverence toward Energy is a general, a cultural, prejudice of James' epoch; focus of that energy on the idea of the French Revolution is Henry James' specialty. Granted, it takes some perspicacity and patience to perceive and interpret, beneath the subtlety of prose stylistics—and other ostensible topics —these connections of art and violence, of revolution and war and creativity in the various arts (home furnishings included), but it can be done; take the following typical passage, for example:

> She occupied, his hostess, in the Rue de Bellechasse, the first floor
> of an old house to which our visitors [Strether and Chad] had had
> access from an old clean court. The court was large and open, full
> of revelations, for our friend, of the habit of privacy, the peace of
> intervals, the dignity of distances and approaches; the house, to his
> restless sense, was in the high homely style of an elder day, and
> the ancient Paris that he was always looking for—sometimes in-
> tensely felt, sometimes more acutely missed.

Concentration on certain strings of verbal association leads to certain
readings: old-old-ancient-elder is one, clean-large-open-high is another, revelations-privacy-peace-dignity-distances a third. After a
sufficient pause for the enjoyment of these, we may finally come to
notice the concluding reference to an ancient Paris as sometimes felt
and sometimes more acutely missed; then, suddenly, we know where
we are again, we have heard that note before, sensed and to a degree
comprehended its agony; we recognize the rhythm of the phrase, we
are even willing to let ourselves be haunted by its melody, "The
palace was gone, Strether remembered the palace," the appositional
structuring of *gone-Strether* contained within the enveloped repetition
*palace-palace*. You can have all kinds of different interpretation to that
cited passage, depending on where you place your italics, but that
particular placing has *my* recommendation, it hooks so well with so
much else.

Some description of the de Vionnet flat is of course nonpolitical
(but not less laudatory): a "wide waxed staircase" (not slippery, as at
Strether's hotel), medallions and mouldings, mirrors (not obscene,
as at the Pococks' hotel), all, we suppose, "hereditary cherished
charming." Suddenly we discover another hook, namely, that the
point, the value of a quiet peaceful inheritance of things is related by
antithesis to the violence of their initial coming into the world, as if
to say that we respect and even honor the events of the past, blood,
terror, and all that, which led to so much *apertura* for humanity,
European and generally, yet we should on the whole prefer not to
have further revolutions if they can be avoided; looking back from
the time of *The Ambassadors,* James was aware that they had not been
avoided; looking ahead, he might still hope for the best. Looking
back to the origins of Marie de Vionnet as hereditary cherished

charming he naturally saw "some glory, some prosperity of the First Empire, some Napoleonic glamour, some dim lustre of the great legend" which as we know from the Deathbed Dictation was his private obsession; I mean the letter of 12 December 1915 addressed to William, dead since 1910, and Alice, dead since 1892, beginning "I call your attention to the precious enclosed transcripts of plans and designs for the decoration of certain apartments of the palaces, *here,* of the Louvre and the Tuileries," emphasis added, and signed Napoléone.[11] Thus at Madame de Vionnet's we find—not, in the last analysis, surprisingly—objects comparatively trivial or even ridiculous emanating from Napoleonism, such as "consular chairs and mythological brasses and sphinxes' heads and faded surfaces of satin striped with alternate silk," and we also find "the post-revolutionary period, the world he [Strether] vaguely thought of as the world of Châteaubriand, of Madame de Staël [author of *Corinne*], even of the young Lamartine," remnants of literature, then back again to "harps and urns and torches," and on and on the description continues with glass cases holding mementoes military (swords and epaulettes) and diplomatic (snuffboxes) and *excelsior!* "copies of works presented, with inscriptions, by authors now classic," but not, we are bound to think, *very* classic, not contemporary with the Sun King, much less Euripides, in fact some of these works would be less than a century older than *The Ambassadors,* less than three-quarters of a century older than *The American*—what price relativity!

Strether's curious mind, like James', is never entirely free from the "faint far-away cannon-roar of the great Empire. It was doubtless half the projection of his mind." It was entirely the projection of his mind, their minds, yet not the less "there," in the text, consequently, without escape, there for us. It is "here" that Strether hears the sounds of Paris commencing a revolution, "here" that he smells the public temper as the smell of blood, "here" that he fancies Marie de Vionnet resembling Madame Roland on the scaffold. All for Chad? Is he worth it? Or are there other, perhaps deeper reasons for the Napoleonizing of Marie de Vionnet? Is she really, as text pretends, one of the "luxurious few" who possesses "the chance, on a great occasion, to be natural and simple"? What in fact *is* her chance? To lose a man with whom she probably ought not to be in love but is, a man younger and undeserving, who appears to be falling out of love with *her?* What is so natural and simple about that? What, about it, is so good? Tolerable, even? What if, instead, we began to think about Marie de Vionnet along the lines of France Heroinic, France Dominatrice of the Arts, France S. Jeanne d'Arc (secularized) of Modern Civilization, France Henry Jamesed, Henry James Frenched at last— and simply wallowing in, as I have presumed to call it, *Gloire Complète?*

Descending from the thin air of such elevations, we might want to ask how these interiors of Paris are specifically or uniquely Parisian; the answer is that they are Parisian variously. The interiors of Notre Dame, the Louvre, the Théâtre Français, are not to be matched anywhere in the world, nor anywhere else even in Paris. There is less distinction as we come down to cafés and restaurants; in "An International Episode" we are entertained by French waiters at New York hotels. Gloriani's garden space is blocked out (or in) by hôtels in a different sense of the word and might be hard to locate outside of Paris, but little Bilham's Left Bank Bohemian studio might be found in any large city of the time (Dreiser would have put it in Chicago); it is in Paris because *The Ambassadors* is, and in honor of the Tourist Reader who in 1903 still thought of Paris as an emblem of art's ardors. The hotels of *The Ambassadors* are still less exclusively Parisian, the same kind of hotel was increasingly found all over the world. So with the Gostrey and Newsome holdings (collectibles). Their apartments happen to be furnished with objects presumably French because they happen to have been purchased, mostly secondhand, in France, but it is difficult not to suspect that pretty much the same sort of second-hand artifacts might have been found in London or Boston. Indeed, there is little or no guarantee that the prize objects so rapturously pounced upon in Paris weren't first manufactured in one of those Godforsaken places, Woollett even.

## 4. Who Speaks What

Who speaks what is obviously and always a matter of interest in, to, and for the international theme, the Tourist Novel, as, long since, in *The Portrait of a Lady:* " 'I am sure you understand everything, and that differences of nationality are no barrier to you,' Ralph went on. Miss Stackpole gazed at him still. 'Do you mean the foreign languages?' " Long before the first French word is dropped by Maria Gostrey—she is especially good at it—French has come up in connection with her calling card. To her name "was attached, in a corner of the card, with a number, the name of a street, presumably in Paris, without other appreciable identity than its foreignness." Presumably in Paris, yes, but even more presumably in France, and certainly in some "French-language area." It makes a nice opening— subtle and distanced, the exchange of calling cards occurring in Chester, where, and later in London, there is talk of Americans abroad, of "Europe," and even one slight reference to Paris. But almost to the end of England there is nearly no French until Maria suddenly bursts out with her typical Comment donc, *bon, milieu,* voilà, *parti,* and again *Bon!* (Either she or text moves casually in and out of italics.) The opening notes of French are so simple, so easy, so superficial as almost to seem like an additional system of punctuation, a sauce unnecessary yet welcome.

Other functions of French in *The Ambassadors,* particularly as practiced by Anglophones in Paris, are more operational. They tend to be ladled out one at a time, with many pages in between, quite a different textual effect from that of *The American,* where French words and phrases steadily flowed forth from beginning to end. Regardless of what language is ostensibly spoken by the major personages—and for the most part it is English and is given as English (*The Ambassadors* is written in English, not French; in French translation, the interpolated French fillips would lose their point)—the world's first and foremost language, according to the French, a sentiment in which James seems to concur, swirls around the topographical landmarks of Paris, in and out of the Paris weather, in and out of the ears of the Tourist Reader. But it is seldom referred to explicitly, issues are seldom made of it, no one takes French lessons. Indeed, after Maria Gostrey's opening notes there is no further attention to the fact of French until Book Second, when Strether on his Great Walk finds himself in the Rue de la Montagne Saint-Geneviève, where Chad used to live, for his curious reasons. The curious reason for *us* is that the location is not only topographic but linguistic. "This was the region—Chad had been quite distinct about it— in which the best French, and many other things, were to be learned at least cost." Chad had further been distinct, for home consumption, that the inhabitants there are "a much more profitable lot to be with . . . than the 'terrible toughs' (Strether remembered the edifying discrimination) of the American bars and banks roundabout the Opéra." At a stroke the clever young man alleges himself to have moved to the Left Bank (aristocratic), cut his connections with the sort of Americans who stay in hotels on the Right Bank spending their spare time drinking up the proceeds of moneys sent out from the States, and put himself in position (like Isabel Archer) to perfect his French; he also makes it difficult, if not impossible, for his family to check up on him. But soon, as Strether also remembers, that phase came to an end: "The son and brother [!] had not browsed long on the Montagne Sainte-Geneviève—his effective little use of the name of which, like his allusion to the best French, appeared to have been but one of the notes of his rough cunning," for in fact the Montagne Sainte-Geneviève is no mountain at all, only a slight eminence and an undistinguished street behind (east of) the Sorbonne, near the Pantheon. In or about that street, Strether infers, Chad has had his various little Parisian girlfriends, one of whom, no doubt, "had determined the second migration, the expensive return and relapse, the exchange again, as was fairly to be presumed, of the vaunted best French for some special variety of the worst." In plain English, Chad has moved back to the Right Bank, where we find him. The Boulevard Malesherbes is long, extending from 8ème well past Parc Monceau into 17ème and we shall never know, lacking a street number, how far "out" (northwest) to place him; but we rather suppose him to consort neither with the American Colony nor with the terrible toughs.

No more of Chad's wanderings in pursuit of the best French but after overhearing Strether's "Merci, François!" (he says it "out quite loud when his fish was brought" by the waiter at his hotel) we are presented the mystery of Miss Barrace the paradigmatic Parisienne, "mature meagre erect and eminently gay, highly adorned, perfectly familiar, freely contradictious," whom some readers will take for American, others for French, and which no word of text will ever determine. Instead we have undecidably suggestive information that she once saw a man resembling Waymarsh (also resembling Daniel Webster, who was never the representative of his government in

Paris) "who used when I was a little girl in the Rue Montaigne to come to see my father and who was usually the American Minister to the Tuileries [thus in the Second Empire] or some other court." To the undoubted Americans Strether and little Bilham she speaks as if she were none of them—"You're so wonderful, you people . . . for not feeling those things"—but the locution of second-person otherness proves nothing about her own nationality, it is such a common form of American or English speech behavior vis-à-vis the continent. Miss Barrace, who also lacks a first name, is an apparition of international interlinguistic confusion, as is Strether's easy assumption that he and Chad may speak English on the streets of Paris without being understood. " 'Do you think one's kept only by women?' His [Chad's] surprise and his verbal emphasis rang out so clear in the still street that Strether winced till he remembered the safety of their English speech." In *Paris*—of all places?

As with Madame de Cintré and the Bellegardes in *The American* (and the Proberts in *The Reverberator*) who had to speak English in order to provide easy linguistic access to interloping aspirant Christopher Newman (and his bland successor Francie Dosson), so in *The Ambassadors* Marie de Vionnet and her charming jeune fille daughter Jeanne are for the convenience of Lewis Lambert Strether supplied with bilingual accomplishments and an explanatory binational background.* Of Madame de Vionnet's verbal habits we hear first from Chad, uncertain whether to tell Strether that his friends are French or English (in every respect but ability to converse with Strether they are pure French), "their English was the most charming in the world, so that if Strether were wanting an excuse for not getting on with them he wouldn't in the least find one." Then Maria Gostrey having been to school with Marie (another old James device found also in *The American, The Wings of the Dove, The Golden Bowl*, schoolgirls supplying from their common past expository information otherwise difficult to get at) tells of her "chattering French, English,

---

*James' binational bilingual arrangements for such personages as Claire de Cintré and Madame de Vionnet seem to me primarily expediential and even ponderous; to other readers they are expressively characteristic. Thus Madame de Vionnet's linguistic gifts lead Eileen T. Bender, in " 'The Question of His Own French': Dialect and Dialectic in *The Ambassadors*," *The Henry James Review* (1984), 5:128–34, to speak of "the precarious nature" of her "pose," the "ambiguity" of her "stance," the "sacrifice of individual integrity that may be the price of such a polyglot sensibility" (p. 131). This is all very fashionable, of course, but the overall implication of the Jamesian œuvre is just the opposite, especially as to French.

German, Italian," the latter two languages not called on in *The Ambassadors* but the same as those utilized or referred to in *The Princess Casamassima* and *The Tragic Muse,* with the result that "It would doubtless be difficult to-day, as between French and English, to name her and place her," which is, of course, precisely where the author is virtually required by his fable to name her and place her, precisely on the linguistic border between his two favorite languages. Again like Claire de Cintré's English, Marie de Vionnet's is a little special, different, "unlike any other he [Strether] had ever heard," the textual (phonetic) transcription of which we are blessedly spared (no *"expray,"* no *"prenny"*).

At Gloriani's polyglot garden party, possibilities of cosmopolitan converse (and mystification) abound. James typically represents but few, one, for example, a typical party incident: "Madame de Vionnet greeted her as 'Duchesse' and was greeted in turn, while talk started in French, as 'Ma toute-belle'; little facts that had their due, their vivid interest for Strether," and surely not less for the Tourist Reader as reader *of* Strether (who furiously "reads"). Strether observing all, and making his perpetual inferences, often erroneous, an unidentified "gentleman" now breaks in to talk with Madame de Vionnet and "His French had quickly turned to equal English, and it occurred to Strether," as he fades in and out of one language or the other or out of language entirely, "that he might well be one of the ambassadors," that is to say one like himself. Such it is to live abroad for a period of some months, slightly adrift; such it is to read about such a one. At the same party, Jeanne de Vionnet speaks sweetly to Strether, language not specified except for "the faint sweet foreignness of her 'Au revoir, monsieur!' " Later she tells him, with emphasis, how English she is—"almost American too."

Much the most brilliant, original, daring use of French in *The Ambassadors,* way beyond any foreign-language effects James had achieved in his earlier French fictions, is found in the great revelation scene, placed as an excursion into French ruralism (which is also a painting, also a play)—it is the great comic scene in all James for the learning and speaking of French. The comicality is intrinsic to the Tourist Novel, for if folks had just stayed at home and had to do with people who spoke their own language, as the locution of location would have it, none of these problems would ever have arisen, but neither would we have the excitement and pleasure of their solution, however partial and temporary; we must remind ourselves, perhaps for one last time, that the international theme is internationally political, having to do with communication among peoples; for its very instauration, it is necessary that persons cross over from their own language to that of others; it is taken for granted that such crossings may well be uneasy, nervous, and, in one or another degree, failed.

The first use of French in Strether's rural retreat—there is naturally no place name given—is entirely in his imagination. The textual tone is romantic and precise, graced with visions of an evening meal "fried and felicitous," i.e., alliterated, "washed down with *authentic* wine" (emphasis added), white tablecloth, sanded floor, and afterward a native driver, straight out of Maupassant and significantly garbed, with, naturally, "the genius of response." James' 1888 essay on Maupassant had objected to his overemphasis on sexuality, which is what this scene is also about. Still altogether imagining, "Strether heard his [own] lips, for the first time in French air . . . emit sounds of expressive intention without fear of his company. He had been afraid of Chad," whose acquired French has become so good, and likewise of Maria Gostrey "and of Madame de Vionnet," who came by her French more effortlessly. Oddly enough, as may first appear, he had been most afraid of Waymarsh, "in whose presence, so far as they had mixed together in the light of the town, he had never without somehow paying for it aired either his vocabulary or his accent." Strether's fear of Waymarsh is just this side of incredible, Waymarsh's Connecticut mangling of French being just this side of unimaginable. The explanation of Strether's anxiety about Waymarsh's opinion of his own certainly better French must surely reside in Waymarsh's status as homefolks. Waymarsh is the displaced judgment of *there,* now in its mindless out-of-country intransigence terrorizing Strether *here,* that is in and out of Paris, for Waymarsh, who dominates Strether's retrospective linguistic fears, is not, of course, physically present in the scene of French ruralism. Strether's difficulties with French, not previously mentioned, are dropped in at the last minute of the novel and we are evidently invited to think our way back into deeper depths of certain earlier anxieties, the retrospection somewhat resembling the retrogressive structure of *The Tragic Muse.*

In the course of the scene, Strether makes two quantum leaps in his language acquisition, one up and one back. During the wanderings of the day he has "conversed with rustics who struck him perhaps a little more as men of the world than he had expected," less as simulacra of Maupassant Norman peasants; thanks to his new humanistic outlook, he has "acquired at a bound a fearless facility in French" (more f- alliteration). It is a curious point, and worth pondering, that Strether is fear*less* now conversing with French persons who almost certainly know no English but fear*ful* when conversing with Americans presuming on the sophistication of their cosmopolitan attainments, which may well be near-perfect with Maria Gostrey, something decidedly less than that with Chadwick, and virtually nonexistent with Waymarsh. It is obviously a matter of tone and attitude, of social relation, a question of who uses French on whom and for what purpose. The real French "rustics" (natives) clearly have no reason for linguistic-social maltreatment of Strether, and so he perceives no maltreatment, and, for a miracle, there *is* none.

Strether's second and last quantum leap in French, perhaps more accurately his adjusted measurement of how far he has leaped the first time and how short he fell, derives from Madame de Vionnet, who suddenly and instinctively reverts to idiomatic French, leaving Strether far in the rear again, "the wonderful woman's overflow of surprise and amusement was wholly into French, which she struck him as speaking with an unprecedented command of idiomatic turns, but in which she got, as he might have said, somewhat away from him, taking all at once little brilliant jumps that he could but lamely match," and yet he appears to be still talking—*French!* It is now that we first learn how "The question of his own French had never come up for them," with her he had, during all those many pages, been hearing, and we, vicariously, hearing, "the charming slightly strange English he best knew her by." At that time, by romantic exaggeration, she was a creature "with a language quite to herself, the real monopoly of a special shade of speech," but now, realistically, she is what we all are, a limited communal user of language, according to Strether losing her identity even, her spoken French "shifting her back into a mere voluble class or race to the intense audibility of which he was by this time inured," as well as to its (for the most part) intense incomprehensibility. By being more fully what she has been all along, she suddenly becomes "foreign." She is, for another miracle, by no means what he had been acting as if she were the whole time even while he knew better, she is not, that is to say, another slightly eccentric American compatriot somehow resident in Paris, she is not, God help us in our belated revelations, in the least an American, she is, when you come right down to it, *French!* Thus finally and with some abruptness American aspirations and even the best will in the world are brought up sharply against their limit, as who should say: thou shalt not, be thy motives never so noble, be other than what thou art, nor shalt thou conceive persons not-thyself as other than what *they* are, i.e., as other. It is the moral lesson of differentiation and acceptance which structures the Jamesian œuvre.

In his earlier novels and tales, perhaps most conspicuously in *The American,* a French word or phrase was often followed by the interpolated phrase "as they say here," e.g., in Paris. In *The Ambassadors* even the provincial locutions of New England receive similar treatment, the speech of home, now that Strether is away, coming to seem "foreign." Strether shares this habit of mind with narrative authority; of five references to the locutions of Woollett, three are Strether's and two are in the voice of the omnipresent and virtually omniscient (despite what critics say) "third person." These references might seem to reverse the general flow of narrative from New England to France but in fact they are part of the flow in its backward eddying, again not entirely unlike the retrogressive structure of *The Tragic Muse* but more subtle, perhaps related to the nearly inaudible wail of nostalgia which you can hear if you listen for it in almost every sentence of *The Ambassadors.* Such phrases as these are what I have in mind: "I feel it [being from Woollett] so that I certainly must look it, speak it, and, as people say there, act it" (Strether to Gostrey); Strether remembers a "private pledge of his own to treat the occasion [his first visit to Paris] as a relation formed with the higher culture and see that, as they said at Woollett, it should bear a good harvest"; narrative voice reports a Strether meditation at Gloriani's, "Did he [Chad] wish to spring them [his exotic ladies], in the Woollett phrase, with a fuller force [?]"; Strether's inability to agree with Mrs. Newsome "didn't at all, as they say, suit her book" (Strether to Gostrey); Strether musing, after the river revelation, assumes that Madame de Vionnet "had so sized-up, in the Woollett phrase, their necessity," hers and Chad's, of a certain judicious concealment. It is

entertaining, and instructive, how Strether puts to himself this delicate matter in the not very delicate language of his old home, the
language of manufacture, metaphorically abundant with commercial
quantification, the weights and measures.

There is vastly more French in *The Ambassadors* than I am able to
glance at, though much less than in the other great French novels,
one more respect in which James has grown subtler with the years.
Almost all of *The Ambassadors'* French, as might be anticipated,
involves Strether—he speaks about half of it or it is spoken to him
—while the other half is in third person and is about him. It is a basic
vocabulary not to task the attainments of the beginner in French
(much simpler, to revert to that novel once more, than the French of
*The Tragic Muse*). And so we have, for those with a grain of patience
left for yet one more word list, with explanation as necessary (but
none for the presence or absence of italics, the use of which seems to
be quite unusually chaotic): Comment donc, *bon, milieu,* voilà, *Bon!,*
*parti,* atelier, consommation, cafés, porte-cochère; Merci, François;
salle-à-manger, patronne, concierge, troisième (oft repeated), déjeu-
ner, *succès fou* (Waymarsh!), salon, entresol, bibelot, Quoi donc;
what they call here a *fait accompli; tout bêtement,* as she [Maria Gostrey]
often said; coupé, *ces dames, hôtels, cher confrère, gros bonnets, femmes du
monde* (often), *Il faut en avoir, en exil* (Waymarsh!), *vous allez voir;* Ma
toute-belle (as quoted, one of the few French remarks in *The Ambassadors* neither by, to, or about Strether, but of course he hears it);
*Impayable,* as you say; Au revoir, monsieur; *Ces gens-là* (a thematically loaded Frenchism, the ever present *là*), *en province, voyons, Allez
donc voir, boiseries, sabots, petit salon, jeune fille, notre jeune homme, Je
suis tranquille, bien aimable, nous autres, omelette aux tomates* (famous,
with bottle of straw-colored Chablis), *salon de lecture; Marchons, marchons* (irrepressibly Chadwick); *parti pris, en dessous, raffiné, comme
tout, vieille sagesse,* coquette, *cul-de-sac, nuance,* what you call here
*difficile* (Strether to Bilham), carafe, *lingère, banlieue, carriole, auberge,
côtelete de veau à oseille, agrément* (these last five examples pertaining
to French ruralism), *invraisemblance, là-bas* (again *là*), *Comme cela se
trouve, petit bleu, Postes et Télégraphes, corps de logis, batteau-mouche, à
quoi se fier, chambre d'ami,* sou, and *c'est un monde.* Twice James
ventures into Latin, not far: *Omnes vulnerat, ultima necat; panem et
circenses.* Unless *bock* is also German—it is surely French—there is

no German. There is no Italian. The foreign language of *The Ambassadors* is a well-nigh perfected, short, and easy French word list suitable to the tastes and capacities of the perfected Tourist Reader, insouciant of titillated desire and the simpler satisfactions.


## 5. Weather

Yet one more (the fifth?) analogue of the surface-depth dyad, the absence-presence dimension, that centralizing reversible internalized image of *The Ambassadors,* is found in the curious exchanges of outdoors and indoors, together with emphasis on passage (normally of air) between them. These exchanges additionally make for subversion of Tourist Fiction stereotypes, one of them being the outsider's pathetic exclusion from home and hearth in the country visited. Perhaps as a sop to such pathos Providence kindly arranged that Paris should be of all cities the one most notoriously (in good weather) *en plein air*—except for hotel rooms, *en plein air* is where the tourist is most likely to be, as the Tourist Reader will remember. Lacking invitations to people's houses, the Tourist Reader can always go to a sidewalk café with the other Parisians, no more and no less at home than his or her veritable alienated self. Lambert Strether, to be sure, is blest among James' Americans in Paris by the number of houses or apartments he penetrates and the decency with which he is received. That was the topic of a previous chapter. Now our concern is with air inside and out, weather in the most inclusive sense, weather, of all things, literary.

Outdoors-as-in, indoors-as-out: in which of these two conditions (or are they so exchangeable as to be the same?) shall we imagine Strether and little Bilham when "at the Louvre"? The Louvre is a building which divides outside space from inside space. To be *at* the Louvre normally means to be *in* the Louvre. (It is not an open-air swap-meet.) But Strether seems unable or unwilling to make such discriminations. The facts of little Bilham's life in Paris, as Strether thinks of them at the Louvre, in whatever gallery, "figured for him as an unseparated part of the charged iridescent [same adjective as for Paris-jewel] air, the glamour of the name, the splendour of the space." Bilham is part of the "air" of Paris, *double entendre,* and so he and the air both may be conceived as being inside as well as out, both sides of the walls. Splendor and the space being so ambivalent, the Louvre might as well be a street scene. Or put it that the weather of Paris invades and makes itself at home indoors. Space is thereby reversed from its usual associations of emptiness to opposite associations of plenitude at the same time as outdoors is discovered to be in a place opposite to where we assume it naturally to belong. Again at Gloriani's party the text of *The Ambassadors* subtly causes outdoors and indoors to exchange. The guests are, for the most part, outdoors, in the garden. Some pass in and out of the house, not including Strether. In the garden, indoors-outdoors equations are once more complicated and even reversed by the existence of a small pavilion offering yet another set of possibilities for ingress and egress, for being "in" or being "out." The garden itself is the ultimate reversal. Despite the usual complement of trees and birds, its air (always that ubiquitously circulating and equalizing common noun) "was in such conditions all a chamber of state"; its sense of spatial clôture further reminds Strether of a convent. The governmental or spiritual functions of state chambers or convents are normally conducted inside of edifices. Gardens, on the other hand, are notoriously outdoors (indoors they change their name to "conservatories" or "planters").

Passage or stasis, as well as reversal, of outdoors and indoors, is in *The Ambassadors* generally rendered in terms of windows, that rather obvious two-way reversible device permitting relational motion between the two conditions of outside and inside, or alternatively permitting us to observe the lack of such relational motion. (A window is also an "absence," a square or rectangular area of a wall which may be most simply defined as "not-wall.") What moves through windows is for the most part air but it may also be warmth (persons less often), air and warmth also going in either direction, the direction in turn expressing the relative temperatures within and without. In Book Sixth, Strether makes a first visit to Madame de Vionnet, and if we are attentive we shall be rewarded with certain information derived from the fact that she sits near the fire, which has burned down to ashes, while one window stands open "to the mildness" (temperature about the same both sides of the wall) and "stillness" (air not moving much).

In Book Seventh Strether and Madame de Vionnet are at lunch, quayside, Left Bank, restaurant not named but well-known, especially to Strether, a habitué there as at Notre Dame, and again we are asked to attend to the relation of temperatures, the movements of the air, and much else (the advance of the season, the advance of social intercourse), back and forth and inside and outside, "in the mere way the bright clean ordered water-side life came in at the open window," that is to say it is the fact and function of windows which are at the moment open to which we are first of all invited. "Situation," with its two meanings, one of which is "place," consequently is and is not identical with setting, just as Madame de Vionnet's "grey eyes moved in and out of their talk," as if talk were also a place into and out of which you could move, but her eyes do even more than that, they move "back to the quarter of the warm spring air," quarter now in its turn being interchangeably a place or a condition or an epoch, a part of the "air" (air, always) "in which early summer had already begun to throb." Summer for *The Ambassadors* is less a word on the calendar than it is the touch of the air (warm), the status of the window (open). The air and the window are also the validating adjuncts of one more inside-outside exchange amounting to a virtual collapse of distinctions. Which is in, which is out, as we listen to "the tone of their words and the clink of their glasses . . . the hum of the town and the plash of the river"? If the hum and the plash can come in through an open window, the tone of voice and the clink of glass can just as well go out (the window is still open), not to mention Madame de Vionnet's glance, her eyes moving in and out of conversation, in and out of weather, in and out of narrative and setting, in and out of everything but text.

And now text shows us how space is also time. Her eyes' spatial motion, our delicately perceptual awareness of that motion, informs us that it is early summer; informs us also, should we have failed to notice, that the timepiece of *The Ambassadors* is the weather of Paris, conceived as reasonably predictable and regular in its progressions, well known to the Tourist Readership and indeed to the whole civilized world, and glamorized by association with the city of Paris as the center of the civilized world, by no means of France alone; Paris weather is consequently felt to be typical weather, classical weather, normal weather, golden-meter weather, weather as it ought to be, and whether it is or is not (it sometimes rains, even in *The Ambassadors*). Writing from Paris to Mrs. Edmund Gosse in London, where Gosse was sick, James in a 21 March 1893 letter from Paris half-seriously half-jocosely plays on these notions of the Paris ambience, meteorological division: "Paris will create within him afresh all the finest pulses of life. It is mild, sunny, splendid—blond and fair, all in order for his approach. I allude of course to the specious allurements of its exterior. The state is odorously rotten—but everything else is charming. And then it's such a blessing, after long grief and pain, to find the arms of a *climate* around us once again! Hasten, my dear Edmund, to be healed." [12] England lacks a climate because England is where you live. Other places have climates. Paris has the best climate of all.

Weather as timepiece for *The Ambassadors* helped James resolve what he frequently referred to as the hardest thing for the novelist, e.g., in a letter of 23 December 1903 to Millicent, Duchess of Sutherland, "to give the impression and illusion of the real *lapse of time, the quantity* of time, represented by our poor few phrases and pages." [13] Turning the pages of *The Ambassadors* we discover Strether arriving in Paris on a beautiful spring day and taking his Great Walk on the day following, equally beautiful, a "prompt Paris morning," the word *prompt* immediately obscure and manifold. Just as promptly we are brought *au courant* of how and why Paris weather is so indescribably wonderful, not least through being so entirely at one with all other aspects of setting and narrative, now so magically blent: "the air had a taste as of something mixed with art, something that presented nature as a white-capped master-chef." (Properly to estimate James' malpractice of English grammar, so brilliant and virtuoso, so wanton and provoking, would require another book; let it pass.) On the previous page, making much of little, master-chef of text told us how Strether slipped Woollett letters into the pocket of his "loose grey overcoat," which is how warm-cold it is, what color of cloth he prefers or is obliged to wear, and perhaps how less rotund he has become during his courtship of Mrs. Newsome, or just after. Even when master-chef grudgingly vouchsafes the name of a month the name is well-nigh smothered in sensuous apprehension; thus Chad's third-story window takes the March sun while simultaneously (as a consequence or all by itself?) the ambient air turns violet, a visual effect we remember to have seen in paintings of Paris if not in the actual streets. Later we are told it is the month of June and at least twice we are reminded that three months have passed (in fact, more); overall we are secure in the knowledge that much time has passed; Maria Gostrey refers to Chester and London (the opening pages) "as of far-off things and as if they had spent weeks at the places she named," yet in real life it was only a few pages back and not long since. These are some of the myriad meanings compounded, confused, and concealed in facile phrases like organic unity.

Still comparatively early in the spring (in the narrative, in the setting conceived as temporal), Strether and Chad leave their café (Avenue de l'Opéra), pass out "into the mild bright night" to be met by, well, what would you suppose? only "people, expressive sound, projected light," for in Paris the sound of the people never ceases, never even much diminishes (the Tourist Novel tells us so) and what the people do (talk, mostly) is always done abroad in the full light of simply the best (brightest, most famously) illuminated city center humanity has ever been pleasured by. (Still it is fickle spring and in a few pages "it had sadly begun to rain.") A few pages more (opening sentence of Book Fifth) and "The Sunday of the next week was a wonderful day" (Gloriani's garden party)—"spring at last frank and fair." Soon we are having *omelette aux tomates* and Chablis at the quayside restaurant and then in the next chapter it seems to be three days later, at or near the solstice (22 June) but instead of the actual date we are once again swamped and seduced by sensuous suggestion, "daylight was long now," which is explicit enough, "and Paris more than ever penetrating," which is not, "The scent of flowers was in the streets, he had the whiff of violets perpetually in his nose," a considerable exaggeration, surely, and then the passage collapses into a totalized phantasmagoria of sense and association particularly attributed to just this place, which in turn contains just this narrative, now hinted at as "vibrations of the air, human and dramatic, he imagined, *as they were not in other places*" (emphasis added) and surreptitiously doubling as fictive chronology "as the mild afternoons deepened" (stayed light later), "a far-off hum, a sharp near click on the asphalt, a voice calling, replying, somewhere . . ." It is effectively the end of spring, which occupies slightly more than half of *The Ambassadors*.

By cunning transition we move into summer (as it was in *The Ambassadors*) and a distinctly different meteorological milieu quite exactly reflecting the disintegrative narrative—disintegrative in two senses, there is less and less of it and what remains is worse and worse, until finally the two senses vanish together and there is nothing at all. In Book Eighth it is still "early summer . . . a vast warm fragrant medium," phrases which leave much (nearly everything) to the imagination. Then at the Pococks' hotel we have a belated quasi-facsimile-repetition of the earlier outdoors-indoors exchanges, "the shutters were bowed upon the summer morning . . . [but] the far-spreading presence of Paris came up in coolness, dimness and invitation," cool from the Tuileries gardens, dim because coming up from several floors below, invitational just because of Paris.

Suddenly it is summer, literary summer, defined as the act of vacating or of being vacated, emptying or being emptied. Except for Strether and Maria Gostrey, even the Americans withdraw, while Chad and Madame de Vionnet are increasingly out of town. Paris emptied—so unnatural!—appears in the compacted image of a vacated hotel room, "the room looked empty as only a room can look in Paris, of a fine afternoon, when the faint murmur of the huge collective life, carried on out of doors, strays among scattered objects even as a summer air idles in a lonely garden." The room looks more empty there because Paris is elsewise so full; people (Strether) are more lonely there than any place else because of their contrasted situation vis-à-vis "the huge collective life." We notice in passing where it is carried on and how; we notice once more "air" and "garden." But the weather continues to change as the narrative climaxes and falls away: "The night was hot and heavy and the single lamp sufficient [in Chad's troisième]; the great flare of the lighted city, rising high, spending itself afar, played up from the Boulevard [Malesherbes]," comparatively deserted save by spots of sight and sound, by "the wide late life of Paris." You can almost taste the loneliness, plus its minimalistic compensations: "after their day of great and premature heat, the midnight air was delicious." By Book Eleventh, deliciousness, like the pleasure of Paris, is gone in heat; Paris is spent. "It's getting late, as you see," Maria Gostrey tells Strether, late in the year, late in the social season, late in life, late in *The Ambassadors*, late in the literary career of Henry James (all this at a conspicuously early point in the twentieth century), "and Paris turning rather hot and dusty. People are scattering." A few pages later still, Strether answers as Strether must and as no one else could "I think I shall like it." Paris is his own draining diminishing time, naturally with its occupations, Maria Gostrey specifying them in terms of the locale possessed, "the empty town, with plenty of seats in the shade, cool drinks, deserted museums, drives to the Bois in the evening," and, *spécialité* of this particular novel, "our wonderful woman all to yourself," except she isn't invariably or reliably there. So Strether lingers under "awnings as wide as avenues," an odd hyperbole even if awnings were over avenues as obviously they aren't.

Strether's final visit to Madame de Vionnet is lurid with narrative, with setting, with weather, with France Napoleonic, with France imperial, France powerful, France violent, France revolutionary, France creative and destructive, France ultimately the grandest thing that ever was. Consider, after all, the climatological tone and what is made of it: "The day had turned to heat and eventual thunder," which never seems to arrive, while Marie de Vionnet comes dressed in white ("Madame Roland must on the scaffold have worn something like it"), there are no lamps but only candles, and, mainly, the windows are open again to "the vague voice of Paris. . . . Thus and so [Strether imagining], on the eve of the great recorded dates, the days and nights of revolution, the sounds had come in, the omens, the beginnings broken out. They were the smell of revolution, the smell of the public temper—or perhaps simply the smell of blood." Is it all in his imagination? Is it partly in the represented literary weather? Is it to be blamed upon, or credited to the account of, "organic unity"? Strether and the Tourist Reader take one last lingering look at Madame de Vionnet's "things" (apartment, rooms, flat, house, with its objects, contents): "he might never see them again . . . and he should certainly see nothing in the least degree like them. He should soon be going to where such things were not," the land of negation, of the missing links, material, associative, literary, aesthetic, and historical (everybody is at the office).

As if they were Adam and Eve at the opposite end of time, the only two persons left alive in the city of Paris, Strether proposes to Maria Gostrey local amusements out of his new-won expertise: he will take her to shops, to the Bois, on a *bateau-mouche,* to dine outdoors "on one of the terraces, in one of the gardens, of which the Paris of summer was profuse," if not of inhabitants. One of our last visions of Paris, and one of our best, is the remnants of Chad's late supper—for these are indeed "long hot days"—romantically "a supper of light cold clever French things," we are not told exactly what and are left to wonder how things to eat can in France manage to be "clever"—it must be owing to the genius of the French language— all which "one could see the remains of there in the circle of the lamp, pretty and ultra-Parisian." How wonderful, now that everything else has been taken away forever, that it should be *French food* and a *French lamp* that are left and that it may not be possible to determine whether it is the food or the lamp which is ultra-Parisian, beyond Paris itself, should such a thing be imaginable, but on second thought we think it is probably the light of the lamp—this comes to us a few pages later on as we notice that the food, just before or just after our closing the back cover of the book, has already begun to turn into something else, as regularly happens to organic matter disintegrating. Soon it will be no more, that represented food, and that represented Strether, and that Henry James who represents them. *The Ambassadors* is not a hymn to death, exactly, but it is a long careful thoughtful deeply felt rendition of what a poet calls "the always coming on / The always rising of the night" (Archibald MacLeish, "You, Andrew Marvell"). "But not the praise," as Phoebus is quoted as saying to another poet (Milton, "Lycidas"). The text survives as the representation of dying.

# VIII.

# A Henry James Retrospective:
# Six Canvases

There used to be, and perhaps still is, a pleasant American commercial custom known as Add-A-Pearl, whereby you gave, especially if you were of the non-fair sex, to mother or sister or daughter or wife or girlfriend (if you expected to continue) or even mother-in-law, an originating set of basic beauties on a string, further items to be added as funds permitted and occasions prompted, until the poor thing, weighted down to the ground, could scarcely walk. A book about Henry James is like that, but it ought not to be too much like that. And still, with a corpus so vast and so variously entertaining, omission comes hard. A while back, I listed James' French tales regretfully passed over in favor of major monuments and hinted that we might return to some of them. Now in a concluding chapter I propose modest attention to six of the hitherto neglected *morceaux*.

Five of them providentially present themselves as having seen original publication at four to five year intervals from the very beginning in 1864 down nicely to 1883, thus making a convenient survey-review. The sixth is very very late, however (1909), and must instead do double duty as a coda to *The Ambassadors* and indeed to James' entire career in the fictive representation of France and French. Each of the six tales, *as* a tale, is of course by virtue of genre discrete and self-contained, complete in its own right, owing little more either to the other tales or to the major monuments than may be derived from the fact that the same person wrote them all. I shall accordingly take these six tales as much as possible one at a time, on their own terms, and with a minimum of cross-reference.

*A Tragedy of Error* (1864). This is James' first tale—indeed his first publication—known to be extant. It was published anonymously in an abolition magazine in 1864, the year Lincoln was reelected and Sherman marched to the sea. James was living with his family in Boston and had not been to Europe since 1860. The tale contains no Americans, if we exclude the author and the undoubted influence of Edgar Allan Poe. It is lurid and slick and improbable: a beleaguered adulterous French wife hires a French boatman to murder her returning husband but by a "tragedy of error" he murders her lover instead. " 'Baffled! baffled!' hissed Madame,"[1] as *thirteen years later* the Marquis de Bellegarde will hiss at Christopher Newman in Parc Monceau. Like *The American,* "A Tragedy of Error" exhibits in extreme form a disjunction of narrative and setting. The narrative is melodramatic to the point of impossibility, the setting is realistic. The narrative, we say, might take place any place; or we say it more likely might not take place at all. The Tourist Reader is bid to the contemplation of sensational events in "a French seaport town" identified only as H——, presumably Havre; C——, presumably Caen, is nearby. This French seaport town comes with a harbor, quays, an ancient quarter, a "crowded region" of fishermen and boatmen, a bridge which opens and closes, a cemetery and a lighthouse—a meagre list of items, perhaps, but rich indeed in comparison with the protagonists and their questionable doings.

In our retrospective, what is more striking is James' early use of the French language for local color and vraisemblance. But as all the personages are French there is no question of linguistic difficulty. There are references to Spanish people as well, but no Spanish is quoted (*Watch and Ward* will show a few scraps of Spanish). The reference is internationally thematic rather than linguistic, Spanish people being held to be more forthright in their homicides:

> "In South America and those countries, when a man makes life insupportable to you, what do you do?"
> "*Mon Dieu!* I suppose you kill him."
> "And in France?"
> "I suppose you kill yourself. Ha! ha! ha!"
> By this time they had reached the end of the great breakwater, terminating in a lighthouse, the limit, on one side, of the inner harbor. The sun had set.

That passage wonderfully reveals in little the basic split of the tale's text, as after the "Ha! ha! ha!" we are quickly returned to the specificities of time and place. The tones are completely different and appear to have nothing to do with each other.

Within that dichotomy of narrative and setting young James lavishly sprinkles his bits and pieces of French. Most of them come from the mouths of the personages but in literary effect they belong, for realism, to setting rather than to narrative; they are an evident attempt to anchor the unbelievable action in a believable locale. As will tend to be James' practice lifelong, doubtless convergent with editors' and publishers' house-style habits, he gives French words in italics, but some words which might be either French or English are out of italics and should probably be taken for English. The French vocabulary of "A Tragedy of Error" is a simple vocabulary of brief phrases, most of them quite common and easy, a bit more colloquial than the comparable French vocabularies of James' later French fictions. There are a couple of Latin and Italian words which somehow wandered in. Thus we have, some of them more than once: *congé, bon jour, n'est-ce pas?, terra firma, détour,* boudoir, *migraine, tisane, Allons, Allez, empressé, C'est comme ça, La bonne idée!,* sous (out of italics), *là-bas, moi, sabots, Pardio, Pardon, Mon Dieu!, ma foi!, Ventrebleu!, Parbleu!, commissionaires, sergent de ville, fournisseur, que si!, ces messieurs* (but monsieur and madame are out of italics, given as

English), *Eh bien!*, *Allons donc*, *Sapristi!*, *Nom de Dieu!*, *Mais oui*, *Tenez*, *Il faut fixer la somme* (the longest French quotation by far, and the most thematic), *Songez donc*, *Pas si bête!*, *Voyons, hein?*, *Tiens!*, *chez monsieur*, and *savoir faire*. If the last phrase can be imagined as going down the American throat in that grim year 1864, I suppose we may think the tale as a whole made good reading in relief from the miseries of the war. How much nicer to be someplace else, for example in a French seaport town, probably on the way to Paris, clucking over the well-known immorality of the French while at the same time vicariously enjoying the heavenly delight of *good talk* (in, of course, French).

*Gabrielle de Bergerac* (1869). Mere *opinion* should never prevent our return to items unfashionable in the James canon, not even James' opinion, who notoriously wrote in a 28 June 1869 letter to his mother that the tale struck him "as the product of a former state of being,"[2] his, I take him to mean, not that of France, and then in a 31 August 1869 letter to his sister Alice that it struck him (he is fond of the phrase) as "amusingly thin and watery."[3] No such thing! "Gabrielle de Bergerac" is wonderfully illuminating on a number of critical Jamesian points, among them these, in no special order: (1) European nobility and the American response to it (Italian nobility is at issue in *Roderick Hudson*, *The Princess Casamassima*, and *The Golden Bowl*, English nobility in *The Portrait of a Lady*, *The Awkward Age*, and *The Wings of the Dove*, German nobility in *The Europeans*, French nobility in *The American* and *The Ambassadors*—and many other texts besides); (2) the *ancien régime* as a necessary precondition of that French Revolution which looms so large in James' fictions—"Gabrielle de Bergerac" is his only fictional representation of it; (3) his fierce objections to rigid, impassable, legalized, or inherited class discriminations, such social systems or attitudes as I have been in the habit of calling "totalitarian"; and (4) the connection between the American and the French Revolutions—as an American writer "attaching" French Literature, this connection could hardly be for him a matter of indifference. All four of these points figure largely in "Gabrielle de Bergerac," and recognition of them is instrumental to the better comprehension of James in general, not to mention that "Gabrielle de Bergerac" may be sufficiently entertaining even to such readers as take no interest in matters of instructional value.

"Gabrielle de Bergerac" is a love story about modern France coming into existence, a love story of a noblewoman and a commoner, a love story with a happy ending (marriage) and an unhappy ending (the scaffold), told by an old man (the youthful Chevalier of the tale) to a young auditor (*not* Henry James), with overtones of lapsed time and bygone violence: "The old man fixed his eyes on the fire, and laid his hand on mine, as if his memory were fain to draw from both sources," fire and young blood. Gabrielle's portrait, by her lover Pierre Coquelin, shows a nature combining "revery, affection, and repose" with a capacity for action "and even of heroism. Mlle de Bergerac died under the axe of the Terrorists." Plebeian Coquelin, a tutor, a writer, and an artist, is also a revolutionary democrat who has served three years under the Marquis de Rochambeau in "the aid of the American insurgents." At the dinner table de Bergerac he answers questions about "the history of the American War," Gabrielle's mother expressing surprise "to find in a beggarly pedagogue a perfect *beau diseur.*" Coquelin has made "a series of illustrations and reminiscences of his adventures with the American army, and of the figures and episodes he had observed in the Colonies. . . . There were sketches of the enemy too, whom Coquelin apparently had not been afraid to look in the face." The love affair between Coquelin and Gabrielle represents a crossing of class lines; it would seem to follow that the American Revolution, already in progress, and the French Revolution, now preparing, make a single sequence of two acts against two enemies—privilege and the British —who are and are not one.* Signs of sympathy with the old order in "Gabrielle de Bergerac" are few; they sound obligatory. The words *"Noblesse oblige"* are quoted. There is talk, unconvincing, about the honor of one's name (title). The morals of the story are that love conquers all, and that nothing much matters except personal merit, especially literary-artistic merit. Finally in Paris and to stay, Coquelin "painted portraits and did literary work," the most

*Many years later James in Washington, D.C., enthused about the newly erected memorials to Lafayette and Rochambeau, for reasons—if one may say so—rather more French than American: "Artful, genial, expressive, the tribute of French talent, these happy images supply, on the spot, the note without which even the most fantasticating sense of our national past would feel itself rub forever against mere brown homespun. Everything else gives way, for me, I confess, as I again stand before them; everything, whether as historic fact, or present *agrément,* or future possibility, yields to this one high luxury of our old friendship with France," including, as one easily makes out, the luxury of a French word. *The American Scene* (1907), ed. Leon Edel (Bloomington: Indiana University Press, 1968), p. 356.

important kinds. A touching scene shows Gabrielle commiserating with the peasants (as in something by Mark Twain). In another scene Coquelin scales (thus conquering) a ruined castle. He and Gabrielle considerably discuss the past, for which she attempts a kindly word, but then she comes round to his viewpoint, which is contemptuous, and sails her fan across the parapet. " 'There goes the name of Bergerac!' she said." Narrative authority anachronistically and sardonically remarks that "the taste for ruins was at that time by no means so general as since the Revolution (when one may say it was in a measure created)."

"Gabrielle de Bergerac" is written in English for an Anglo-American audience—need I remind us? (I sometimes think so.) But no more than "A Tragedy of Error" is it the full-blown international interlinguistic theme with characters from two distinct nationalities speaking two different languages. Here all the personages are French. They live permanently in France. With the exception of Coquelin, they have never been out of France—where should they go? They speak French without difficulty. They have always done so. They know no one who does not. They never notice these facts, not any of them. Nonetheless, Tourist Readers *will* have their *frissons* Francophiliac and cosmopolitan and so by the introduction they are led to believe that the narrative was first uttered viva voce in French and is subsequently changed over into written (printed) English, to which deceitful end French words and phrases are liberally provided as the tale goes along, including a fair amount of meaningless profanity and expostulation and a few words designed to send Tourist Readers back to the dictionary, *veneur* huntsman, *jabot* frills to a blouse, *agaceries* flirting, but most of the time it is nice easy going with good old friends like *bonhomie, blasé, châteleine,* and mademoiselle, which is given both as French and as English, so that, if you are in an Isabel Archer mood, you can choose.

*Madame de Mauves* (1874). For the literary historian as well as the common reader in a developmental mood, "Madame de Mauves" has the bifold merit of being not only eminently readable but of pointing the way to grander accomplishments in the future, most obviously *The American*—and even *The Ambassadors,* distant by nearly thirty years. Even more than *The Reverberator,* it makes brilliant use of what you might call the banlieue-centre axis, Saint-Germain-en-Laye and Paris, commuter-type dialectics. For its early date in the progress of James' international productions, "Madame de Mauves" is blessedly realistic and, as a consequence, blessedly non-melodramatic. It features a pair of unusual yet perfectly credible experiences of Americanism expatriate or touristic and penetrant into France, an international marriage and a response to that marriage. James' comparisons of French and American civilization, generally and in some detail, his keen sense of their similarities (at times, their identities) and not merely their differences, are sensitive, informed, exact, expressive, judicious. There is no flag-waving patriotism; no uncritical adulation of French superiority; no American hatred of everything American. And of his French performances prior to *The American,* "Madame de Mauves" is surely the prize example of James spectacularly playing his English-French bilingualism, his making almost too much but not quite of language difference construed as the unavoidable entry port to confrontational conflictual issues conceivably more profound, one of them held in eternal suspension, love-adultery-marriage narrowly averted in the evenly balanced deadlock between "tenderness" and "a feeling for which awe would be hardly too strong a name" (concluding sentence).

The banlieue-centre axis is the enabling act for visions of the eye (city from suburb, not the other way), for conversational reference to the one place from its obverse, for frequent goings back and forth by suburban train. From under and within "the starlit silence of the town and the forest" you can perfectly well make out, 17 km. away, "distant Paris, as it lay twinkling and flashing through its hot exhalations" like the iridescent jewel of *The Ambassadors.* Longmore speaks of Paris—"and he tossed his head toward the distant city." For their different reasons, disreputable and virtuous alike, M. de Mauves and Longmore run into town and out. In the opening paragraph we find Longmore refreshing himself at Saint-Germain-en-Laye but already thinking he might "go to Paris for the evening, to dine at the Café Brébant"—the same to which Chad will take Mamie Pocock? it is hard to be sure, things change—"and to repair afterwards to the Gymnase"—definitely where Strether goes with Waymarsh—"and listen to the latest exposition of the duties of the injured husband." Instead next day he visits his friend Mrs. Draper at Hôtel de l'Empire,

Rue Neuve St. Augustin 57, a hotel according to Bædeker among "the best-situated and most respectable"[4] (unlike James, Bædeker can never forget the respectability of social class, meaning money), where he learns all about Madame de Mauves. There he is, then, in Saint-Germain, whiling away his time; he "lounged on the terrace and walked in the forest, studied suburban street life," quite limited, "and made a languid attempt to investigate the records of the court of the exiled Stuarts." History unavailing, he meets with Madame, in forest, on terrace, at house, the places are few, and in chapter 5 he is in Paris, "lingering irresolutely on the deserted boulevards"—it is summer now—and then he walks the "long villa-bordered avenue," Avenue du Bois de Boulogne in 1874, now Avenue Foch, to the Bois, where in a restaurant ("how much better they ordered this matter in France," dining not love affairs) he observes Monsieur with his *belle brune*. In chapter 7 Longmore abandons city and suburb both in favor of country (and the first version of the great revelation scene in *The Ambassadors*): "Longmore thought he had never seen anything so characteristically French; all the French novels seemed to have described it, all the French landscapists to have painted it," and at least for the moment we are comfortably aglow in the delusion that no other novelists or landscapists exist or can ever exist. There is also the usual inversion of the Jamesian or Tourist Fiction, namely that the representation (novel, painting, "Madame de Mauves") is the original rather than the copy, so that if you were able to visit the allegedly actual, real, originating place you would know it as a mimesis of what you had already read about or seen in a frame. At length (back in Saint-Germain), "He must certainly go [not to any of these places but far off], and yet it was hideously hard. He compromised and went to Paris to spend the rest of the day," boulevards, window-shopping, Jardin des Tuileries, boulevards again, table at a café, where, of course, is M. de Mauves—and back to Saint-Germain. But now the tale of fluctuations is told and Longmore may only say to Madame: "I shall go to America. I have done with Europe for the present." We do not know if Longmore will be back. What we do know is that Tourist Writer and Tourist Reader will be back, not all the hosts of heaven and hell having power to restrain them. How could you possibly help yourself, and why should you want to, faced with the opening moments of such a tale as "Madame

de Mauves" (in all their alluring present-tense travel-writing mode)?
"The view from the terrace at Saint-Germain-en-Laye is immense
and famous. Paris lies spread before you in dusky vastness, domed
and fortified, glittering here and there through her light vapors, and
girdled with her silver Seine." With what lust you might have read
that, sitting in deadly boredom on your piazza in San Diego, New
Mexico, an imaginary spot at which we shall soon arrive, perhaps to
find it more diverting to read about than if we were actually there.

But of course if you *will* go to Saint-Germain-en-Laye to torture
yourself with the near accessibility of wonderland you *may* have
trouble with your inability to speak—to speak really well, to command—more than a single tongue. Like Mrs. Tristram, Claire de
Cintré, Maria Gostrey, Marie de Vionnet, Maggie Verver, Charlotte
Stant, and other James women, Madame de Mauves has attended a
French school; she has married a French man and a French title; her
French must be presumed excellent, even if only acquired; it is never
remarked upon. Longmore, by way of contrast, is distinctly less
fluent in French, and text desires to make much of his lack: "For
reasons involved apparently in the very structure of his being,"
reasons having partly to do with native Americanism out of its native
sphere, "Longmore found himself unable to speak the language tol-
erably." Or perhaps he is insecure. "He admired and enjoyed it, but
the very genius of awkwardness controlled his phraseology." Longmore's linguistic ineptitude also reflects a doubtful relation to the
woman he loves and to her husband. Arriving at Saint-Germain
from Paris, that husband greets that wife, "and having bowed to
Longmore, asked her several questions in French." She introduces
Longmore as a "fellow-countryman," and M. de Mauves shifts to
"very fair English." Longmore is promptly squelched by "the light
which M. de Mauves's good English cast upon his own bad French."
Especially the French personages of "Madame de Mauves" regularly
employ their linguistic capabilities for the discomfiture, coercion,
control, wounding, or destruction of others, poor Longmore being
the regular victim. With Madame Clairin, not strong in English, he
naturally speaks his own bad French, once achieving a miniscule
breakthrough: " *'Allons donc!'* cried Longmore, in the best French
he had ever uttered." In the scene of French ruralism, the tavern hostess almost certainly has no English and her conversation with

Longmore naturally proceeds "in French"—we do not know how bad, it is not very complicated—even if it happens to be, in fact, in English.

Place names are naturally Englished, even retaining accent marks, as are common forms of address. But many French words, normally found in italics, boldly appear in "Madame de Mauves" in roman type, as if they were either "English, after all, you know," or "such old friends that why would we bother?"—examples are gentilhomme, tête-à-tête, la vieille galanterie, bon-bons, Voyons, some of these words clearly more "English" than others, however capaciously that language be conceived. Most French words are of course in italics so that we may know how French they are, how "foreign," how exotic; then we can be humble and admire, or, alternatively, join in with a certain self-satisfied jubilation, decent or not, depending on our character. Perhaps the uncertainty with respect to typeface is only a specific aspect of the general linguistic mystification practiced by the internationalized Tourist Fiction, the assumption that things are "really taking place" in French when obviously we are droning along quite comfortably in English. Conversation between Longmore and tavern hostess is a classic case of such harmless mystification:

> "Don't trust to it, monsieur! Those artists,—*ça n'a pas de principes!* . . . I know them, *allez*. I've had them here very often; one year with one, another year with another."
>
> Longmore was puzzled for a moment. Then, "You mean she's not his wife?" he asked.
>
> She shrugged her shoulders. "What shall I tell you? They are not *des hommes sérieux,* those gentlemen! They don't engage themselves for an eternity. It's none of my business, and I've no wish to speak ill of madame. She's a very nice little woman, and she loves her *jeune homme* to distraction."

The passage is constructed to offer extra pleasure if you know a little French, yet to be clear enough if you know not a word. We are easily seduced into thinking ourselves involved with a genuinely French experience, and maybe, insofar as we seriously address ourselves to the sounded presence of the French language, as well as the ostensible French places and French people, we are. We have at least come to the threshold of literary internationalism, which is about as far as literature alone can carry us.

*A Bundle of Letters* (1879). Around this time James wrote three international comedies, the others being "The Pension Beaurepas" (1879) and "The Point of View" (1882). A few "characters" (the term perhaps claims too much) appear in more than one tale, each of which has Americans, English, and French. There is a German in "A Bundle of Letters" only; no Italians anywhere; the Swiss are French-speaking and count as French. Two of the three tales are situated in *pensions*—"The Point of View" is the exception—and two of them are epistolary—"The Pension Beaurepas" is the exception. It would seem that "A Bundle of Letters" is the most centrally representative performance of the set. Its location *en pension* is of course largely owing to James' passion for Balzac, whose Pension Vauquer in *Le Père Goriot* he never wearies of mentioning. That novel and Balzac are a very great deal mentioned in the letter from Louis Leverett to Harvard Tremont in "A Bundle of Letters," along with much esteem for Madame Hulot of *Les Parents Pauvres*.

We readily understand why the *pension* is so propitious a fictive locale for the conspectual mingling of internationally differentiated personages: it automatically brings them together within unity of place, seldom a nagging concern in James' longer narratives but increasingly a value to clutch at as the pieces get shorter. The "Bundle of Letters" epistolers comprise three Americans (two New England, one New York; two female, one titularly male), one English girl, one French man, one German—what shall we call him? Some, not all, of these people are engaged in learning French and that is why they live where they do. But if the *pension* structuration makes for unity, that of the epistle flies away in the opposite direction. The nine letters of the tale emanate from the same place but they are dispatched to quite different places, Bangor (Maine), New York, Boston, Brighton, Lille, Göttingen. These places thus become implied, indirect, or secondary settings while the recipients of the letters become implied, indirect, or secondary characters. *How* the letters come to be bundled together as we find them is not explained; by some kind of occulted transaction they are imagined more or less to exist rather at the point of departure, or even of composition, than at the point of reception, excluding ours.

Petty amours and petty animosities abound in such places inhabited by such types. One animosity is not petty at all, however, that of the German professor who studies French character in preparation for the next German assault. All the other letters are dated 1879 and they run from 5 September to 22 October but the mind of the German letter writer is fixated on the year 1870, one of the years so carefully occluded in *The American*. The German letter (assuming no textual error) is *not dated*—no year, no month, no day of the month, no day of the week, as if its time of inscription were to be read as "pretty much all the time." The acuity of its denunciation by no means diminishes the ugliness of its attitude: "The French are so exclusively occupied with the idea of themselves, that in spite of the very definite image the German personality presented to them by the war of 1870, they have at present no distinct apprehension of its existence." The hindsight of two world wars gives us an easy irony. A more profitable reflection, then and now, might be a certain resemblance of the German and American tempers, each so avid for admiration in excess of desert and each so willing to compensate the absence of admiration with mere assertion of power. But in "A Bundle of Letters" Germany alone is singled out for explicit disapproval. Americans and other nationals who appear in the tale are equally but not uniformly depicted as absurd but harmless. The tone is of a lofty amused derision which is not what you would call loving.

The saving grace of so much derision is of course self-satire. "A Bundle of Letters" is rich with James' delighted delightful assaults on himself both as a person and as a writer. He appears, to a knowing eye, in more than one place, perhaps most self-evidently self-mockingly in the letter by Louis Leverett—sensitive, aestheticized, experience-mad, cosmopolitan, Francophiliac-Anglomaniac, *un délicat, comme qui dirait,* Henry James indulging a purely absurdist view of himself. Sentimentalists overly impressed with Strether's empty exhortations "to live" in *The Ambassadors* might moderate their credulity by prolonged contemplation of Leverett, who happens to be of the identical opinion and who is not a whit less expressive—indeed he is doubly expressive, in two languages: "The great thing is to *live,* you know. . . . There are times, my dear Harvard, when I feel as if I were really capable of everything—*capable de tout,* as they

say here. . . . Oh, to be able to say that one has lived—*qu'on a vécu,*
as they say here." Not only are the sentiments Strether's (and
Christopher Newman's and Isabel Archer's and Milly Theale's and
lots of other folks') but the slightly over-affectionate slightly-over-
bearing condescension-impressment tone of the epistolary style is
quite Henry James' own, as readers at all attentive to the nuances of
his correspondence will recognize and appreciate. Such readers may
also enjoy the "as they say here" formula, familiar to them as a
stylistic mannerism of *The American* and other inter-locational texts
by Henry James.

All of which is somewhat obvious, perhaps; less obvious, surely,
is the self-ridiculing self-portraiture concealed within the satiric portrait of Miranda Hope from Bangor, Maine, who writes four of the
nine letters comprising the bundle (I, II, V, and IX); her very name
refers us to *The Tempest* and to the theological virtue sometimes
graciously bestowed upon a nation with all its future greatness yet in
store, and it should soften our scorn for her free-wheeling, aggressive, liberalistic, sloganeering American fatuity. There may have
been a family joke, now lost, about Henry and her or a fellow
townsperson. A letter from James to his mother of 31 October 1880
speaks of "the news of my engagement to the young lady in Bangor,
etc." as "a slight mistake."[5] The reason for thinking the Bangor girl
a family joke is that the sentence fragment just quoted follows family
references to Alice James and William James. Miranda Hope's pert
mock-contemptuous indirection vis-à-vis her boyfriend at home "(you
can get William Platt to translate this, he used to tell me he knew so
much French)" is virtually the same as that of a younger Henry
James to Thomas Sergeant Perry (the message to be passed along by
William): "P.S. Since T. S. Perry is so hard at work on philology,
ask him the Persian for a faceless and perjured friend!"[6]

Miranda Hope's apparently preposterous desire, Paris weather being
"dull and damp," to be "braced up" by some nice cold weather *à la
Maine* is unarguably a crotchet displayed by James himself in a series
of letters from Italy in the spring of 1873: to his mother, 24 March,
Rome, he wishes the weather had "a little snap and lift to it"; to
William, 9 April, Rome still, "The want of 'tone' in the air is
altogether indescribable"; to Alice, 25 April, from Albano, "I had
grown rather unstarched with the lovely relaxation of the Roman

Spring"; to his parents, 4 May, Rome again, "The weather has been abnormally cold . . . but it has tuned me up comfortably"; to his mother again, later in May, from Florence, "I find just now a rather heated and heavy atmosphere in Florence which if it continues, will not be just the thing to tone me up."[7] If Miranda Hope sounds like a naive self-suffering devotee of cold snaps, she comes by it honestly.

Like her compatriot Louis Leverett she is also the innocent indefatigable transatlantic seeker of foreign culture and deliberated alienation whom nothing will ever change. At tale's end, having "done" Paris, she is off, not knowing which country to choose (it will be Italy, we may be sure) but anyhow "to meet plenty of fresh experiences." If her French is not perfected, it is probably improved, and she can use it on William Platt long winter nights in Boston, which she is saving to "finish off" with, and where she intends to "reside" for the rest of her natural life. While in Paris, she rejoices at being "in *foreign parts*" where she meets so many Americans rejoicing in the same privilege. She transfers herself from hotel to *pension* for the sake of learning French. The bookkeeper at the hotel, her only Parisian friend, spoke English to her, the chambermaid was Irish, the waiters German; the French spoken at the theater was too fast "and, besides, there are a great many vulgar expressions which it is unnecessary to learn." At Théâtre du Palais Royal, "a small but very popular theatre for vaudevilles and farces of a character not always unexceptionable,"[8] as Bædeker has it, she overhears a conversation (in English) about how to learn French by living *en pension,* where again she naturally finds other Americans "here for the same purpose as myself," among them Miss Violet Ray of New York, with mother. Father, milked of money, is back at the New York office, presumably pleased that his loved ones are acculturating themselves in Paris on his behalf; he particularly wishes that his daughter shall, precisely, "perfect" her French, which, in *her* view, is "quite as perfect as I want it to be," wanting only in a certain security about genders and idioms. Her letter contains a few French words in evidence of her prowess. It is from her that we learn how Louis Leverett refers to Paris weather as "a real Corot day." At the *pension* Miranda Hope talks all the French she can, especially reveling in conversation, that quintessentially French *art.* Departing Paris, she declares herself possessed of "a good knowledge of the language." Her correspondence hardly bears her out. Except for quotation of other people, and the single word *salon,* her letters have no French. It is what I meant, among other things, by her being indefatigable.

*The Siege of London* (1883). An amusing recent article by George Monteiro calls to critical attention James' "rather embarrassing errors of geography" in "The Siege of London" and reprints a rather typical-of-the-times paragraph from the *Overland Monthly* of June 1883 lampooning "Mr. James, who can hardly be expected to have very clear notions of the geography of a country so remote from London and Paris as California."[9] Monteiro tends to think it must have been for very shame James corrected his ignorance when revising the tale for the New York Edition, the most conspicuous error being the placement of San Diego in the Southwest, specifically New Mexico. But New Mexico was not of course a state in 1883 or even in 1908 at the time of revision; California had been, since James was about seven years old. The first third or so of the *Overland Monthly* paragraph is not in fact about James at all but about general slovenliness in American misuse of the term "West," a common vexation to California-dwellers, then and now.[10] Monteiro reminds us that in 1905 James visited San Diego, almost unavoidably acquiring a new geographical sophistication, and he conjectures that it might have been this fresh awareness, rather than or in addition to, remembered shame which prompted his textual changes—these mainly amounted to deleting San Diego and for it inserting an innocuous San Pablo, perhaps in emulation of how cleverly his friend Howells had in *A Modern Instance* (1882) disposed of an unwanted personage at Whited Sepulchre, Arizona, also not a state; these non-states, as may be imagined, must have been wonderfully hard to find.

In the original version, the San Diego-New Mexico confusion was at first attributed to Rupert Waterville's ignorance of American geography but then the confusion crept into other people's speech and into the text itself, as if one explanation of confusion could cover a whole series of extended confusions including the author's own. It seems unlikely that James cared much about it. Wittingly vague or slightly erroneous or contemptuous references to what he conceived as the general emptiness and vulgar monstrosity lying westward of Manhattan are common in his writings; a hundred years later comparable jokes can still be found in *The New Yorker.* Most of the time James got away with his vagueness: extension of transatlantic-transcontinental reference from Europe to California is not unique to "The Siege of London" but is also found in such texts as *The American, Confidence,* "The Point of View," and "Mrs. Temperly." And despite his change of San Diego to San Pablo, some of the vagueness and indeterminacy he stuck to. In both the 1883 and 1908 versions, Mrs. Headway alludes to her past life "in Arizona, in Dakotah, in the newly admitted States," somehow related to "the Rocky Mountains" and the "Pacific slope" (the designations are in all conscience ridiculous enough). Once she locates her past in Texas, like California a state for many years. As text preposterously remarks, "in that spacious civilization the locality was large," a natural context for San Diego as "a town where it would have been ridiculous to be difficult to please," a passage which was let stand with San Diego removed. It hardly matters: the main point of the *nouvelle* is that people are not always reducible to the places they come from. Because of "the way she picked up ideas," Mrs. Headway is Parisian.

"The Siege of London" is generally formed upon the same plan as *The Tragic Muse,* Paris first and England after, with a certain amount of Parisian retroaction in England. But in "The Siege of London" England is also retroactive at Paris along with San Diego and there is none of the *Tragic Muse*'s invidious comparison at the expense of the English, animus being grandly displaced upon the American West. "The Siege of London" comes in two equal halves, rather than one-third and two-thirds proportions, and in fact Part II or England commences with Mrs. Headway telling in *London* how in *Rome* the country round about reminded her of *San Diego.* (I am of course quoting the 1883 version and shall continue to do so.) But once the flood of Paris-referring starts it is hard to stop and it resembles in little the same operations in *The Tragic Muse:* "Don't you remember how I told you in Paris[?]"; "Don't you remember the play we saw in Paris?"; "Do you still hold to that theory you propounded in Paris?"; "I told you that in Paris"; "I told you in Paris you could help me"; "as Littlemore had said of old, in Paris"; "I told you that in Paris, don't you remember?"; and indeed the denouement, alluding back, "He had suddenly become conscious of the need to utter the simple truth with which he had answered Rupert Waterville's first question at the Théâtre Français. 'I don't think Mrs Headway respectable,' he said." There are many fewer such passages than in *The Tragic Muse,* of course; "The Siege of London" is much shorter; it is also less bitter, less Flaubertian. The tone is that of a highly sophisticated observer from overseas amusedly disdaining what he knows all too well is hardly worth the trouble of deciding whether it merits a laugh or a yawn.

From early James, present-tense travel-writing convention lingers for representation of *actualités* likely to whet the pleasure of the Tourist Reader. "In the month of September the audience at the Théâtre Français is comparatively thin. . . . The boxes are far from the stage." Then, later on, "The little American colony in Paris is rich in amiable women," as we always knew but are gladly reminded of. Major scenes in the Paris part of "The Siege of London" are ascribed to the Théâtre Français, Hôtel Meurice (Rue de Rivoli 228, expensive, and I believe still in existence), the gallery and garden of the Luxembourg. The first narrative sentence includes description of "the curtain of the Comédie Française," the second sentence informs us that the house "had lately been cleansed of its historic cobwebs," the ones you noticed the last time you were there, and the third sentence tells us that the play being watched by the American protagonists is Emile Augier, "L'Aventurière," the same to be recited in a few years by Miriam Rooth. We might as well be there; we might as well be they; *en effet,* we are. Then sitting at "the Grand Café, on the Boulevard de la Madeleine," we think again of "L'Aventurière," and of "Le Demi-Monde" (Dumas) as well, both plays showing "the justice to be meted out to unscrupulous women who attempt to thrust themselves into honorable families." To this thesis "The Siege of London" renders a satiric answer, as we might have guessed from all the talk about Voltaire at the Comédie, where his statue, by Houdon, is "gaped at by visitors obviously less acute," and Mrs. Headway kindly designates: "And this is Voltaire, the celebrated writer."

Hôtel Meurice adds little in the way of local color, a hotel room being at best the interior of a six-sided cube, within which conversations of two or more personages may be physically contained. Mrs. Headway and Waterville go to the Luxembourg Museum over the river from the hotel and along the Rue de Seine, she with her Murray (not Bædeker) ever in her lap, she ever vulgar and ever perceptive. "Waterville was sure that before she left the gallery she knew something about the French school. . . . She [also] had quite seized the difference between the old Paris and the new." She thoroughly appreciates the "romantic associations" of the Latin Quarter. She even knows to prefer French life glimpsed in the garden to mere pictures in a gallery. "It's more of a picture. . . . I like France!" The woman is sound, and will be saved, but the *nouvelle* in which she finds herself, and which is the means of her saving, is regrettably slight.

*The Velvet Glove* (1909). This late lusciousness of James' is not quite his last word on France and French—*A Small Boy and Others* (1913) and *Notes of a Son and Brother* (1914) were still to come, with other, lesser, and lessening notes—but it is his last great fictive word on France and French, immensely comical, self-jeering, bristling with *maîtrise* open and covert, suggesting in at least a marginal way irrepressible irrepressibly Francophiliac Edith Wharton *elle aussi*, flaunting resurrections (Gloriani for certain, conceivably Christina Light), spectacular night scenes of Paris, and Olympian laughter issuing from ironic fractures of Olympian romance.

Biographical interpreters claim to see in "The Velvet Glove" a great deal more of Edith Wharton than I do. They are especially keen that she *be* "the Princess" of the tale. The case rests on such phrases, easily matched outside the tale, as "chariot of fire" for Wharton's car. The case rests also on James' letter to her of 9 May 1909: "the whole thing *reeks* with you . . . and with *our* Paris."[11] It may, indeed, so reek but it does not follow that the Princess is Edith Wharton; in fact, it quite inescapably follows that the Princess is *not* Edith Wharton for the reason that she is some one else. In his letter James addresses Wharton as "you" and refers to the Princess as "her." *You* and *she* are obviously two different people and there must be an explanation of why the latter should be in quotation marks.★ Further evidence against Edith Wharton being the Princess is found in the main data of the tale. Princess has no name. Her *nom de guerre* (pen name) is Amy Evans, which recalls (if one *must*) Mary Ann

---

★It is possible that the pronoun in quotation remarks is Edith Wharton's car. See Percy Lubbock's note in *The Letters of Henry James*, 2 vols. (New York: Scribners, 1920), 2:197. It is possible that the pronoun is Christina Light. It is possible that the pronoun is both.

Evans, George Eliot, not Edith Wharton. Her frequent identification as an American by biographers in zeal[12] is non-substantiable by anything in the text, and unlikely, virtually excluded by her depiction of herself as one who writes in English, as if to do so were somewhat odd, in that English language "which I love, I assure you, as much as you can yourself do"—a practiced author would never say such a thing. Nor would an American whose nationality was unquestioned go on to say "and which gives one (doesn't it? for who should know if not you?) the biggest of publics. I 'just love'—don't they say?—your American millions." These are the kind of remarks one might expect from a person of multiple languages and mixed nationality.

If the Princess is clearly not Edith Wharton, who is she? Not so clearly, but more than just possibly, she is Christina Light the Princess Casamassima. In the previous year James had written, in the New York Edition preface to *The Princess Casamassima,* how Christina Light was "left on my hands" after *Roderick Hudson,* with an insistence upon being revived: "To continue in evidence, that had struck me from far back as her natural passion," driven as she is, from text to text, by "a restless vanity" and by James' evident adoration of it. "I was to have looked for her—quite *off* and away."[13] Here she is again, off and away one last time, no longer the *femme fatale* with white poodle of *Roderick Hudson,* no longer the amateur revolutionist desirous of death by hanging of *The Princess Casamassima,* but an aristocratic popular novelist in search of a flattering preface for the sake of sales. Perhaps she is dragged back, or they drag each other, by Gloriani, he too making a third and final appearance (from *Roderick Hudson* to *The Ambassadors* to "The Velvet Glove"), his chamber-of-state-conventual garden now transcended by a veritable "studio." The first two-thirds of "The Velvet Glove" takes place at a party in Gloriani's studio, the last third *en voiture dans les rues de Paris.* Surely it is entertaining to contemplate Edith Wharton driving Henry James around Paris (but not being refused a preface she never asked for, she says she did not, and it isn't at all like her; but it is just like Christina Light). It is far more entertaining to contemplate Henry James mocking an imaginary Henry James contriving to snatch a good night kiss from his favorite heroine, this to be his last gesture as writer of French-international novels and tales from the American point of view. "The Velvet Glove," modestly reduced to more modern scale, is his *Tempest*.

John Berridge is as ridiculously successful as nearly 66-year-old Henry James knew he had never been, although plenty deserving. Like a stationary comet, he is "the new literary star that had begun to hang, with a fresh red light, over the vast, even though rather confused, Anglo-Saxon horizon." And more: "every one in the world (so far had the thing gone) was reading *The Heart of Gold*"—as every one in the world was by no means reading *The Golden Bowl,* and never had been, and never would be, either—that "prodigious 'hit.' " More still: *The Heart of Gold* is none of your limited constricted pinched and doomed-to-indecent-brevity-by-outside-malefactors (editors, publishers) production but it is, of all things, "slightly too fat." Still more: this fat novel is sensationally doubling as a "fifth-act too long play," most of James' plays being three acts, because of exigencies and not because of art. And more, and more, James piling it on: "the queer world of his fame was not the mere usual world of the Anglo-Saxon boom," oh no, "but positively the bottom of the *whole* theatric sea," to wit, footlights German (the Germans now forgiven), French (where James learned his theatric wiles), Italian (the beloved country), Russian (for Turgenev), Scandinavian (James now latching onto Ibsen). Paris, of all places, "really appeared for the hour the centre"—he gives it a French spelling—"of his cyclone," plus all the appurtenances of fame and fortune, "reports and 'returns,' to say nothing of agents and emissaries, converging from the minor capitals." Ironically, his work has failed to suffer the "critical excoriation" in London which "it had received at the hand of supreme authority, of that French authority which was in such a matter the only one to be artistically reckoned with," and so, of course, he knows his play is no good, especially the fourth act, James himself having come to theatrical disaster with the second or next-to-last act of *Guy Domville.*

The middle of "The Velvet Glove" develops in beautiful romantic and romantic-parody prose John Berridge's fantasies about the sort of rich and leisured people met at parties and for the moment envied. The mode is mock-pastoral mock-mythological, the rich and leisured people figuring as gods and goddesses condescending down from Olympus upon Endymion-type shepherds, particularly *she* the

Princess, "Olympian herself, supremely, divinely Olympian." If "she" is indeed the Princess Casamassima, she has not aged since 1886 but is the same as when last glimpsed with Schinkel in Hyacinth Robinson's squalid room. Berridge knows her and he doesn't: "What Princess, or the Princess of what?" Our answer is, the Princess of the Jamesian œuvre, first and last, 1875–1909, sporadically. She is also the Ideal Reader, or says she is: "I've read everything, you know, and *The Heart of Gold* three times." If *he* were an Olympian, Berridge thinks, "he would leave his own stuff snugly unread, to begin with." So utterly infatuated as to want her to love him for himself—she wants the same thing of him and even uses the phrase—Berridge reflects on his "acted clap-trap," his "printed verbiage." Under a false name (" 'You didn't perhaps know I'm Amy Evans,' she smiled"), she has just published *The Top of the Tree* and has gone on to write *The Velvet Glove,* "an object as alien to the careless grace of goddess-haunted Arcady as a washed-up 'kodak' from a wrecked ship." Her prose style, generously quoted, leaves much to be desired.

Berridge's aversion to the idea of the Princess as a writer, his insistence that she be and be only Romance, a female to be adored and not a female to be competed with, a female to write about, a female as external object but never a female as subject, is easily misread as Jamesian misogyny, an interpretation quite impossible in view of his long-standing if troubled discipleship to George Eliot and his even longer-standing more-than-fond overestimation of George Sand. What seems to be going on, instead, is James at play with the notion of a represented personage, *his,* impossibly coming to life and daring to write when, as is well known, represented personages by definition get themselves written *about*. She might even write about *him!* he who gave her her textual existence in the first place. Already, on the spot, she is probably plotting his fictive epiphany, gathering foolish party material with which to immortalize him in her deathless prose. It is not to be imagined that Christina Light, taking up the pen in her later years, would be the world's worst novelist; but it is decidedly to be supposed that she would be top-of-the-head slap-dash, excessive and undisciplined, brilliantly contemptuous, totally irresponsible, and rather grand.

Paris by night is what you might call under-represented: the huge iridescent jewel is perceived as visual and suggestive, nothing but darkness, bright lights, and romantic associations. There are no recognizable landmarks, nothing has a name or a designated location, we do not know where we are, we do not care where we are, so long as we are in Paris, that heaven in which we are more than pleased to find our ultimate touristical alienation: "in spite of his constantly-prized sense of knowing his enchanted city and his way about," Berridge like the Tourist Reader positively palpitates in a new ecstasy as he "ceased to follow or measure their course." He hangs over Paris, instead, "from vague consecrated lamp-studded heights," as if lofted up in a balloon, or perhaps only looking down from Montmartre, taking it all in sweepingly but non-topographically, for "spread below and afar" what we see is simply "the great scroll of all its irresistible story," the story of modern man (American and European version, nineteenth century, early twentieth century), "river and bridge and radiant *place* . . . quays and boulevards and avenues . . . monumental circles and squares," nothing but *lighted shapes,* "a thousand things understood and a flood of response conveyed," the James text sounding like Whitman, the writer at Paris resuming the grief-stricken bird in foreign parts. And as he hangs over Paris, Paris obligingly reciprocates, "splendid Paris hung over them, as a consecrating canopy, her purple night embroidered with gold."

Then the Princess begins her plaint, "Ah, of course you don't allow that I *am* literary," and then she begins her plea, just for the "lovely, friendly, irresistible log-rolling Preface that I've been asking you if you wouldn't be an angel and write for me." Now they are back at her house, address not given. Her *porte-cochère* is closed. He gets out of her car. They argue. He still refuses to write her preface. He will never see her again. He may never so much as mention her again, in print or otherwise. "Then you don't like me—?" . . . "I adore you." He kisses her. The *porte-cochère* opens. She in her chariot of fire is driven in. He stands outside, waving his hat, "as she passed to disappearance in the great floridly-framed aperture whose wings at once came together behind her." John Berridge is fictively excluded but the France and French of Henry James are well inside, where all texts find their abiding place as the represented recorded past.

# Notes

**PREFACE**

1. Adeline R. Tintner *The Museum World of Henry James* (Ann Arbor: UMI Research Press, 1986) pp. 204, 232.

2. These books are Marie-Reine Garnier, *Henry James et la France* (Paris: Librairie Ancienne Honoré Champion, 1927); Alberta Fabris, *Henry James e la Francia* (Rome: Edizioni di Storia e Letteratura, 1969); Jeanne Delbaere-Garant, *Henry James: The Vision of France* (Paris: Société d'Editions "Les Belles Lettres," 1970).

3. Henry James, *A Small Boy and Others* (London: Macmillan, 1913), pp. 57–58.

4. *The Diary of Alice James,* ed. Leon Edel (New York: Dodd, Mead, 1964), p. 163.

## I. *CONTES DE LIEU ET DE LANGUE*

1. *The American Scene* (1907), ed. Leon Edel (Bloomington: Indiana University Press, 1968), pp. 291–92.

2. *Essays on Literature, American Writers, English Writers* (New York: The Library of America, 1984), p. 610.

3. *Henry James Novels 1881–1886* (New York: The Library of America, 1985), p. 971.

4. *French Writers, Other European Writers, The Prefaces to the New York Edition* (New York: The Library of America, 1984), p. 49.

5. *Essays on Literature,* p. 275.

6. *French Writers,* p. 217.

7. *The American Scene,* pp. 431, 275.

8. *The Tragic Muse* is quoted from the edition by Leon Edel (New York: Harper, 1960), the other novels from the New York Edition (New York: Scribners, 1907–09).

9. *Essays on Literature,* p. 55.

10. *Henry James Letters,* 2:419.

11. *The American Scene,* p. 391.

12. *The American Scene,* p. 366.

13. Percy Lubbock, ed., *The Letters of Henry James.* 2 vols. (New York: Scribners, 1920), 2:11.

14. *Henry James Letters* 2:221, 3:259; then 1:82, 160, 187, 201, 305, 484; 2:355; 3:157, 159, 435, 473. Leon Edel and Lyall H. Powers, eds., *The Complete Notebooks of Henry James* (New York: Oxford University Press, 1987), pp. 238–39.

15. Harry R. Warfel and G. Harrison Orians, *American Local-Color Stories* (New York: American Book, 1941).

16. *Henry James Letters,* 2:417.

17. *Henry James Letters,* 1:183.

18. *Henry James Letters,* 2:50.

19. The 1902 essay, *French Writers,* p. 97.

20. *Essays on Literature,* p. 327.

21. *Henry James Letters,* 2:308, 315.

22. *Complete Notebooks* p. 22.

23. *French Writers,* p. 583.

24. *French Writers,* pp. 1279–80.

25. *The American Scene,* p. 242.

26. *Henry James Letters,* 2:166.

27. Leon Edel, *The Conquest of London* (Philadelphia: Lippincott, 1962), p. 105; *The Master* (Philadelphia: Lippincott, 1972), p. 131.

28. John Carlos Rowe, *The Theoretical Dimensions of Henry James* (Madison: University of Wisconsin Press, 1984), p. 62.

29. *Henry James Letters*, 1:54.

30. *French Writers*, p. 40.

31. *French Writers*, p. 75.

32. *French Writers*, p. 78.

33. *French Writers*, p. 87.

34. *French Writers*, p. 44.

35. Leon Edel, "Introduction: Colloquies With His Good Angel," *"The Sea Chest"*—in *Complete Notebooks*, pp. ixf.

36. *Notebooks*, pp. 188, 119, 166–167, 172, xiv.

37. *Henry James Letters*, 2:161.

38. *A Small Boy and Others* (London: Macmillan, 1913), p. 98.

39. *French Writers*, p. 423.

40. *The American Scene*, p. 234.

41. *Henry James Letters*, 4:603.

## 2. THE AMERICAN

1. Citations of *The American* are from the Norton Critical Edition of James W. Tuttleton (New York: Norton, 1978), which gives the 1879 London Macmillan text, with variants from the Boston Osgood text of 1877, none of which appear to affect the present topic; the first American book edition of 1877 appears in *Henry James Novels 1871–1880* (New York: The Library of America, 1983). Casual collation with the "late text," i.e., that of the New York Edition (New York: Scribners, 1907), plus bemused contemplation of the facsimile *Version of 1877, Revised in Autograph and Typescript for the New York Edition of 1907* (London: Scolar Press, 1976) reveals comparatively little change in the French portions of *The American*. There are more additions of French than deletions; generally, James let well enough alone, and wisely, for when he rewrote he marred as much as he mended.

2. John Carlos Rowe, "The Politics of the Uncanny: Newman's Fate in *The American*," *Henry James Review* (1987), 8:80. Even more dazzlingly, at p. 89, n.2, Newman seems to be charged with ignorance of French political conditions in 1875–76.

3. *French Writers, Other European Writers, The Prefaces to the New York Edition* (New York: The Library of America, 1984), p. 472.

4. Leon Edel and Ilse Dusoir Lind, eds., *Parisian Sketches: Letters to the New York Tribune, 1875–1876* (New York: New York University Press, 1957), passim.

5. *French Writers*, p. 11.

6. Karl Bædeker, *Paris and Northern France*, 3d ed., "revised and augmented" (Coblenz: 1872), pp. v–vii.

7. *Galignani's New Paris Guide for 1872* (Paris: 1872) p. i. On the title page, the preface is subtitled, in parentheses, *"(Important to the Stranger)."*

8. Karl Bædeker, *Paris and its Environs*, 4th ed., "remodelled and augmented" (Leipzig: 1874), pp. v–vi. *Paris and its Environs* is a new revised edition of *Paris and Northern France*, with a change of title, not a new work.

9. *Parisian Sketches*, pp. 10–11.

10. Galignani, p. 330.

11. *Parisian Sketches*, p. 6.

12. *Roderick Hudson* is cited from *Henry James Novels 1871–1880*.

13. *Henry James Novels 1871–1880*, p. 1283.

14. *The Novels of Henry James* (New York: Macmillan, 1961; rpt. in Tuttleton), pp. 426f.

15. *Parisian Sketches*, p. 7.

16. Examples of living near the rose, *la plus belle fille,* and *abondant dans le sens de* are variously cited from Tuttleton's *American; Henry James Novels 1871–1880; Henry James Novels 1881–1886; The Complete Tales of Henry James,* ed. Leon Edel, 12 vols. (Philadelphia: Lippincott, 1961–64); the New York Edition; Leon Edel, ed., *A Little Tour in France* (New York: Farrar, 1983); *The American Scene* (1907), ed. Leon Edel (Bloomington: Indiana University Press, 1968); *Henry James Letters,* 4:202, 2:51; Leon Edel, ed., *The Complete Plays of Henry James* (Philadelphia: Lippincott, 1949).

17. Leon Edel and Lyall H. Powers, eds., *The Complete Notebooks of Henry James* (New York: Oxford University Press, 1987), p. 53.

18. "Henry James," *Literary Essays of Ezra Pound,* ed. T. S. Eliot (Norfolk, Conn.: New Directions, 1954), p. 320.

19. *The Middle Years* (Philadelphia: Lippincott, 1962), p. 238.

20. *Notebooks,* pp. 40–43.

21. Citations of *The Reverberator* are from the first English edition (London: Macmillan, 1888).

22. As Henry Haynie calls it: "even as Washington is the Federal city of our national Union, so may Paris some day become the Federal city of the United States of Europe"—along with the so much more that it already was. *Paris: Past and Present.* 2 vols. in 1 (New York: Frederick A. Stokes, 1902), 1:12.

## 3. ITALIANATE FICTIONS

1. Citations of *The Portrait of a Lady* are from *Henry James Novels 1881–1886* (New York: The Library of America, 1985).

2. The shorter fictions are quoted from Leon Edel, ed., *The Complete Tales of Henry James,* 12 vols. (Philadelphia: Lippincott, 1961–64).

3. Citations of *Roderick Hudson* are from *Henry James Novels 1871–1880)* (New York: The Library of America, 1983).

4. *The Wings of the Dove* and *The Golden Bowl* are quoted from the New York Edition (New York: Scribner's, 1907–09).

5. Henry James, *A Little Tour in France,* Leon Edel, ed. (New York: Farrar, 1983), p. 110.

## 4. *THE PRINCESS CASAMASSIMA*

1. *French Writers, Other European Writers, The Prefaces to the New York Edition* (New York: The Library of America, 1984), p. 653.

2. Mark Seltzer, *Henry James and the Art of Power* (Ithaca: Cornell University Press, 1984).

3. Adeline R. Tintner, *The Book World of Henry James* (Ann Arbor: UMI Research Press, 1987).

4. Citations of *The Princess Casamassima* are from the first edition (London, 1886).

5. Percy Lubbock, ed., *The Letters of Henry James,* 2 vols. (London, 1920), 1:95.

6. Leon Edel, ed., *Henry James Letters,* 4 vols. (Cambridge: Harvard University Press, 1974–84), 1:258.

7. Henry James, *A Little Tour in France,* Leon Edel's edition (New York: Farrar, 1983).

8. S. Gorley Putt, *Henry James, A Reader's Guide* (Ithaca: Cornell University Press, 1966), p. 178.

9. *Henry James Letters,* 2:287.

10. *Henry James Letters,* 4:418.

11. *Henry James Letters,* 4:196.

## 5. *THE TRAGIC MUSE*

1. Leon Edel, ed., *Henry James Letters,* 4 vols. (Cambridge: Harvard University Press, 1974–84), 3:223.

2. Citations from *The Diary of Alice James* are from Leon Edel's edition (New York: Dodd, Mead, 1964).

3. Percy Lubbock, ed., *The Letters of Henry James,* 2 vols. (New York: Scribner's, 1920), 1:42.

4. *French Writers,* pp. 56–57.

5. Citations of short fiction are from Leon Edel, ed., *The Complete Tales of Henry James,* 12 vols. (Philadelphia: Lippincott, 1961–64).

6. *French Writers,* p. 421.

7. All citations of *The Tragic Muse* are from the edition by Leon Edel (New York: Harper, 1960) of the original 1890 text.

8. Leon Edel, ed., *The Complete Plays of Henry James* (Philadelphia: Lippincott, 1949), p. 696.

9. "Socialism and Civilization," in *Moralism and Christianity* (1850), rpt. F. O. Matthiessen, *The James Family* (New York: Knopf, 1948), p. 56.

10. Leon Edel and Lyall H. Powers, eds., *The Complete Notebooks of Henry James* (New York: Oxford University Press, 1987), pp. 48, 46.

11. *Henry James Letters,* 4:417.

12. *Notebooks,* p. 216.

13. See Edel, *Complete Plays,* p. 40.

14. Since January of 1870, according to Leon Edel in *The Untried Years* (Philadelphia: Lippincott, 1953), p. 320.

15. F. O. Matthiessen and Kenneth B. Murdock, eds., *The Notebooks of Henry James* (New York: Oxford University Press, 1947), pp. 92–93; Edel, *Complete Plays,* p. 40; Edel, *The Middle Years* (Philadelphia: Lippincott, 1962), p. 253.

16. *Henry James Letters,* 1:203.

17. "Ladies are not admitted to the orchestra seats." Karl Bædeker, *Paris and its Environs,* 9th rev. ed. (Leipzig, 1888), p. 29.

18. Henry Haynie *Paris Past and Present,* 2 vols. in 1 (New York: Frederick A. Stokes, 1902), 2:73–74.

19. *Paris guide par les principaux écrivains et artistes de la France,* 2d ed. (Paris, 1867), p. 800.

20. Henry James, *A Little Tour in France,* Leon Edel's edition (New York: Farrar, 1983), p. 90.


## 6. ENGLISH PERIOD

1. Leon Edel, ed., *Henry James Letters,* 4 vols. (Cambridge: Harvard University Press, 1974–84), 4:367.

2. *Henry James Letters,* 3:284.

3. Except for *The Sacred Fount,* where the first edition (London: Methuen, 1901) is quoted, citations of James' novels in this chapter are to the New York Edition (New York: Scribner's, 1907–09); citations of shorter things, including "The Turn of the Screw" and "In the Cage," are to Leon

Edel, ed., *The Complete Tales of Henry James,* 12 vols. (Philadelphia: Lippincott, 1961–64).

4. *Henry James Letters,* 3:213.

5. *French Writers, Other European Writers, The Prefaces to the New York Edition* (New York: The Library of America, 1984), p. 468.

## 7. THE AMBASSADORS

1. Leon Edel and Ilse Dusoir Lind, eds., *Parisian Sketches: Letters to the New York Tribune, 1875–1876* (New York: New York University Press, 1957), p. 3.

2. Leon Edel, ed., *Henry James Letters,* 4 vols. (Cambridge: Harvard University Press, 1974–84), 1:7.

3. Citations of short fiction are from Leon Edel, ed., *The Complete Tales of Henry James,* 12 vols. (Philadelphia: Lippincott, 1961–64).

4. Leon Edel and Lyall H. Powers, eds., *The Complete Notebooks of Henry James* (New York: Oxford University Press, 1987), pp. 140–42.

5. *French Writers, Other European Writers, The Prefaces to the New York Edition* (New York: The Library of America, 1984), p. 849.

6. Citations from preface and text of *The Ambassadors* are to the New York Edition (New York: Scribner's, 1909).

7. *Notebooks,* p. 216.

8. *French Writers,* p. 222.

9. Karl Bædeker, *Paris and Environs,* 13th rev ed. (Leipzig, 1898), p. 32.

10. *French Writers,* p. 50.

11. *Henry James Letters,* 4:811.

12. Percy Lubbock, ed., *The Letters of Henry James,* 2 vols. (New York: Scribner's, 1920), 1:201–02.

13. *Henry James Letters,* 4:302–03.

## 8. HENRY JAMES RETROSPECTIVE

1. All citations from James' short pieces are to Leon Edel, ed., *The Complete Tales of Henry James,* 12 vols. (Philadelphia: Lippincott, 1961–64).

2. *Henry James Letters,* ed. Leon Edel, 4 vols. (Cambridge: Harvard University Press, 1974–84), 1:126.

3. *Henry James Letters,* 1:132.

4. Karl Bædeker, *Paris and its Environs,* 4th ed., "remodelled and augmented" (Leipzig, 1874), pp. 4–5.

5. *Henry James Letters*, 2:310.

6. *Henry James Letters*, 1:186. Letter of 27 December 1869 to William James.

7. *Henry James Letters*, 1:356, 365, 370, 376, 387.

8. *Paris and its Environs*, p. 47.

9. George Monteiro, "Geography in 'The Siege of London,' " *The Henry James Review* (1983), 4:144–45.

10. In *Frontier: American Literature and the American West* (Princeton: Princeton University Press, 1965), pp. 3–4, I cite several examples of earlier nineteenth-century American confusion and frustration over the term "West."

11. *Henry James Letters*, 4:521. Whartonian interpretation begins with Adeline R. Tintner, "James's Mock Epic: 'The Velvet Glove,' Edith Wharton, and Other Late Tales," *Modern Fiction Studies* (1971–72), 17:483–99. In *The Master* (Philadelphia: Lippincott, 1972) Leon Edel has a whole chapter entitled "The Velvet Glove," all about James and Wharton, hardly a word about France and French, "our Paris," or James' French career. The latest biographical reading is Jean Frantz Blackall, "Henry and Edith: 'The Velvet Glove' as an 'In' Joke," *The Henry James Review* (1985), 7:21–25.

12. For example, Leon Edel's note 1 in *Henry James Letters*, 4:522.

13. The *Princess Casamassima* preface is cited from *French Writers, Other European Writers, The Prefaces to the New York Edition* (New York: The Library of America, 1984).

# Index

# DATE DUE

PRINTED IN U.S.A.